To Friedlieb Ferdinand Runge
(1794–1867)

who discovered caffeine and began its scientific investigation,
and to the vast majority of the men and women throughout
the world, who already enjoy caffeine, most of them
nearly every day of their lives

Contents

Foreword

THE BOOK NOW in your hands can truly improve your life. In *The Caffeine Advantage*, Weinberg and Bealer explain how the judicious use of caffeine can provide a safe and strategic advantage to living the good life. In the popular imagination, caffeine is possibly the most misunderstood of all substances. While conducting my own studies on its effects, I have been surprised by how often individuals express an almost automatic disapproval of its use. I am glad the authors have done such an effective job of reflecting the countless misunderstandings and misconceptions about the actions of this ubiquitous substance. Caffeine is in fact a wonderful aid to health and achievement. More than just being a tonic to wake you up, it has benefits for intelligence, mood, physical performance, weight control, and, in many cases, disease prevention.

Weinberg and Bealer have already been widely acclaimed for the fascinating, rich history of caffeine in their scholarly book *The World of Caffeine: The Science and Culture of the World's Most Popular Drug*. The present book presents a briefer, more practical application of the scientific knowledge detailed in their longer text and adds the results of groundbreaking new research. Through factual reporting, specific advice, careful warnings, entertaining self-tests, and lively narration, the authors demonstrate that caffeine is a true boon to humanity. Clearly, the authors have done a masterful job in bringing to the general public a wide array of research on the benefits of caffeine in its popular sources, including coffee, tea, chocolate, caffeinated soft drinks, and caffeine pills.

Perhaps the most valuable service performed by this book is the apt debunking of three great myths about caffeine: that it is necessarily bad for your heart, that moderate consumption increases anxiety and sours mood, and that caffeine causes dehydration. As Weinberg and Bealer carefully explain, these myths arose from historical prejudice and the misuse of caffeine.

The oft-quoted ancient Greek advice "Know thyself" is rightly paired with the saying "Nothing to excess." Accordingly, an important principle of this book is the Yerkes-Dodson Law, a tenet of physiological psychology that reminds us that for each person there is an optimal level of consumption to achieve the caffeine advantage. Too little or too much caffeine obviates the clear advantage, and it is important to pay attention to the guidelines for sensible consumption. Physical dependence on caffeine and potentially undesirable consequences of excessive caffeine use are explicitly and repeatedly documented in this balanced appraisal of caffeine's effects.

The reader who heeds the caveats and exhortations to consume in moderation will achieve caffeine's benefits and avoid any negative consequences of overindulgence. The benefits are numerous: improving sleep quality as well as overcoming fatigue, combating jet lag, elevating intelligence and memory, enhancing creativity, improving mood and dispelling boredom while increasing sociability, raising physical performance and endurance, aiding weight loss and dieting, and preventing aging while counteracting disease. Indeed, caffeine appears as an elixir of life to the informed user.

The reader will find accurate, up-to-date scientific information from authoritative sources to confirm the many benefits of caffeine. Of considerable interest and value are the tables of caffeine content of beverages and medications and food and drug interactions in the appendices.

So, make time to enjoy this enlightening, useful guide. It should prove an indispensable introduction to the fascinating world of caffeine. I believe a copy should be placed in every café and teahouse. It is an energizing work of popular, accurate science that is a pleasure to read, not unlike drinking a gourmet coffee made from freshly ground beans. Enjoy this helpful book—it deserves a wide audience and praise for its efforts to bestow upon the reader the undeniable benefits of caffeine.

PAUL J. KULKOSKY, PH.D.
Professor of Psychology
University of Southern Colorado, Pueblo, CO

Introduction

The World of Caffeine

What is it in man's devious make-up that makes him round on the seemingly more wholesome and pleasurable aspects of his environment and suspect them of being causes of his misfortunes? Whatever it is, stimulants of all kinds (and especially coffee and caffeine) maintain a position high on the list of suspicion, despite a continuing lack of real evidence of any hazard to health.

Editorial, *British Medical Journal*, 1976

I S THERE A SUBSTANCE that enables you to run farther and faster, think more cogently and fluently, feel happier, more self-confident, and more relaxed, eat less, and that even acts as a powerful antioxidant? One that is also the favorite recreational drug of the twenty-first century, a pop icon? Yes, there is. It's caffeine. Throughout this book, we will see examples of the ways in which caffeine, by heightening our mental and physical capacities and enhancing our moods, enables us to realize our hidden potential and achieve our goals and in the process helps to shape and drive the progress of the modern world.

Using caffeine is more of an art than a science. Caffeine safely offers a wider range of benefits than any other drug in the pharmacopoeia. The very scope of these benefits requires us to learn something about the scientific studies that describe these effects if we are to use it strategically. And because the range of individual responses to caffeine is so great, we also need experience, self-testing, and reasoned judgment to enable us to enjoy all the benefits caffeine offers. Caffeine's benefits are very real, and yet they are complex and variable. When using caffeine, the guiding motto must be "Know thyself."

You may wonder, If caffeine has so many wonderful benefits, why haven't I heard about scientific studies being done to confirm these claims? The answer is simple. Research *is* being done about caffeine, but quietly. Ironically, caffeine, the most useful stimulant ever discovered, is a sleeper. As scientists in the field have repeatedly regretted, especially when talking about caffeine's potentially valuable uses in treating and preventing depression, gallstones, and Parkinson's disease and other degenerative conditions, no one has a financial incentive to promote caffeine's benefits.

Because caffeine is a generic drug, the profit on the sale of each caffeine pill or capsule is low. Therefore no company can afford to pay for the extensive testing and paperwork that would convince the Food and Drug Administration (FDA) to permit it to make broader claims on caffeine's behalf. Caffeine has been consistently included by the FDA on the list of substances Generally Recognized As Safe (GRAS) for over twenty-five years. That is the reason it can be legally added to foods and drinks. But the FDA, while acknowledging that caffeine is safe, allows caffeine to be promoted only as an "alertness aid." People who sell products that include caffeine as an ingredient aren't legally permitted to make any other claims for it. They can't tell you how caffeine makes you smarter, faster, stronger, more relaxed, and more confident. But we can. We can tell you the full story of the amazing facts about caffeine discovered over the past ten years by serious scientists from all over the world.

Unfortunately, not only do people not know about all the good things caffeine can do for them, they actually fear the harm they believe caffeine causes. Despite caffeine's astounding benefits and valuable place in society, a large number of people worry about using it and think that it is somehow to be avoided. The overwhelming majority of the people we talk to say things like, "Unfortunately, I use a lot of caffeine," or "I drink six cups of coffee a day, but I'm planning on cutting down," or "I used to drink five cups a day, but I've cut it down to two."

Such fears are fueled by poorly informed physicians and health care information and advocacy groups that have warned the public against caffeine for years and continue to do so. If you go to the Web and put the word "caffeine" into a search engine, you'll receive a flood of hits from sites advising that caffeine is dangerous because it causes hypertension and other cardiovascular problems, harmful because even small to moderate amounts of it commonly increase anxiety, and bad for athletes because it causes dehydration. When it comes to using small to moderate doses tailored to each person's needs, there is no truth in any of these statements. These are the caffeine myths, and it is part of the purpose of this book to dispel them.

Exploding Three Myths

Three persistent myths make people hesitant or even afraid to use caffeine.

Caffeine and Anxiety

A common misconception links caffeine use to increased anxiety. In fact, most people who use caffeine demonstrate lower levels of anxiety than people who do not. Although very large doses of caffeine can slightly increase anxiety levels in some people, small to moderate doses, tailored to each individual, usually have a relaxing or tranquilizing effect. So, if you're on edge, don't skip the coffee. Relax and have a cup.

Caffeine and Your Heart

Most studies show that in the hours after a person takes caffeine, blood pressure can increase slightly, especially in people who haven't used caffeine recently. The critical question, however, is not whether there is or is not a small transient increase in blood pressure, but whether the use of caffeine causes or contributes to the development of hypertension, heart attack, or other cardiovascular pathologies or the risk of death or disability that arises from these conditions. The best way to evaluate these risks is to follow large numbers of high-risk people over long periods of time to see if their caffeine use correlates in any way with the onset or exacerbation of heart conditions. Several studies have examined tens of thousands of men in their forties, fifties, and sixties—peak candidates for developing hypertension and other heart conditions—and they have demonstrated unequivocally that caffeine use and the level of caffeine intake does not contribute to the incidence or course of high blood pressure, congestive heart failure, or heart disease of any sort.

In addition, whatever small effects caffeine may have on blood pressure, these effects are probably altogether absent in habitual or regular caffeine users. Most studies have shown that all effects on blood pressure vanish within five days or less.

(continued on next page)

Interestingly, the consumption of hot beverages, even when they do not contain caffeine, has been shown to increase both diastolic and systolic blood pressure and heart rate temporarily, producing a significantly greater increase than that produced by caffeine ingestion alone. And even the act of raising a cup to your mouth repeatedly has been shown to increase blood pressure. Such effects as these may in part account for some reports attributing transient blood pressure effects to caffeine.[1]

Caffeine and Dehydration

Sports and fitness gurus in print and on the Internet almost universally advise athletes to beware of caffeine because of its dehydrating effects. Research has proven, though, that caffeine does not dehydrate people and has no diuretic effect at all on people who are exercising and almost no diuretic effect on people who are resting. This myth probably arose because drinking hot fluids like coffee does have a diuretic effect, although the caffeine in coffee does not contribute in any way to it.

You can also judge, even from the titles of recent books like *Caffeine: Warning It Can Be Hazardous to Your Health,* by Laura Deni, *Danger: Caffeine,* by Patra McSharry Sevastiades, and *Caffeine Blues: Wake Up to the Hidden Dangers of America's #1 Drug,* by Stephen Cherniske, that books share responsibility for worrying people unnecessarily about caffeine's effects.

Beyond the bad advice being offered to the public, there are two deeply rooted attitudes that discourage the use of caffeine: antidrug sentiment and the idea that you should feel bad about feeling good, notions that seem to be ingrained in many Americans. Drugs like heroin, cocaine, and even alcohol are looked on with disfavor, and caffeine, because it is a mood-altering drug that supports a physical dependence, is often lumped in with this unsavory crowd of dangerous substances. This creates a kind of guilt by association. And then there is the notion that anything that makes you feel good, especially if it's a "quick fix" or an "easy way out" or, even worse, if it's a drug, is immoral, a "crutch," and bound to bring about divine retribution in the form of bad physical or mental side effects. The idea is that if something is too easy, you're going to pay for it—to your sorrow—sooner or later.

The sneaking suspicion that you can't get something for nothing underlies a great deal of the skepticism about caffeine's benefits and worry over its possible dangers. As long ago as the beginning of the nineteenth century, Samuel Christian Hahnemann, the founder of homeopathic medicine, asserted that the extra energy provided by caffeine has to come from somewhere, and he argued that caffeine depletes us of our stores of vitality, making us energetic for a while but causing energies to plummet after we have metabolized it. There is, however, no scientific reason to accept this unfavorable interpretation of caffeine's actions. Making muscles and neurotransmitter systems work better doesn't necessarily involve draining our energy resources in any way. For example, the *British Journal of Medicine* reported that caffeine causes "rapid release of calcium ions in muscles, enhancing muscle contractions and making them more efficient."[2] No problems, immediate or remote, are caused by this process. Besides, the body gets its energy by burning food, and one of the ways caffeine increases energy is by increasing our metabolism and the rate at which we burn fat. There is really no problem with that either, especially in a country where most people overeat. As long as the caffeine you're using isn't interfering with your sleep, there is no intrinsic downside to using it for extra energy. And far from upsetting our balance, the way Hahnemann thought it did, caffeine is a great restorer of the balance of our neurotransmitter systems.

Such superstitious thinking fosters the pervasive belief that caffeine is harmful and should be avoided, and if it can't be avoided entirely, it should

Caffeine and the Military: Safely Sustaining Performance

The Committee on Military Nutrition Research of the Institute of Medicine's Food and Nutrition Board was asked by the U.S. Army Medical Research and Material Command to prepare a brief report to assist the Department of Defense in using the results of civilian caffeine research in military applications. The result was *Caffeine for the Sustainment of Mental Task Performance: Formulations for Military Operations* (2001), which concluded that caffeine is effective in maintaining cognitive performance and physical endurance and that its use under conditions of sustained military operations would not appear to pose any serious health risks, even when increased doses are indicated.[3]

be limited as much as possible. This belief creates a constant climate of guilt about using something that gives so much to our lives and poses so little risk. But there's no reason to feel guilty about using caffeine. On the contrary, caffeine gives us a safe, almost magical tool for releasing our hidden potential and achieving our goals.

Despite all the misgivings about caffeine, its attractions are so great that over 85 percent of Americans use substantial amounts on a regular basis, so it seems inevitable that it should have had a profound effect on people individually and as a society. In his 2001 article, "Java Man: How Caffeine Created the Modern World," Malcolm Gladwell, leading social commentator and critic for the *New Yorker* magazine, explains that caffeine is more than simply an alertness aid or recreational adjunct. Referencing our previous book *The World of Caffeine: The Science and Culture of the World's Most Popular Drug,* he points out that caffeine is responsible in part for the movement to sobriety in Europe.[4] In medieval times, peasants and tradesmen drank alcohol morning, noon, and night, and chronic alcohol intoxication was the rule, not the exception. The introduction of coffee, tea, and chocolate, the "great temperance drinks," each of which brought with it the benefits of caffeine, helped to replace incapacity with efficient self-regulation of time and energy. These benefits helped bring about the industrial revolution, and they are also driving us into the future of the information-intensive, fast-moving world of cybertechnology. Gladwell claims that caffeine actually produced the modern personality. As he says, "The modern personality is, in this sense, a synthetic creation: skillfully regulated and medicated and dosed with caffeine so that we can always be awake and alert and focused when we need to be."

Is this a good thing? Gladwell thinks it is. "On a bet, no doubt, we could walk away from caffeine if we had to," he comments. "But what would be the point? The lawyers wouldn't make their billable hours. The young doctors would fall behind in their training. The physicists might still be stuck out in the New Mexico desert. We'd set the world back a month." Caffeine, he says, is the best and most useful drug because it enables us to take control of our minds, bodies, and moods and enables us to become what we want to become. Gladwell concludes, "Give a man enough coffee and he's capable of anything." And that is a pretty fair summary of what caffeine does. By releasing our hidden potential, it helps us achieve whatever it is we want to achieve.

In Chapter 1, "Getting Started with Caffeine," we explain the principles of strategic caffeine use and give you the basic information you need to understand the dynamics of caffeine's effects, controlling dosage, and issues relating to side effects and physical dependence. We reveal the remarkable Yerkes-Dodson "less is more" curve of caffeine's activity and explain why a small to moderate dose of caffeine can do you more good than a larger one. We also explode a few major caffeine myths and provide an account of caffeine sources, including one you may not have considered: caffeine pills.

It's often said that the clock is an unmerciful, omnipotent despot and that no power on earth can alter its decrees. But as we will see in Chapter 2, "Caffeine and Your Body Clock," caffeine enables us to defy the clock by working longer and maintaining our alertness, speed, and diligence. The advantage we gain can help us succeed at work and even save our lives on the highway. When Edison invented the light bulb in 1879, he caused an upheaval in human sleep patterns. This invention, which brought about both late nights and the stretching of our natural 24-hour daily rhythm into a 25-hour cycle, is one of the major factors in shaping the modern world in a way that benefits from caffeine. Most people do not realize that their body actually operates on a twenty-five- rather than a twenty-four-hour schedule, and caffeine can enable us to fit in more comfortably with the demands of the clock.

In Chapter 3, "The Jet Lag Program," we teach you the secret of overcoming jet lag by using caffeine's power to help regulate your cycles of waking and sleeping and quickly and painlessly adjust to a new time zone without missing a beat.

In Chapter 4, "Sharpening Your Mind," we explore caffeine's astounding power to make us smarter. By improving abstract reasoning, reaction time, memory, and the ability to concentrate, caffeine enables us to exceed our normal levels of intellectual attainment and accomplish more in our work and our personal lives.

Caffeine has been used for hundreds of years by many great artists and scientists to boost their creativity. In Chapter 5, "Enhancing Your Creativity," we present an overview of the contribution that caffeine has made to the production of the arts and sciences and suggest ways it may help you to become more creative in your own life.

We all have moments when we feel stuck in a bad mood. In Chapter 6, "Getting in a Good Mood," we present caffeine's mood-enhancing powers, including the ability to make you more optimistic, clearheaded, upbeat, dynamic, forceful, relaxed, and friendly.

In Chapter 7, "Relaxation and Meditation," we explain the truth behind the coffee break: how caffeine, at the same time as it increases energy levels, also increases calmness, tranquility, and serenity and may even foster an improved ability to meditate.

The Greeks knew the wisdom of aspiring to a sharp mind in a fit body. In Chapter 8, "Improving Your Athletic Performance," we review the proven improvements caffeine can make in virtually every kind of athletic activity, including endurance sports, sprinting, and strength training. In Chapter 9, "How Much to Take and When to Take It to Boost Athletic Attainment," we show you how to use caffeine strategically to get more out of your workouts and even to become a winner in competitive events.

Carrying on the theme of physical fitness, in Chapter 10, "Weight Loss," we show you how you can use caffeine to curb your appetite and burn fat, so you can lose weight faster and keep it off.

Caffeine delivers a host of immediate benefits to your mind and body. However, that is not the whole story of its amazing powers. In Chapter 11, "An Elixir of Life? Caffeine and Staying Younger," we describe the ways caffeine actually works to keep us younger longer. And in Chapter 12, "Caffeine and Good Health," we explore the many ways caffeine can contribute to our health and help us fight disease, and we also fully consider the few caveats that attend its use.

The scientific and cultural sources of our information are extensively noted at the end of the book, where you will find references to many of the most important journal articles and books we consulted.

As you read this book, consider that you are getting to know an old friend better—an old friend who, it turns out, can do a great deal to help you lead a happier, healthier, more productive life.

1

Getting Started with Caffeine

CAFFEINE IS A VITAL PART of the daily lives of billions of people around the world, the overwhelming majority of whom use it every day. Most of us think of it as a drug that helps us stay awake and alert. But recent ground-breaking scientific studies confirm what many soldiers, weight lifters, long-distance runners, novelists, chess players, mathematicians, and mystics have known for years: that caffeine produces an astonishing, nearly endless variety of special beneficial effects for the mind, body, and spirit. It may seem incredible, but it's a fact that in healthy adults, caffeine improves mood, speeds reaction time, boosts memory, focuses attention, sharpens reasoning ability, increases muscular endurance and lung capacity, relieves pain, reduces appetite, and speeds fat burning. It also has an impressive array of actual and potential therapeutic applications, including relieving migraines and asthma, preventing Parkinson's disease and gallstones, and even helping people to function mentally and physically as if they were much younger than their chronological age. Best of all, it accomplishes these things safely, without increasing the likelihood of death or disease and with minimal unwanted side effects.

Neurotransmitters:
How Caffeine Does All Those Wonderful Things

Within minutes after you drink your coffee or tea, your bloodstream carries caffeine to all your organs and virtually every cell in your body. Because caffeine is fat soluble, it passes easily through all cell membranes. It is quickly and completely absorbed from the stomach and intestines into the bloodstream, which carries it to all the organs. Caffeine permeates the organs more rapidly than most other drugs, but not more rapidly than alcohol. And because there is no significant physiological barrier that hinders its passage through tissue, the concentrations attained by caffeine are virtually the same throughout the body and in blood, saliva, and even breast milk and semen.

Many of caffeine's powers depend on its power to pass into the central nervous system (CNS). To enter the CNS, caffeine must cross the blood-brain barrier, a defensive mechanism that protects the CNS from biological or chemical exposure by preventing viruses and other large (and most small) molecules from entering the brain or its surrounding fluid. Even when injected into the bloodstream, many drugs fail to penetrate this barrier, and others enter it much less rapidly than they enter other tissues. However, caffeine passes through the blood-brain barrier as if it did not exist.

All psychoactive drugs, including caffeine, achieve their effects by imitating or altering the release or uptake of neurotransmitters, the chemical messengers that direct how the neurons of the CNS interact with each other. Neurotransmitters are altered by drugs in a variety of ways, including increasing or decreasing their synthesis; inhibiting or enhancing their transport; modifying their storage or release or the way they are degraded; or directly mimicking their activity or, alternatively, blocking their action at the receptor site.

Caffeine achieves many of its effects by blocking the activity of adenosine, a neurotransmitter that affects almost every bodily system. Because one of the primary actions of adenosine is to make us tired or sleepy, caffeine, by blocking the uptake of adenosine, keeps us from feeling the effects of fatigue. But scientists have learned that largely as a consequence of its blockade of adenosine receptors, caffeine also has profound effects on most of the other major neurotransmitters, including dopamine, acetylcholine, serotonin, and, in high doses, norepinephrine. By affecting these other neurotransmitters, it is able to deliver a major boost to our capacities even when we are well rested, something that could not be explained by the inhibition of adenosine alone. By increasing the transmission of dopamine, caffeine improves our mood and may protect brain cells from age- and disease-related degeneration. By increasing the activity of acetylcholine, caffeine increases muscular activity and may also improve long-term memory. By raising and adjusting serotonin levels, caffeine relieves depression, makes us more relaxed, alert, and energetic, and relieves migraine headaches.

The full story of caffeine's intricate mechanism of action is only partially understood by pharmacologists and physicians. And although caffeine is probably the most widely studied drug in history, the effort to penetrate its mysteries continues today. Animal studies are problematic, because rats, mice, cats, dogs, and monkeys process caffeine very differently from each other and very differently from human beings. Human studies are sometimes bedeviled by the individual differences in quality of responses to caffeine and differences in the rate at which it is metabolized by different people and at different times. Finally, there is the unique problem that because almost everyone already uses caffeine, it is difficult to determine what they would be like without it. However, even if we don't know all the answers about how caffeine works, we can classify the two major effects caffeine has on our neurotransmitters:

• Caffeine alters the production or uptake of many neurotransmitters so as to increase mental and physical energy and enhance performance.

Caffeine's Benefits

Caffeine, by acting to modify and regulate a host of the body's neurotransmitters, enables us to tap into our hidden potential in four major areas:

Cognitive: Sharpens reasoning, memory, verbal fluency, concentration, and decision making and heightens sensuous perception

Affective: Enhances moods, increases relaxation, relieves boredom, and boosts self-confidence

Physical: Improves speed, endurance, energy output, strength, and reaction time and increases thermogenesis, that is, fat burning and metabolic rate

Therapeutic: Protects body cells and especially brain cells from some kinds of long-term damage and delivers many other specific therapeutic benefits, including pain relief and protection from the pulmonary complications of smoking and the damage from strokes

• Caffeine regulates the balance of many neurotransmitters in ways that enhance moods, kill pain, suppress appetite, and even protect brain cells from damage and disease.

How Caffeine Affects Different People

You don't have to know every scientific detail of how caffeine does what it does in order to enjoy its benefits. What is necessary is to learn how to customize your use of caffeine to implement the scientific strategies for achieving these benefits in your own life.

It is vital to understand, for example, that in the language of science, caffeine's effects are "task and situation specific."[1] That is, the nature and extent of caffeine's benefits are different in different areas. For example, caffeine helps increase your ability to concentrate on two things at once, such as your ability to follow the story line of a movie on TV while taking a phone call, but has little effect on your ability to concentrate in the face of distractions, like construction noise outside your window. Furthermore, different doses of caffeine are required to achieve different kinds of benefits. For example, 100 mg of caffeine might be the right amount to enhance your mood, 200 mg may be a perfect dose to help you solve computer problems or reduce your appetite, and you might require 300 to 400 mg to achieve the maximum improvement in your cycling time. To estimate how much caffeine you are getting, see the table of typical caffeine values.

What Is a Cup?

Conventionally, a cup of coffee is said to contain about 100 mg of caffeine. But this value, approximately correct for a 6 ounce cup of instant coffee, is much lower than a typical cup of filter drip, which has about 150 mg in a 6 ounce cup. And remember that most cups are 8 or 10 ounces or even more.

For simplicity, in this book, a cup of coffee will be considered to contain about 150 mg, and we will frequently give our instructions in terms of cups of coffee. A roughly equivalent amount of caffeine is found in three to four cups of black tea or four 12 ounce cans of caffeinated soda.

Typical Caffeine Values

6 oz. cup of instant coffee	100 mg
6 oz. cup of filter drip coffee	150 mg
8 oz. cup of filter drip coffee	200 mg
Vivarin tablet	200 mg
12 oz. can of Coca-Cola, Pepsi, Dr Pepper, and other caffeinated soft drinks	c. 40 mg
6 oz. cup of green tea	15 mg
6 oz. cup of black tea	50 mg
6 oz. cup of hot chocolate	10 mg
Hershey's milk chocolate bar (1.58 oz.)	12 mg
Hershey's dark chocolate bar (1.3 oz.)	36 mg
Häagen Dazs coffee ice cream (8 oz.)	64 mg

Another complicating factor is that people demonstrate a wide range of sensitivities to caffeine. Some people can detect the stimulating power of 1.8 mg of caffeine. Others can't tell when they've been given 180 mg of caffeine. That means that some people can detect the caffeine in an eyedropper full of coffee, and others can't feel a buzz from even a full cup. In addition, individual sensitivities to caffeine vary with your state of health, whether you're an introvert or an extrovert, whether you're well rested or fatigued, and several other factors. The effects of caffeine are also proportional to your body weight, which means that, all other things being equal, a 100 pound person will have twice the exposure to any given dose of caffeine as a 200 pound person. Further, people metabolize caffeine at enormously different rates. This means that, for example, an identical dose of caffeine will maintain a given level of activity in one person's body for 3 hours, while in another person's body, it will still be going strong after 6 hours. Also, the effects of caffeine are conditioned by the foods and other drugs you are taking. Taking oral contraceptives and certain antibiotics, smoking cigarettes, and even drinking grapefruit juice or eating charbroiled meats or some vegetables will alter the way it is metabolized by your body. (See Appendix B.)

Caffeine's effects are complicated by the fact that they generally exhibit what scientists call a biphasic curve of activity. This means that the graph of most of caffeine's effects can be charted as an inverted U. Consuming a little caffeine has a small effect, consuming more has a greater effect, but con-

Everyone Is an Individual When It Comes to Using Caffeine

The dosage of caffeine that is right for you will be determined by the following factors:

- Your individual sensitivity to caffeine (determined by genetics, personality type, state of health, and other factors)
- The rate at which you metabolize caffeine
- The benefit you are trying to achieve from caffeine

suming still more has a smaller effect again. But what is "a little caffeine"? That depends on your individual sensitivity to caffeine at any given time. If you have an average sensitivity to caffeine, 200 mg, or the amount in about an 8 ounce cup of filter drip coffee, is a small to moderate dose for you. However, if you are unusually sensitive to caffeine, 200 mg may be a fairly hefty dose. It's impossible to say what any given amount of caffeine will do to any person, or whether more or less caffeine will increase or decrease the effect of caffeine on that person without first determining the person's individual caffeine sensitivity level. Let's say that two people are each drinking a cup and a half of filter drip coffee (containing about 200 mg of caffeine). If the amount is increased to two cups of coffee (or about 300 mg), will that increase or decrease caffeine's effects on them? It depends. If one of them has average sensitivity, increasing the dose will increase the effects. If the other has high sensitivity, increasing the dose will tend to reduce the effects.

Psychologists explain these "up then down" dynamics by referring to the Yerkes-Dodson curve of caffeine activity. The theory is "that there is an optimum level of arousal for efficient performance."[2] Other scientists explain the "up then down" dynamics by theorizing that higher doses of caffeine have additional effects on the body that suppress performance. The important point to remember is that as you increase your dose, the positive effects of caffeine increase until you reach a certain level, at which time these effects begin to reverse themselves.

Finally, because caffeine can cause side effects, you must become aware of what, if any, undesirable effects caffeine has on you and what you have to do to minimize them. For example, many people think that if they use

Where Do You Stand on the Dosage Curve?

Let's compare two people's responses to different dosages of caffeine in order to understand the variable dynamics. Let's say that both Sally and John are taking 200 mg of caffeine. What will happen if each increases the dosage to 300 mg?

Sally is very sensitive to caffeine because of genetic factors and because she is an introvert. She is feeling well today. John is less sensitive to caffeine because he is an extrovert. He is very tired and is coming down with a cold. If Sally increases her caffeine dose from 200 mg to 300 mg, the curve of caffeine's benefits—that is, the level of caffeine's effects on her performance—goes down. If John increases his dose from 200 mg to 300 mg, the curve of benefits goes up. (More details on this "up then down" curve of caffeine activity are found in Chapter 4.)

caffeine during the day, it will keep them up at night. The truth is that each person has a caffeine cutoff point, which could be anything from 10 A.M. to midnight, after which time caffeine will interfere with sleep, but not if it is taken earlier. (See Chapter 2.) A very small number of people may be so sensitive in undesirable ways to caffeine—for instance, it makes them edgy—that they should avoid it entirely. Others only *think* that they must avoid caffeine; in fact, they should simply reduce their dose in order to enjoy its benefits and be comfortable taking it.

To get the most out of this book, you will have to do a little experimenting to find out just what caffeine does for you and to you. You could try to do this haphazardly by experimenting with different amounts of caffeine in different situations. But if you want more precise answers, we offer self-tests. Caffeine pills can be very helpful in taking these tests, because they deliver an exact dose of caffeine all at once, making the effects easier to evaluate. Of course, you can accomplish a similar result with coffee or any other caffeine source, provided you consume a standardized preparation and do so promptly at the time required for the test. Because of the complexities of caffeine's effects and the numbers of variables involved, it is worthwhile to take these tests if you want to get the most out of using caffeine.

One word of caution: Caffeine isn't for everyone. A minority of people become agitated, experience palpitations, or can't sleep well if they consume even a small amount of caffeine. And although caffeine is remarkably safe for healthy adults and long-term studies of tens of thousands of people have proven that it does not contribute to cardiovascular disease, cancer, or mortality from any cause, you should definitely consult your doctor before undertaking the programs described in this book if you are being treated for any medical condition. None of the advice or information in this book is intended for children.

Dosing: When to Use It and How Much to Use

Because 100 mg, the amount in half a caffeine tablet or about the amount in a 4 ounce cup of filter drip coffee, is enough caffeine to produce sustained benefits in mood and cognition in most people, we regard 100 mg as the basic dose of caffeine, that is, the dose you can take when you are beginning to experiment with using caffeine to improve your mind and brighten your outlook on life. You will want to determine your personal

Driving Success with Caffeine

You're out on the highway, driving through the night and hoping to make it home by dawn. You're tired and groggy, and your faculties are at a low ebb. If you take the right dose of caffeine, your vigilance will increase, your reaction time will pick up, your visuospatial reasoning will sharpen, your ability to make fast choices will improve, your mood will be enhanced, and you will feel clear-headed, calm, and alert. Such improvements in performance levels can help get you where you want to go, safely and on time.

Driving requires a complex of skills, and in order to drive safely and reach your goal, you need to maximize your performance levels in all of these areas. Many of these skills are the same ones that we need to succeed at work and play. Just as caffeine can activate high performance levels on the road, it can help us uncover our hidden potentials in life, enabling us to sharpen our minds and boost our physical attainments in ways that can make the difference between falling short and successfully reaching our goals.

Think Small: The Caffeine Advantage Basic Dose of 100 mg

You don't have to use a large dose of caffeine in order to enjoy its benefits. In fact, taking too much of a good thing can even result in losing the benefits you get from lower doses. In addition, although caffeine has infrequent and few adverse side effects, most of them are experienced only with large doses. For these three reasons, when you start to experiment with caffeine, try 100 mg. Smaller doses still, in the range of 25 mg to 50 mg a day—what you'd get in two or three cups of green tea or 6 to 12 ounces of caffeinated soda—can provide many people with all the benefits of caffeine they desire.

pickup dose of caffeine—the amount it takes to provide you with significant mental and mood benefits when you are well rested, for example, when you first get up in the morning. If you find that you are comfortable taking 100 mg of caffeine when you are well rested, you may want to increase your dose to 150 mg or 200 mg. Most people find that 200 mg is a large enough individual dose to get all the mental and mood benefits they can from using caffeine when they are well rested. However, you can continue to increase your dose by 50 to 100 mg as long as you aren't experiencing any adverse effects, such as difficulty falling asleep. If you experience such effects, you know that you are taking too much caffeine and should reduce your dose to a comfortable level. Once you have found your comfortable personal pickup dose, you can experiment with repeating this dose two or even three times throughout the day, being careful not to take any after your caffeine cutoff point, the time after which caffeine use interferes with your sleep (more about this in Chapter 2).

More caffeine is usually required when you want to overcome fatigue or improve athletic performance or lose weight, so we recommend that you consider starting your experimenting in these areas at about 150 mg of caffeine, the amount in a 6 ounce cup of filter drip coffee, or 200 mg of caffeine, the amount in most caffeine tablets. Then you can apply the same procedure outlined above of increasing your dose by 50 to 100 mg until you find your own personal sweet spot: the amount of caffeine that maximizes benefits but is comfortable to take and produces no unwanted side effects.

The key recommendations prepared by the Institute of Medicine (IOM)

Daily Dose Guidelines

We recommend a total daily intake of no more than 500 mg to 600 mg, the amount of caffeine in three to four 6 ounce cups of filter drip coffee, divided into at least two doses of no more than 300 mg each. Especially if you are taking caffeine pills, which seem to deliver the most punch per milligram of caffeine, this amount is probably enough to achieve virtually any benefit from caffeine you are looking for.

More is okay—as long as it agrees with you. We all know people who drink six or even eight cups of coffee or more a day, and there is no reason to believe that even such large amounts of caffeine will cause any health problems in people in normal health. However, if you have trouble sleeping or experience an increase in tension, remember that higher doses of caffeine may have this effect in some people.

Remember that even very small doses of 25 mg to 50 mg a day can confer considerable benefits on sensitive people or those who have no tolerance to caffeine.

for use by the U.S. military state that 100 mg to 600 mg of caffeine can be effective in maintaining speed of reactions and visual and auditory vigilance, which in military operations could be a matter of life or death. The IOM states that 200 mg to 600 mg is effective in sustaining physical endurance. The Committee on Military Nutrition Research concluded that a delivery vehicle that provides caffeine in 100 mg increments is most appropriate for use in sustained operations. It also concluded that caffeine is safe and should be the compound of choice for counteracting cognitive deficits. Finally, the committee recommended that members of the military should be given an in-depth training program on the benefits, directions for use, and potential side effects of caffeine.[3]

Overall, moderation is the key to caffeine dosing:

- Low doses have sustained beneficial effects on mood.
- Low doses improve reaction time, attention span, logical reasoning, and memory.
- Moderate doses confer the maximum athletic benefit.

- Moderate doses reverse the decrements induced by fatigue and sleep deprivation.
- Low to moderate doses minimize the chance of any adverse side effects, including sleeplessness.
- Low to moderate doses avoid the risk of taking too much, which might reverse the benefits.

Two Dosing Strategies for the Two Different Ways Caffeine Works for You

Caffeine has two very different sorts of effects on our energies and abilities: When you're fatigued or bored, it restores your energy and attention to normal levels; when you're fresh and alert, it augments your abilities so that you can perform at higher levels than usual.

Although many controlled experiments have been done on caffeine's effects since the start of the twentieth century, until recently few researchers had thought to compare these two effects in a single study.[4] In one of the earlier studies comparing these effects, undertaken in 1994 and yielding results that were later confirmed by other research, it was determined that caffeine delivered profound benefits in both situations, but that its effect on most performance levels was generally even greater when people were impaired by fatigue or lack of sleep. For example, caffeine's effects on shortening reaction time are the same whether you are fatigued or well rested. However, in many other areas, "the enhancing effects of caffeine on performance are most pronounced when functions are impaired or suboptimal."[5] In fact, some researchers have asserted that although caffeine has selective effects that vary by task, the most important variable in the power of caffeine is the freshness or fatigue of the subject.

Once-a-Day Minimum Dosing Routine

If you can tolerate caffeine and are more concerned with its benefits than the pleasure of drinking coffee or tea, take a 100 mg tablet every morning. It will help your mood and memory—and maybe your other cognitive functions—all day long. It will also probably provide long-term benefits as an antioxidant, protect the brain against degeneration and stroke damage, and reduce your chances of contracting Parkinson's disease.

But there is another difference between what we can expect from caffeine when we are fatigued as opposed to when we are well rested: When you are fatigued, sleepy, or ill, you will need more caffeine to achieve the same benefits you received from a smaller dose taken when well rested. For example, when you get out of bed after a good night's sleep, even though you may at first feel groggy, 200 mg of caffeine will probably kick-start your day, heighten your powers, and get you rolling. In the late afternoon, when fatigue has set in, 200 mg may just about bring you up to par, but not actually increase your abilities to above-normal performance levels. If you want to increase your performance still more, you will probably require an additional dose of caffeine.

How Much Are You Getting? The Caffeine Conundrum

One of the bedeviling facts about caffeine is that it is very difficult to know how much you're actually using. A "cup" of coffee, which can be from 4 to 16 ounces, can contain anything from 75 mg of caffeine to 300 mg or 400 mg or even more, depending on how it is brewed and what sort of beans you are using. A similar uncertainty surrounds the question of how much caffeine is found in a cup of tea.

Sometimes, such as when you are training for or competing in an athletic event or implementing a program to prevent jet lag, you need to know how much you are taking. That's one reason caffeine pills or capsules can be a good idea. A single Vivarin pill, for example, contains 200 mg of caffeine, which is an optimal dose for maximizing many of the mental and physical benefits of caffeine, while keeping any unwanted side effects to a minimum.

Less conventional sources, such as caffeinated mints, caffeinated chewing gums, caffeinated vanilla ice cream, and caffeinated waters, are becoming increasingly available as the interest in caffeine grows. However, they frequently fail to reveal how much caffeine they contain, so there is no way even to estimate it. We suggest you avoid any products that simply say they contain caffeine, without providing an amount if you want precision in dosing. An exception is carbonated soft drinks, because it is easy to find out (see Appendix A) how much caffeine they contain. Most soft drinks contain about 40 mg in a 12 ounce serving, about a quarter to a third of what you get in a 6 ounce cup of filter drip coffee. Caffeine is a drug, although a healthy one, and if you are going to take it, you want to know how much you are taking.

Caffeine Dosing: Everything Is Relative

Whenever we specify a dose of caffeine, unless it is otherwise qualified, we are thinking of the typical dose required by a 150 pound person with average caffeine metabolism. To approximate what the equivalent dose would be for you, adjust the dose in proportion to your weight. For example, if you weigh 200 pounds, which is one-third more than 150 pounds, then you must increase the dose to about 250 mg in order to get the same effect. If you weigh 120 pounds, you would decrease the dose to about 150 mg.

Caffeine's effects are proportional to your body weight. This means that all other things being equal, the less you weigh, the more effect a given dose of caffeine will have on you, and the more you weigh, the less effect it will have on you. Caffeine doses are measured in milligrams, or 1/1,000s of a gram. Body weight is usually given in kilograms; 1 kilogram is equal to 2.2 pounds. One average cup of coffee has 150 mg of caffeine, which thus yields a relative dose of 2 mg per kilogram in a 150 pound person. The table provides the amounts that people of different weights would have to consume to achieve this same amount of caffeine in proportion to their body weight.

Amounts of Caffeine Equivalent to 150 mg for a 150 Pound Person

Body Weight	Dose Equivalent to 150 mg per 150 Pounds of Body Weight (mg of caffeine)	Equivalent Number of Ounces of Filter Drip Coffee
100 lbs. (45 kg)	100 mg	4 oz.
120 lbs. (54 kg)	120 mg	5 oz.
150 lbs. (67.5 kg)	150 mg	6 oz.
175 lbs. (79 kg)	175 mg	7 oz.
200 lbs. (90 kg)	200 mg	8 oz.
250 lbs. (112.5 kg)	250 mg	10 oz.
300 lbs. (135 kg)	300 mg	12 oz.

Timing Your Dose: When to Take Caffeine

Most studies demonstrate that blood levels of caffeine peak at about 60 minutes after ingestion, but findings vary between 30 minutes and 90 minutes. However, caffeine levels usually reach 75 percent of their maximum values after only 15 minutes.[6]

The mean half-life of a moderate dose of caffeine is about 3 to 4 hours, which means that in 3 to 4 hours, about half of the caffeine you took will have been eliminated from your bloodstream. Its strongest effects usually last about the same time. However, genetics, other drugs you are taking, even the foods you are eating, and many other factors determine the actual half-life in any person at any given time. Factors that slow the metabolism of caffeine and extend the amount of time during which it exerts its effects include drinking alcohol, taking oral contraceptives, being pregnant, obesity, or liver damage. Factors that speed up the metabolism of caffeine include smoking cigarettes. (For more about factors that affect caffeine metabolism, see Appendix B.)

When you take larger amounts of caffeine, an additional factor comes into play. Caffeine exhibits what is called dose-dependent pharmaco-dynamics. This means that the length of time it remains in your system will vary with the amount you take. This is not true for most drugs. Generally, drugs have a half-life with a fixed length, and after this interval of time, half of the drug will have been eliminated from your system.

In one study, participants were given different amounts of caffeine in proportion to their body weight. For example, a person weighing 150 pounds received 150 mg, 300 mg, or 600 mg of caffeine. The half-lives of the drug were found to vary radically with the dose. The half-life of the drug in the people receiving the lowest dose of caffeine averaged 4.7 hours, close to the average half-life of caffeine that is reported in most studies. However, the half-life of the group receiving twice as much caffeine was 5.4, and the half-life of the group receiving four times as much was 6.4 hours.

As your dose of caffeine increases, this factor can have a striking effect on how long caffeine will continue to exert its effects. Consider an example. Let's say that when 150 mg of caffeine is circulating in your bloodstream, you are able to increase your cycling speed by 10 percent. If you take 300 mg of caffeine right before a race, assuming you have an average caffeine metabolism, 150 mg will still be active in your system 4 hours later. The effects of caffeine will begin to wane after that. However, if you take 600 mg of caffeine, 150 mg will still be active in your system 13 hours later.

Side Effects: How Much Caffeine Is Too Much?

Although caffeine is remarkably safe for healthy adults and does not increase the likelihood of heart disease, cancer, or death from any cause, and small to medium doses relax you, too much caffeine can give you palpitations and cause insomnia and even anxiety and jitteriness. How much caffeine is too much? Whenever the amount of caffeine you are consuming makes you feel uncomfortable, you know you have taken too much. One of the interesting things about caffeine ingestion is that it tends to be self-limiting. That is, unlike dangerous psychoactive drugs such as heroin and cocaine, the usage level of which tends to increase without bound, the amount of caffeine people are inclined to consume is limited by the onset of unwanted side effects.

In order to minimize side effects and help you better manage your caffeine use, we suggest that you keep an accurate log of the amount you are consuming. At least during the early stages of your experimentation with caffeine, write down how much you take and when you take it.

How Do You Take Your Caffeine?

The primary source of caffeine in America is coffee, a tropical glossy-leafed evergreen shrub or bush belonging to the genus *Coffea.* The earliest known and cultivated species is *Coffea arabica,* "the coffee shrub of Arabia." This is the coffee that is grown in Latin America today and accounts for 75 percent of all coffee consumption worldwide. Because it makes the most flavor-rich drink, it is used exclusively in making gourmet coffees. Different varieties of arabica contain slightly different amounts of caffeine, but they average about 1.1 percent caffeine by weight. *Coffea robusta,* which

Time to Cut Down on Caffeine?

Consider reducing the amount of caffeine you take if you experience these symptoms:

> Insomnia
> Rapid heartbeat[7]
> Agitation
> Restlessness
> Dysphoria (bad moods)
> Anxiety

accounts for the remaining 25 percent of worldwide consumption, has twice the caffeine content by weight, averaging about 2.2 percent. *Coffea robusta* is more bitter and less subtle in taste and is used only in the cheapest blends. In giving the caffeine content of a cup of coffee, we assume that the coffee you will be drinking is made from arabica beans, and it probably will be. However, you should be alert to the fact that if you get slipped some coffee prepared from robusta beans, it will have *twice* the caffeine content of the same sized portion of the coffee you are used to drinking.

Sources other than coffee predominate in some parts of the world. In England and Asia, for example, tea, a single plant whose leaves are cured to become green, red, or black, is by far a greater source. Cacao prepared as a hot beverage is a major source of caffeine throughout South America. And for tens of millions of South Americans, maté, brewed from the leaves of a Brazilian holly tree, and guarana, brewed from the seeds of an Amazonian vine, are the main sources of caffeine. Tens of millions of Africans get most of their caffeine from chewing or steeping cola nuts. All over the world, caffeinated carbonated beverages constitute an additional major source of caffeine, one that is growing as a percentage of all caffeine consumed. Caffeine is also found in alertness aids like Vivarin and is commonly the active ingredient in so-called energy boosters sold in health food stores, frequently under an exotic name like "guarana powder." Finally, the FDA's National Center for Drugs and Biologics lists more than 1,000 over-the-counter brands with caffeine as an ingredient, including pain relievers, cold medications, appetite suppressants, and diuretics. It is also found in a number of prescription medications. (See Appendix A for tables of the caffeine content of different beverages and medicines.)

Chocolate contains two substances that can give you a boost: caffeine and theobromine, caffeine's chemical cousin. Theobromine's effects are very similar to caffeine's, but, milligram for milligram, theobromine is much weaker than caffeine. However, theobromine is found in much larger amounts in chocolate than caffeine. Although no one is certain, most scientists believe that the combined stimulant effect of caffeine and theobromine in chocolate is about twice that of the caffeine alone. Therefore, in evaluating the lift you will get from chocolate, you should approximately double the amount of the caffeine it contains. Except for dark chocolate, the amount of caffeine in most candy is relatively small.

Guarana and maté, common components of over-the-counter "natural" weight loss or energy-boosting preparations, are often touted as natural stimulants that offer an alternative to caffeine. However, the only active ingredient of guarana and maté supplements is caffeine itself. Typically, these products do not reveal how much caffeine they contain, so avoid them if you intend to use caffeine strategically.

Caffeinated soft drinks, such as Coca-Cola, are a major source of caffeine that many people forget about. Be aware that the 40 mg of caffeine in a 12 ounce soda is enough to give many people a significant boost, especially if they are not accustomed to drinking coffee or are naturally sensitive to caffeine.

Nontraditional sources of caffeine may grow in importance in the years ahead. An example of a promising caffeine product is caffeinated chewing gum. Under military field conditions, coffee and caffeinated soft drinks may be hard to find. That is why Stay Alert, a brand of caffeinated gum manufactured by a subsidiary of Wrigley Brothers, which contains 50 mg of caffeine per stick, was tested by Garry Kammimori, Ph.D., of the Walter Reed Army Institute of Research (WRAIR) in Silver Spring, Maryland.[8] He evaluated the effects of one, two, and four sticks of gum on vigilance tasks performed at all hours of the day and night by both rested and sleep-deprived subjects. Not surprisingly, he found that the gum effectively restored alertness and dramatically increased performance levels. Studies by the manufacturer show that 80 percent of the caffeine in the gum is absorbed in 5 minutes and that it confers a faster mental and physical boost than the same dose of caffeine consumed in a cup of coffee. The gum's advantages are obvious: It's portable, requires no fluids, and delivers caffeine in easily titratable—that is, finely graduated—doses.

Caffeine Pills

If you are primarily concerned with getting the benefits of caffeine, use pills. Coffee tastes great, and it may get you where you want to go, but the pills may be a much more efficient and effective way of reaching your goal.

Vivarin is the leading brand in the United States. There are many store brands, manufactured under the names of different pharmacy chains. These pills tout themselves as alertness aids, because increasing alertness—providing a "mental boost"—is the only claim sanctioned by the FDA. The FDA permits the pharmaceutical companies that make these pills to claim that they increase mental energy. But as we noted earlier, it won't allow them to state that caffeine can boost physical performance in any way, much less claim specific cognitive or mood benefits for caffeine. Perhaps because caffeine is a generic substance—that is, no one company owns the right to produce it—no single company has found it financially worthwhile to spend the tens of millions of dollars that would be necessary in order to secure official approval of caffeine's many benefits that research has already proven. There is a difference between conclusions that have been scientifically proven about a product and the claims that the government permits making on a product's behalf. In the case of caffeine, this difference is all important.

Many of the experiments that have been done to evaluate caffeine's effect on mood and cognition and other benefits have used coffee as the vehicle of caffeine delivery, and studies of long-term effects are invariably based on an evaluation of coffee consumption. The big news is that when caffeine is removed from the matrix of coffee and delivered, for example, in Vivarin or other caffeine pills, it has a far more powerful ability to improve athletic performance and may well be more powerful in its cognitive and mood-enhancing effects as well.

Caffeine pills are used by a very small proportion of people, mostly students, weight lifters, and truck drivers. Most of mainstream America has little experience with them. While most Americans will still prefer the pleasure of coffee, whether at home or in coffee shops, middle-aged and older people have the most to gain from pills, because caffeine can close the gaps in memory and reaction time between older and younger people and can give older people the energy and stamina to perform as they did when they were younger.

If pills have a stronger effect per milligram of caffeine, then we will use less caffeine when taking pills than when drinking coffee. Decreasing the doses of caffeine is a way of ensuring that we avoid even the unusual adverse side effects that caffeine can produce in some people. It is also true that coffee can upset your stomach by increasing acid production, and coffee made in an infusion pot, or French press, that is, unfiltered coffee, can even raise your cholesterol and increase your chances of developing cardiovascular problems. Therefore, pure caffeine delivers the most punch with the lowest chance of any adverse consequences from its use.

Why don't more people know about the extra benefits of caffeine pills? People tend to use pills when very fatigued—students and truck drivers who are pulling all-nighters are regular consumers of caffeine pills—but very few people try them under normal circumstances. Relatively few people have the experience of seeing what the pills can do when they are well rested. In addition, people tend to use caffeine pills episodically, for emergency situations. Therefore, they never get to experience the sustained advantages that pills can provide over coffee.

Most caffeine pills, such as Vivarin, come in doses of 200 mg, although you can sometimes find a drugstore brand with a dose of 100 mg. You may want to buy and use a pill splitter, which you can find at any pharmacy, so you can try a starting dose of 100 mg and titrate, or graduate, your dose in increments of 50 mg or 100 mg. With a pill splitter, you can prepare 50 mg and 100 mg half-tablets of the drug for yourself.

Dependence, Tolerance, and Withdrawal

When certain drugs are used regularly, the body adapts to their presence by requiring more and more to achieve the same effects. This increasing resistance is called a "tolerance." Drugs that create a tolerance generally exhibit a physical dependence, which means that a person who stops using them abruptly will experience withdrawal symptoms.

Users of dangerous drugs like heroin, barbiturates, and amphetamines develop extremely large tolerances, a process that forces them to take ever

How to Benefit from Decaf

If you're concerned with getting the maximum benefits from caffeine, maybe you should try decaf. Some scientists think that the benefits of caffeine to exercise—and perhaps to mood and cognition as well—are partially dampened by a chemical in coffee called chlorogenic acid. Decaffeination removes not only caffeine but also much of the chlorogenic acid. Therefore, if you want to keep enjoying the pleasurable experience of drinking coffee and yet would like to get the biggest boost in performance from caffeine, try using caffeine pills and substituting a really good decaf for your regular coffee.

increasing amounts in order to maintain the same level of effect. In contrast with the open-ended tolerance of these drugs, only limited tolerance develops to many of caffeine's effects, and no tolerance at all seems to develop to others. A person who uses heroin every day for a year may require ten times his initial dose at the end of that year to achieve the same high as he did at the beginning. A person who uses caffeine every day will develop some resistance to some of caffeine's effects—for example, he will require a bit more caffeine to help keep him awake when he is sleepy—but not to others.

Leading caffeine researcher Terry Graham of the University of Guelf explains that some tissues adapt to long-term exposure to caffeine by increasing the number of adenosine receptors, thus creating a tolerance to its effects. However, other tissues do not appear to adapt in any way even to repeated and sustained exposure.[9] Graham found that tolerance does not develop to caffeine's ergogenic, or energy-producing, actions. In other words, all other things being equal, 300 mg of caffeine will give the same boost to an athlete who has never tried caffeine and to one who drinks a pot of coffee every day, and what's more, it will continue to deliver the same boost indefinitely. An example of this lack of tolerance is a scientific study that "found no relationship between caffeine habits and degree of performance response in 1500m runners."[10] In other words, when a person takes a given dose of caffeine, it will tend to improve his running time. And the amount of improvement won't vary if he has never used caffeine before or if he is a heavy daily consumer of the drug.

Other areas in which tolerance does not seem to develop include benefits to memory, reasoning, reaction time, attention span, and mood. The military in its report *Caffeine for the Sustainment of Mental Task Performance* recommends that under demanding conditions, the same doses should be administered to regular and first-time caffeine users, since there is no general agreement about the extent to which a tolerance develops to caffeine's cognitive effects. Whether you will develop a limited tolerance for any given effect of caffeine by using caffeine every day is something we explore throughout the book.

However, although a tolerance doesn't develop to many of caffeine's effects, there is no denying that caffeine supports a physical dependence. When we use any substance that supports a physical dependence regularly and then suddenly discontinue its use, we can experience withdrawal symptoms. The withdrawal properties of caffeine have been well recognized for over a century. In 1893, a researcher published a warning that people who terminated their caffeine use abruptly were at risk of developing a severe headache.[11] We now know that headaches are the most common symptom associated with quitting caffeine too quickly. Other symptoms can include sleepiness, irritability, or even flulike symptoms such as muscle aches and nausea. The nineteenth-century author went on to recommend a regimen similar to the one favored by physicians today: reducing caffeine consumption gradually over a week or more. The ways of successfully "getting off" caffeine and minimizing your problems as you do so are described in more detail in Chapter 2.

The seriousness of the physical and mental discomforts we experience when we suddenly stop using caffeine varies considerably from person to person, depending on genetic constitution and the level of caffeine use. In general, the more caffeine you are taking, the stronger will be your physical dependence and the worse your withdrawal symptoms if you suddenly stop using caffeine. Levels as low as 100 mg a day have been found to support a physical dependence. This means that if you are drinking as little as one cup of coffee a day, you might feel slightly uncomfortable if you quit drinking coffee abruptly and cut out all other sources of caffeine as well.

Scientists disagree about how bad caffeine withdrawal is. Dr. Peter B. Dews, professor of pharmacology at Harvard University School of Medicine, and many other leading caffeine researchers maintain that few withdrawal effects are seen in people who don't know that they are being withdrawn from caffeine. In other words, they say that if you don't expect to feel bad when you stop using caffeine, you probably won't. On average, however, at least 30 percent of people who suddenly stop caffeine use will experience headaches, and a lower percentage will experience the other symptoms. (See the accompanying box for a list of common withdrawal symptoms.)

In addition to a physical dependence, some researchers say that caffeine, because it functions as a reinforcer—that is, people enjoy its effects and want to take it again and again—can create a psychological dependence in a few people. When this psychological dependence combines with a physical dependence to interfere with a person's life, the resulting syndrome is called "caffeinism," a recognized psychiatric condition whose sufferers continue to use excessive amounts of caffeine even though it is adversely affect-

Symptoms of Caffeine Withdrawal

The symptoms of caffeine withdrawal are, in decreasing order of frequency:

> Headaches
> Fatigue
> Sleepiness, drowsiness
> Bad moods
> Difficulty concentrating
> Difficulty working
> Depression
> Anxiety
> Irritability
> Flulike symptoms (nausea, muscle aches,
> hot-cold spells, runny nose)

ing them in some way. For example, a person who persists in taking caffeine late in the day, even though it is interfering with a good night's sleep, might be suffering from caffeinism. Similarly, a person who takes excessive doses of caffeine in an effort to intensify the mood and physical benefits of the drug (even though, as we will see, there is a ceiling to caffeine's benefits that makes this effort futile) might also be diagnosed with caffeinism. This syndrome is uncommon, but, when it occurs, it is a clear sign that the person afflicted should markedly reduce or even eliminate caffeine intake, and seek professional counseling if necessary. As Dr. Roland R. Griffiths, professor of psychiatry and behavioral pharmacology at Johns Hopkins University School of Medicine, one of the world's leading caffeine researchers, wrote to us, "Use caffeine; don't let caffeine use you."

Because caffeine can support a physical and psychological dependence, it is fair to ask if it is addictive. Almost all psychiatrists and pharmacologists today agree that it is not. A drug is addictive only if it causes serious damage to and disruption of people's lives. Drugs like heroin, cocaine, and amphetamines clearly fall into this category. However, no one has ever lost a job, spouse, or house from using too much caffeine.

Some researchers have crusaded against caffeine by advancing the the-

Bug Off with Caffeine!

Caffeine evolved to protect the plants that produce it from insects and microorganisms. Because caffeine is nontoxic to people, it is being used today as the basis for several insecticides. Its power as an insecticide is the reason some gardeners put coffee grounds in rings around their plants. U.S. Department of Agriculture scientists in Hawaii are trying to formulate a clean, environmentally safe pest killer that would replace commercial slug and snail repellants containing chemicals such as metadehyde, banned in crops consumed by people in many countries. They have found that a .01 percent solution of caffeine is an extremely effective slug and snail repellant.

Because of its origin, caffeine, applied locally, has the power to kill some infections, which confirms an ancient Chinese belief in the curative powers of tea for skin ulcerations.

ory that caffeine's benefits are illusory. Because a period of abstinence from caffeine initiates withdrawal symptoms, the supposed "improvements" in performance and mood that we get from taking caffeine are simply the result of feeding our "caffeine jones," or caffeine habit, so that we feel normal and up to par again. Study after study has conclusively demonstrated that this theory is not true. The beneficial effects of caffeine on reasoning, memory, reaction time, athletic performance, and mood cannot be ascribed to alleviating the deficits caused by caffeine withdrawal.[12] The reason is that all of these benefits have been observed in people who do not regularly use caffeine, and therefore cannot be withdrawing from it, and in people who regularly use caffeine but have not been deprived of it prior to the initiation of testing. And although caffeine abstinence can make you tired or depressed, it does not cause any detrimental effects on athletic, mental, or psychomotor performance, so there are no "withdrawal-related deficits" to reduce.[13]

The long and the short of it is that the use of caffeine really does sharpen your mind, boost your athletic performance, and enhance your mood—whether or not you have ever consumed it before and whether or not you have gone without it for any length of time.

2

Caffeine and Your Body Clock

H OW MANY TIMES have you heard someone say, "I just wish there were more hours in the day!" By helping us to control our body clock and restoring our performance to normal levels when we should otherwise have been impaired by fatigue, caffeine can help us overcome an afternoon slump, drive more safely, and even work throughout the night, effectively giving us the extra time we need to accomplish what needs to be done.

As we mentioned in Chapter 1, scientific studies prove that caffeine confers two very different sorts of benefits on abilities and performance levels:

• When given to well-rested people at the peak of natural energy and alertness, caffeine improves cognitive performance, enhances mood, and increases athletic capacity to above-normal levels.

• When given to people who are sleep deprived or fatigued, caffeine acts specifically to restore levels of energy, alertness, reaction time, and mental clarity to their normal waking levels.

To put it simply, caffeine has an amazing ability to make up for the deficits caused by fatigue, and this power is distinct from its ability to improve the performance of well-rested people. So although caffeine helps you whether you're fatigued or well rested, its power to relieve the deficits caused by a sleepless night is even more pronounced and well recognized by scientists than is its power to improve the performance of well-rested people.[1]

How much of a problem is fatigue at the workplace? As it turns out, it isn't confined to people working overtime or on swing shifts. Even in the middle of the day, when people feel as if they are alert, studies demonstrate that "only about 1 in 10 were actually at peak alertness."[2] Multiple Sleep Latency Test (MSLT) scores reveal that nearly 20 percent of those who said they were wide awake were actually so impaired by sleepiness that they posed a serious threat to their own or others' safety. When people are so exhausted that they have become conscious of being fatigued, the impairments they experience and the need to find some way of overcoming them are even greater.

Caffeine works specifically to counter the losses in performance levels occasioned by exhaustion and lack of sleep. When people become tired, alertness, diligence, reaction time, reasoning ability, and memory are severely impaired. In addition, mood suffers; we tend to become depressed, and our overall energy levels decline. Caffeine improves performance levels in each of these areas, bringing them back to normal or close to normal levels, and enables us to function as if we had enjoyed a full night's sleep, even if we might have gone the entire night without so much as closing our eyes. The opposite of a sleeping powder, caffeine is like a magic powder that we sprinkle in our eyes to wake up. In this chapter, we focus on caffeine's ability to take control of the body's diurnal clock, its built-in twenty-four-hour timekeeper, and to combat fatigue and reverse its effects. We shall see how caffeine, strategically used, can help people who must work late into the night or on swing shifts to continue working and performing at normal, rested levels. And because caffeine not only combats the effects of sleeplessness but can be its cause, we discuss how to manage your caffeine use so you don't spoil a good night's sleep.

Overcoming Fatigue

As willing and even eager as we might be to meet the demands of our busy schedules, biological destiny, in the form of our body clock, often gets in the way. According to pioneering sleep researcher William Dement, M.D., we are each subject to a twenty-four-hour cycle of arousal, or energy and alertness levels. These levels rise or fall as a function of our sleep debt, that is, how much sleep we've had or failed to have had recently, and of what is called our clock-dependent alerting, an energy factor that changes with the time of day.[3] This means that our biological clock, based on our sleep load and the time of day, tells us when to wake up and be active and when to rest and go to sleep. The problem is that our schedules and the strictures of our biological clocks are not always well synchronized.

For example, as you drive half the night to make it home from a weekend vacation after getting a call summoning you to attend an unanticipated early morning meeting with your biggest client, your biological clock will be telling you it's time to close your eyes. Your alertness, reaction time, and concentration will begin to suffer serious degradation. By the time you arrive—if you can make it without an accident—you are likely to be lethargic and "punchy" and certainly in no shape to negotiate a major deal.

We don't necessarily have to be the victim of our biology, however. Caffeine has the power to help us take charge of our biological clocks, enabling us to feel refreshed and well rested and to drive an automobile or transact demanding business when our body's timekeeper would otherwise be saying we should be fast asleep. As we shall see, a strategy combining a 15-minute nap with an effective dose of caffeine restores alertness and performance to peak daytime levels for hours.

Caffeine effectively "makes time" by extending the time during which productive work is possible. It does this in three ways:

• Caffeine sharpens specific abilities, including alertness, reasoning, verbal fluency, memory, reaction time, and attention span—the very abilities that are seriously impaired when we become tired or sleepy.

• Caffeine increases muscular endurance and decreases fatigue, increasing the time during which we can do physical work before becoming exhausted.

Effects of Fatigue and Sleep Deprivation Reversed by Caffeine

• Decreased alertness
• Shortened attention span
• Slowed reaction time
• Decreased mental clarity, increased mental confusion
• Depression, lassitude
• Low energy levels

America Wakes Up to Caffeine's Benefits for Fatigued People

In 1912, Harry Hollingworth, a young psychology professor at Columbia University, and his wife and research assistant, Leta, designed and performed the first double-blind experiments on the effect of caffeine on human performance. His conclusions—that caffeine facilitates performance in fatigued people and that daily doses of less than 700 mg will not disturb sleep for most people—are still cited today.

• Caffeine reverses the depression and dissipates the boredom that are caused by fatigue or prolonged sleep deprivation, removing two of the factors that generally impair the performance of tired people.

Using caffeine to dissipate grogginess did not begin with the Starbucks revolution in the 1990s, although coffeehouses have made drinking coffee a far more enjoyable experience than in the past. A World War II retiree from the U.S. Navy told us, "The submarine service ran on two things: diesel oil and joe." An old veteran of the merchant marine recalled how, at the start of every watch, sailors would call out, "Give me a cup of joe, and make it blond and sweet!" and swore they couldn't function without it. What was true fifty years ago is truer today. In its efforts to keep going at full steam around the clock, the military entertains a great thirst for caffeine.

"Modern warfare pushes the limits of human performance," says Colonel David Penetar, Ph.D., of the U.S. Army Research Institute of Environmental Medicine in Natick, Massachusetts. The action on the field of battle no longer stops at sundown. New instrumentation allows wars to be fought 24 hours a day. To help meet rigorous scheduling demands, the role of caffeine in countering the decrements in performance caused by sleep disruption, especially when coupled with heavy physical demands that impair critical decision making and other cognitive skills, was examined at a conference of the National Academy of Sciences (NAS) in 1999. Speakers addressed the Committee on Military Nutrition Research of the NAS Food and Nutrition Board, which will advise the U.S. Department of

Defense about applying the committee's research findings. Presenters at the conference concluded that caffeine is the best agent available to counteract fatigue in battlefield conditions and that "caffeine studies also hold implications for civilian life, for physicians on call, pilots, truckers, rescue workers, and perhaps even for the sleep-deprived general public."[4]

There is no more dramatic proof of caffeine's ability to fight the body's diurnal clock than the U.S. Navy studies of young servicemen. Along with the army, the navy recognizes that alertness can be a matter of life and death. For this reason, it conducted studies on soldiers who were sleep deprived for 72 hours. Caffeine was found to be the best all-around agent for restoring freshness, alertness, and energy to normal levels. Even at the large doses the scientists used in their controlled experiments, there were few complaints about unwanted side effects. The upshot of the naval study was that for critically sleep-deprived persons, a 15-minute nap combined with a dose of caffeine yields alertness and performance on the same level as when well rested during the day.

A series of important caffeine and sleep deprivation studies have been conducted at the Walter Reed Army Institute of Research (WRAIR) in Silver Spring, Maryland. In one study, scientists dosed subjects who had been without sleep for 48 hours with 150 mg, 300 mg, or 600 mg of caffeine (the amount you'd get from, respectively, one, two, or four cups of filter drip coffee). Improvements were observed at all dosage levels. The 600 mg dose improved cognitive performance, alertness, and self-assessments of mood as much as a 20 mg dose of amphetamine did, and caffeine, of course, caused fewer side effects. The benefits were fairly sustained. "The findings suggest," concluded Mary Kautz, Ph.D., the lead researcher, "that caffeine may help postpone sleep up to 12 hours."[5]

Another WRAIR study, this one conducted at the Department of Behavioral Biology in 1992, tested fifty healthy adult men who had gone

Revving Up Your Metabolism

When you're tired and sleepy, your metabolic rate drops. Recent studies have shown that caffeine increases the metabolic rates of sleep-deprived subjects to normal levels, which means it overcomes lethargy and restores you to the levels of well-rested people.[6]

without sleep for two days with varying doses of caffeine, examining the effects of caffeine on mood, as well as alertness and mental clarity.[7] The study found that relatively high doses of caffeine (600 mg, or the amount in about four cups of filter drip coffee) reversed the effects of sleep deprivation on both alertness and mood, restoring objective and subjective scores on many tests to near rested values and achieved these benefits with no increase in self-ratings of side effects. In sleep-deprived people, caffeine reversed changes in the Stanford Sleepiness Scale (SSS), the Visual Analog Scales (VAS), and tests of vigor, fatigue, and confusion. Although peak effects began to wane after about 4 hours, this high dose of caffeine produced significant alerting and long-lasting beneficial mood effects in the sleep deprived that were still apparent after 48 hours. While earlier studies had established the benefits of low doses of caffeine in conditions of shorter-term sleep deprivation, this study proved that higher doses of caffeine actually reverse the effects of prolonged sleep deprivation, producing significant alerting and long-lasting beneficial mood effects in individuals deprived of sleep for 48 hours.

A major civilian study confirmed how well larger doses of caffeine work to help critically sleep-deprived people keep awake and alert without unwanted side effects. This study found that after 600 mg of caffeine, the maximum ability for delaying sleep peaked at about 4.5 hours. Interestingly, it found that the peak of most of caffeine's important mood effects— higher scores in the "vigor" measure and decreasing "fatigue and confusion"—lasted only 2 hours. The best news was that even the large 600 mg dose did not increase ratings of heart pounding, headaches, perspiration, or upset stomach.[8]

The Cure for "Afternoon Slump"

It happens to most people almost every day: You feel fine, but after eating lunch, you go into a slump that makes you feel as if you should be going to bed instead of back to work. It's not just your imagination or the fact that your job isn't as interesting as it used to be. What you may not know is that scientists have documented this syndrome, and recent studies have shown that certain decrements in performance do follow from eating a meal and are independent of time of day. For example, several studies have found that perceptual sensitivity,[9] reaction time, and scores on tasks requiring thinking and paying attention declined after lunch,[10] while there was no change in the performance of subjects who hadn't eaten.

Why does this slump occur? Scientists have speculated that an increase in blood glucose, or a release of gastrointestinal hormones with psychoactive effects, such as insulin, or even a surge in the level of the neurotransmitters cortisol or serotonin is the culprit. No one really knows the answer, but the truth is that eating causes so many changes in the body that it is unlikely that the slump can be explained by any single mechanism. The unfortunate fact is, however, that the afternoon slump, and the inefficiency and the safety hazards it creates, is real. The good news is that although not much is known about the interactions of caffeine and food intake, scientific studies prove that not only can caffeine help you combat the afternoon slump, but, used correctly, it can eliminate its effects entirely.

In one major study of the afternoon slump, twenty-four male and female university students were assessed four times throughout daytime or night shift work. They were asked to perform what scientists call the detection of targets in a cognitive vigilance task. The test used was the Bakan vigilance test, which moves quickly, involves memory, and allows experimenters to measure errors of omission, false alarms, and speed of response. A sequence of digits was presented to the students on monitors at the rate of 100 digits per minute. They were asked to press a button as quickly as they could when recognizing sequences of three consecutive odd or three consecutive even numbers. The results were impressive. The students scored an average of over two-thirds correct hits before eating but managed to get only about half right after lunch.[11]

This same study found that the extent of this impairment in perceptual sensitivity seems to depend in part on whether you are gregarious and easygoing or quiet and intense. People with a low level of anxiety and high extroversion scores on the Eysenck Personality Inventory, so-called stable extroverts, show a significantly greater decline in performance after lunch. Fortunately, these are the same people who tend to benefit the most from using caffeine. (See Chapter 4 for a fuller discussion of personality factors.)

Do you ever notice that after eating your midday meal, your mind has a tendency to wander? Because the tasks that suffer the greatest declines in performance after lunch are those that require sustained attention, studies have been undertaken to see if caffeine can help people to reverse these effects and stay focused throughout the afternoon. One such study evaluated thirty-two university students who were given caffeine tablets equivalent to 3 mg per kilogram of body weight (for a 150 pound man, this is about as much caffeine as in one and a third cups of filter drip coffee). When given the Bakan vigilance test without caffeine, the subjects suffered declines in speed and accuracy after eating. Caffeine improved performance before and after lunch, but produced a much greater improvement after lunch—in the words of the journal article, "totally removing the postlunch dip."[12] On a more difficult test, subjects were shown a letter from the alphabet in a number of different orientations and told to determine as fast as possible whether it was a regular or a mirror-image representation. Again, "caffeine completely removed the postlunch impairment" observed in people who had not taken it.

Surprisingly, breakfast and lunch seem to produce a different pattern of effects on performance, and caffeine seems to interact differently with the declines in performance experienced in each case. The result is that although caffeine can completely eliminate the slump that follows eating lunch, it has no effect on the milder slump experienced after breakfast. As we have seen, lunch decreases alertness and impairs performance on tests requiring sustained attention, semantic processing, and logical reasoning. Breakfast doesn't affect alertness or attention span but does impair logical reasoning. Although caffeine was extremely potent in overcoming the postlunch declines, there were no interactions observed between caffeine and the way people felt after breakfast.[13]

The afternoon slump can also put you in a bad mood. Caffeine delivers relief from this problem as well. After lunch, people who have taken caffeine feel significantly more content, happier, and more interested in their work. And when they have a reasonably substantial breakfast—meaning more than a piece of toast or glass of juice—they feel more tranquil, less tense, and calmer if they have caffeine with the meal.[14] An increase in tension is observed when you take caffeine and skip breakfast, yet another reason not to miss this most important meal of the day.

Evening meals produce much less of a slump and fewer changes in cognitive performance, mood, and behavior than either breakfast or lunch. So although caffeine has been shown to create improvements in all of these areas, you don't really need it after dinner to combat the special form of fatigue that usually follows the earlier meals of the day.[15] This is probably a good thing because many people find that caffeine after dinner interferes with falling or staying asleep.

Safer Driving Alert

Caffeine improves the constellation of abilities that you need to be a safe driver, including shortening your reaction time and increasing your attention span and vigilance. Many scientific studies have conclusively proven that caffeine enables people to drive better, and the contributions of caffeine to safe driving have been recognized for decades.

In 1974, a team of scientists led by Edmund Regina, Ph.D., at the U.S. Department of Health, Education and Welfare (HEW) branch in Providence, Rhode Island, used an elaborate, highly realistic automobile driving simulator in which twenty-four subjects performed actual driving operations while on and off caffeine. The researchers found that 200 mg of caffeine significantly improves driving performance, particularly in relation to sustained vigilance and reaction time.[16] The subjects in this study were well rested. And because these parameters of driving performance drop dangerously when people are tired or sleepy, the power of caffeine to improve them assumes even greater importance when one considers that an abnormally high proportion of traffic accidents occur during late-night driving.

This was an elaborate and ambitious study. Although it was conducted before the age of personal computers, the researchers created a kind of virtual reality environment that produced a high degree of realism. The subjects sat inside a full-sized automobile and "received visual, auditory, and tactile inputs" associated with sitting behind the wheel. Lighting instruments simulated a twilight environment. The exterior was convincingly simulated with the use of "motor sounds, wind effects, and visual field that included onrushing scenery and a continuously moving highway center-line." Accelerating and breaking produced appropriate changes in the scenery, speedometer, and motor noise. Each subject was instructed to follow a model lead car that was driving between 45 and 65 mph and was permitted to overtake the lead car, maintain a constant distance behind it, or fall farther back behind it.

The scientists found that caffeine enhanced driving performance in a way that was "broad in nature, encompassing responses to both gradually appearing signals (changes in the lead car speed) and signals which were discrete (on-off high-beam signals)." An unusual two-stage dosing regimen was followed. Subjects took a 200 mg peppermint-flavored caffeine tablet and a half-hour later began an uninterrupted drive lasting 90 minutes. After a 10-minute break, they took a second caffeine tablet and drove for another 90 minutes. Not surprisingly, a greater benefit over a placebo was found during the second half of the drive, possibly owing to the high blood levels of caffeine achieved by adding in the second dose, or possibly to the increased fatigue from the longer drive. After sophisticated analysis of blood levels and comparing results for the two parts of the test, Regina concluded that there were dependable caffeine-induced benefits to alertness, vigilance, and safe driving, even for people who are well rested and wide awake.

Because it is monotonous, prolonged highway driving at night is impaired not only by sleepiness but also by boredom. Bored people suffer from greatly increased lapses in attention—what scientists call "inhibited response blocking." Studies have clearly proven that 200 mg of caffeine significantly decreased such dangerous attention lapses during the extended performance of a monotonous task and that these beneficial effects persisted for 4 hours.[17] In the real world, this could mean that the sudden change in speed or direction by a nearby car will not go unnoticed, and that extra attentiveness could save your life.

If it is risky to drive a car when you are sleepy, it is even worse to steer a ship or pilot an airplane. One of the most notable examples is that of the oil tanker *Exxon Valdez,* which in 1989 ran aground in clear weather, spilling millions of gallons of oil into the ocean and incurring a $2 billion cleanup bill and untold environmental damage. The news headlines at the time focused on the captain's alcoholism and put it down as the cause of the accident. However, the National Transportation Safety Board (NTSB) blamed the disaster not on too much alcohol but on too little sleep. The official NTSB report recounts that the captain was off the bridge at the time the accident occurred and command had been turned over to the third mate. The third mate had slept only 6 hours in the previous two days. Because his alertness and attention span were severely compromised by lack of sleep, he failed to notice that the autopilot was still on and that the ship had failed to enter a necessary turn. When he finally realized what was happening, it was too late to maneuver to safety.[18] You couldn't find a more dramatic example of the harm from a lapse of attention caused by drowsiness.

It's best to avoid driving cars and steering ships when you are exhausted and have gone without a good night's sleep. Unfortunately, though, life's demands don't always fit neatly into our schedule. It isn't always possible to sleep when we need to the most, and it is sometimes necessary to perform such tasks when our energy and ability to focus are low. When this need arises, caffeine can play a vital part in enabling us to do safely and successfully what we have to do. The greatest oil spill in American history might well have been averted if the officer in question had known to take a dose of 150 mg of caffeine (or more) 15 minutes before assuming control of the bridge.

The Pause That Refreshes: Napping on Caffeine

You may be surprised to learn that sometimes it's a good strategy to take caffeine before you go to sleep. To understand why this is true, consider a driver in the middle of an all-night drive who pulls over for a brief rest in

Save a Life with Caffeine

A survey by the National Sleep Foundation found that nearly 25 percent of respondents acknowledged having fallen asleep while driving during the past year. Nearly 25,000 people a year are killed in accidents caused wholly or partly by dozing off at the wheel. Over one-third of all traffic accidents are blamed on the same cause.[19]

Sleep research has shown that when your sleep debt is high and the time of day puts you at a low point in your 24-hour cycle of arousal, neither loud music nor willpower can enable you to function normally or to avoid lapsing into "micro-sleeps," naps lasting a few seconds to a few minutes. Because it has been proven that caffeine has the power to improve the alertness and reaction time of drivers significantly and effectively reverse the decrements in performance caused by sleepiness, using caffeine when you must drive through the night, or any other time you are tired or sleepy, is a way to avoid accidents and save lives.

the parking lot outside a diner. He intends to take a short nap and then to swig down a large cup of coffee to wake him up before setting out on the road again. Although it may seem logical, this approach is actually very dangerous. When we wake up, whether from a nap or a deep sleep, we feel groggy; our reaction time is extremely slow and attention span is extremely short. Drinking coffee may seem to be immediately refreshing; however, it takes at least 15 minutes for its alerting power to kick in. If you drive during that interval—while you are still groggy after napping but before the caffeine becomes effective—you significantly increase your chances of having an accident.

The best thing you can do under these circumstances is to drink a cup or two of coffee *before* you take your nap, not after. We call this technique the "Loughborough Method," after a study performed by researchers at Loughborough University in Leicestershire in the United Kingdom.[20] Sleep scientists Louise A. Reyner and Jim A. Horne used a driving simulator to test driving performance during the biologically determined afternoon slump, when alertness and reaction time take a major dip. In one test run, the subjects had no coffee and no nap. In a second test run, the subjects had coffee but no nap. And in a third test run, the subjects had 150 mg of caffeine (equivalent to a 6 ounce cup of filtered coffee), followed by a 15 minute nap. In each test, the subjects then spent 2 hours behind the wheel of the driving simulator. The results? Caffeine alone dramatically improved driving performance and greatly reduced the number of incidents in which drivers drifted into adjoining lanes on the simulator. Caffeine in addition to a nap cut down on the number of lane-drifting incidents even more, by nearly 75 percent.

The Loughborough Method makes use of the 15-minute time span before caffeine begins working, and during which driving would still be dangerous, to get some much-needed sleep. With the caffeine alone, you would still be groggy in your first 15 minutes on the road. With a nap alone, you would still be groggy from sleep inertia, or mental fogginess, for the first 15 minutes on the road. But by combining an effective prenap caffeine dose with a short nap, you wake up refreshed, alert, and ready to go.

Will the caffeine keep you from falling asleep? Almost certainly not. The Loughborough University study showed that if you take caffeine before napping, it won't keep you from falling asleep. Once you've taken it,

The Loughborough Method for Safer Late Night Driving

Drowsiness, when your eyelids feel heavy and it's hard to keep them open, is the final warning before the arrival of sleep. If you don't do something to recover your alertness at once—whether you're lying on your couch or driving a car—sleep will arrive suddenly.

When you start to feel drowsy on the road, look for a place to pull over at once. Once you are safely parked and assuming you must continue your drive as soon as possible, follow the procedures developed by the Loughborough Sleep Research Centre:

1. Take a caffeine pill (such as a Vivarin) or drink a strong cup of coffee.
2. Take a 15 minute nap.

You should wake up refreshed by your nap, and the normal drowsiness that follows sleep should have been dissipated by caffeine, so that you are alert and vigilant and have a faster reaction time, better coordination, and increased mental clarity.

however, you will wake up readily after 15 minutes or so, when the stimulating boost of caffeine is nearly fully in effect. (Blood levels of caffeine attain 75 percent of their maximum levels 15 minutes after ingestion.) How much caffeine should you use under these circumstances? As with all other strategic applications of caffeine, you must do some self-testing to see exactly what combination of caffeine and napping works best for you.

Shift Work

Sleepiness and fatigue throughout the night are major problems for night workers, including emergency room physicians and nurses, pilots, truckers, rescue workers, and anyone else whose job requires them to do shift work. Changing from a morning to an evening work shift is like taking a plane across eight time zones. And the "jet lag" that you'll feel is just as real and creates just as many impairments in performance as regular jet lag. In a way, when you arrive for work on a new shift, it's like getting off a plane in another country. However, you won't be able to go to your hotel to sleep—which, as we will see in the next chapter, isn't the fastest way of adjusting to a new schedule anyway. Even worse, you may not be conscious of your diminished capacities until a problem arises that requires your immediate attention. By then, it may be too late.

When you are called on to change your shift from day to night, you are being forced to work at the low point of your energies. You will tend to be inattentive, forgetful, slow to respond, and possibly grouchy as well. To make matters worse, surveys show that shift workers average 2 hours less sleep when they sleep during the day instead of at night. Worse still, because of frequent shift rotation (the typical schedule is one week on each shift), workers never have a chance to become acclimated to any fixed schedule. This weekly shifting, usually from night (11 P.M. to 7 A.M.) to evening (3 P.M. to 11 P.M.), evening to day (7 A.M. to 3 P.M.), or day to night, is analogous to traveling east through several time zones. Just as the workers begin to adjust to their new hours, "another eight-hour phase shift is imposed on their biological clock," keeping them perpetually in the worst state of "jet lag" possible.[21]

Once again, caffeine can come to the rescue. By specifically combating the symptoms of fatigue and lack of sleep, caffeine brings shift workers up to speed at their jobs by making them as alert, sharp-witted, and quick to respond as they are during the day, and it even helps them feel happier about having to work so late.

Although a number of studies had been done demonstrating that caffeine improves physiological alertness during the day, little investigation had been made of caffeine's ability to combat sleepiness and increase alertness at night until the 1980's. A classic study by R. G. Borland in 1986 proved that 300 mg of caffeine significantly improved job performance in experienced shift workers who were tested between 11 P.M. and 8 A.M.[22] In 1989, one of the first major studies of caffeine's usefulness in sustaining wakefulness and reducing sleepiness proved that the beneficial alerting effect of 200 to 400 mg of caffeine is equal to or greater than a 3½ hour nap taken between midnight and 3 A.M.[23]

We know that regular use of caffeine creates a limited tolerance to some of its effects. But what about caffeine's effects on late-night alertness and its ability to keep you from falling asleep? Do people who use a great deal of caffeine build up a resistance to these benefits, so that caffeine either won't work for them any more or they have to keep increasing their dose to achieve the same benefits?

In 1991, James K. Walsh, a leading sleep researcher, wanted to answer these questions—to find out if caffeine's effects on alertness and sleepiness are different for people who use a small or moderate amount of caffeine as compared with those who use a great deal of it. He divided his subjects into two groups: those who consumed two or fewer caffeinated drinks a day and those who consumed five to seven caffeinated drinks a day. He discovered that a dose of 200 mg to 400 mg of caffeine "significantly reduces physiological sleep tendency and improves ability to sustain wakefulness at times of marked sleepiness," and, further, that identical doses of caffeine had a similar effect on both light and heavy caffeine users.[24]

These effects don't peter out after an hour or two. Sometimes workers must sustain performance throughout the night and keep going the next day after missing an entire night's sleep. Walsh showed that the alerting power of a moderate dose consumed shortly after midnight persisted for 5½ hours in light caffeine users and lasted even longer, about 7½ hours, in heavy caffeine users. This is consistent with a half-life of 3 to 5 hours, which is the average for doses in the range used. Remember, however, that larger doses of caffeine will have an even longer half-life and the benefits should last correspondingly longer, even throughout the next day.

Finally, we should mention an extra plus you get using caffeine to help cope with shift work: Caffeine not only increases alertness, energy, and concentration but also increases motivation for work.[25] Although this factor is difficult to quantify, scientists who have used psychological profiling tests tell us that people get a motivational boost from caffeine that enables them to see their way through completing difficult tasks even under adverse conditions. (For more about these sorts of effects, see Chapter 6.)

Getting a Good Night's Sleep

One of caffeine's most universally recognized benefits is its ability to keep you awake when you want to stay awake. Unfortunately, caffeine can also keep you awake when you would like to go to sleep. This interference with sleep has been confirmed in many scientific studies. For example, a study of over 200 women showed that nearly half of those questioned said that a strong cup of coffee before bedtime would interfere with falling asleep.[26] In

Rx for Hospital Physicians and Caffeine

A metastudy conducted by Michael Bonnet, Ph.D., of Wright State University School of Medicine in Dayton, Ohio, and reported in the *Journal of the American Medical Association,* found, in studies of physicians on call at hospitals, that "200 mg of caffeine taken at 1 A.M. preserves alertness through the night" and that another 200 mg at 7 A.M. helps restore alertness into the following day. Bonnet also found that a daytime nap prior to an expected night of sleep loss combined with caffeine "restores nighttime alertness to daytime base levels." [27]

Strategic caffeine use by physicians on shift duty could even save lives in hospitals. It's a shocking fact that "in an anonymous survey, 42% of the house staff in a San Francisco hospital admitted to killing at least one patient by making a fatigue-related mistake." [28] A 200 mg caffeine pill or a strong cup of coffee could well have prevented these fatal blunders.

fact, caffeine so reliably delays falling asleep that scientists use it to simulate the effects of naturally occurring insomnia. [29]

The factors that determine the effect caffeine will have on falling and staying asleep include the dose of caffeine, the time interval before bedtime, the speed at which you metabolize caffeine, your personal general sensitivity to caffeine, and your specific sensitivity to caffeine's ability to induce wakefulness. Another important factor also seems to be how much caffeine you consume daily. People who limit their intake of caffeine are generally the same ones who believe it will keep them from falling asleep at night. The study cited above found that nearly two-thirds of women who drink only one or two cups of coffee a day find a cup consumed shortly before bedtime interferes with their sleep, while only one-quarter of those who drink more than five cups a day reported this interference.

Do people who do not experience insomnia from drinking coffee drink more coffee, especially in the evening? Or do people who are heavy coffee drinkers build up a tolerance to caffeine's effects on sleep, so that they can consume it before bedtime with fewer sleep problems? There is something of a chicken-and-egg question here. Perhaps those who drink a great deal of coffee have markedly fewer sleep problems when they drink coffee before

Caffeine and the Sandman

It would be difficult to exaggerate the range of different effects caffeine has on the ability to fall asleep. In fact, field studies have even turned up a few people (probably fewer than 1 in 200) who use caffeine to help themselves to sleep at night.[30] A forty-eight-year-old record producer from Scottsdale, Arizona, told us, "I never drink coffee in the morning. But my days are so hectic that I need some way to relax before I turn in. That's why I always have a strong cup of coffee before bed—it puts me right out!"

Some people actually sleep too much after consuming caffeine, experiencing a pathological condition called "hypersominia" as a result of consuming it. One researcher wrote in the *American Journal of Medicine* that several of his patients "had severe sleepiness that decreased or remitted after they discontinued caffeine." He concluded that in certain people, "heavy use of caffeine apparently provokes sleepiness."[31]

Keep this remarkable variation in responses in mind the next time someone tries to tell you how you should or should not be using caffeine.

bedtime because they have acquired a tolerance to the drug's effects on sleep, or perhaps the high caffeine users are simply the people whose sleep was not disturbed by caffeine in the first place. No one is quite sure.

Despite individual variations, there is no question that caffeine taken before bedtime generally delays the onset of sleep. But what does "before bedtime" mean? You need to determine at what time of day caffeine consumption begins to interfere with *your* sleep. Then you can eliminate sleep problems that were being caused by caffeine by observing this "caffeine cutoff point" and never ingesting it after that hour.

Determining Your Caffeine Cutoff Point

Determining your caffeine cutoff point is a matter of trial and error. For example, many people can drink several cups of coffee with breakfast and one or two cups more at work before lunch. But if they have caffeine after noon, even just one additional cup of coffee, they'll have trouble sleeping

Sleeping, Aging, and Caffeine

Caffeine delivers more powerful benefits to middle-aged and older people than it does to young people. However, as we grow older, we tend to sleep less. A recent study found that at age twenty-five, the average night's sleep is 7 hours; at age sixty, it is 6 hours; and at age seventy-five, it is only 5 hours. Therefore, as we grow older, it becomes more important than before to make sure that we don't do anything, including using too much caffeine, that might interfere with the amount of sleep we can expect to get.

that night. If caffeine agrees with you, we suggest beginning your evaluation by using it throughout the day and continuing until after dinner, say, 7:00 P.M. If you have trouble sleeping, try stopping your caffeine consumption at 4:00 P.M. If you still have trouble sleeping, stop using caffeine after lunch. And if you're *still* tossing and turning at night, limit your caffeine consumption to the morning hours.

And what if you continue to have trouble falling asleep even though you're drinking coffee only in the morning? Does that mean you have to give up caffeine entirely? Not really. Even if you are highly sensitive to caffeine, you might be able to enjoy its benefits and avoid unwanted side effects such as sleep problems by changing your source of caffeine from coffee to black or even green tea. As we have seen, an average 6 ounce cup of filter drip coffee has about 150 mg of caffeine. A cup of black tea the same size has only about 40 to 50 mg, and a cup of green tea has only about 10 to 15 mg. Caffeinated soft drinks, with about 40 mg of caffeine in a 12 ounce serving, are another relatively low-dose source of caffeine. Persons sensitive to caffeine's effects may become more alert and energetic after drinking a single cup of green tea or 6 ounces of caffeinated soda, but the amount of caffeine they are getting will probably not be enough to disturb their night's rest.

But caffeine doesn't just affect how long it takes to fall asleep. It also can have an effect on the quality of your sleep, for example, whether you're restlessly tossing and turning or out like a log. Use the self-assessment in the next section to help determine what, if any, effect caffeine has on your own subjective assessment of the quality of your night's rest.

You Don't Need Therapy—Just Lower Your Dose of Caffeine!

A twenty-nine-year-old New York woman who had never had sleep problems before was having trouble falling asleep, and once she had fallen asleep, she was having even more trouble staying asleep. She found herself waking up two or three times every night. Going to bed earlier to get more sleep didn't seem to help, and the problem started to interfere with her work because she was exhausted. She consulted a psychologist and began therapy designed to uncover the reasons for her restless nights.

She usually drank four cups of coffee with breakfast, followed by several more throughout the day. One day, she ran out of regular coffee after her first two morning cups, and when she arrived home from work, she drank decaf in the afternoon and evening. Surprisingly, she had a good night's sleep for the first time in weeks. When she told her therapist, he suggested limiting her caffeine to two cups of coffee in the morning and avoiding caffeine entirely for the rest of the day. It turned out that she had recently begun taking oral contraceptives, which can dramatically slow the metabolism of caffeine, keeping it active in the body for much longer than before.

The suggestion worked. She didn't need therapy. She just needed to adjust the size and timing of her dose of caffeine.

Self-Assessment of Sleep Onset and Quality

Most people find that caffeine interferes with falling asleep if consumed within a few hours of bedtime. However, because individual reactions vary, it is important to determine your own caffeine cutoff point—the time after which time caffeine consumption will interfere with sleep, but not if it is taken before.

To determine this point for yourself, take between 150 mg and 200 mg of caffeine, the amount in 6 ounces to 8 ounces of filter drip coffee, between 5 P.M. and 7 P.M., and make sure you take no more caffeine that evening. Repeat this for several days, keeping a record of when you fall asleep each night. If you find that your sleep is being delayed, try taking the same dose an hour earlier for several days. If you find that it is not being delayed, try taking the caffeine an hour later. Continue doing this, moving

From Coffee to Green Tea: For Persons
Who Are Unusually Sensitive to Caffeine

A 6 ounce cup of filter drip coffee contains nearly 150 mg of caffeine. Two large mugs of filter drip coffee could deliver 400 mg or more. If you experience problems that you associate with caffeine—for example, insomnia, jitteriness, or rapid heartbeat—and therefore avoid it, you might consider making the switch from coffee to green tea in order to enjoy its benefits without unwanted side effects.

Green tea does contain caffeine, but the effects of the tiny 10 to 15 mg dose it delivers per cup (7 percent to 10 percent the amount in a cup of coffee) are so small that most people can't feel them. However, if you are unusually sensitive to caffeine, as are a substantial number of people, you might find that a cup or two of green tea provides just the right level of stimulation for you while avoiding the unpleasant side effects that you had experienced with coffee. The only way to find out for sure is to try it.

the time of your last dose earlier or later, until you pinpoint your personal caffeine cutoff point. You will then know exactly how late in the day you can use caffeine without worrying that it will cost you a night's sleep.

If you want to carry your assessment of caffeine's effect on your sleep further, the next morning record an estimate of the quality of your sleep on a scale of 1 to 4, where 1 is uninterrupted rest and 4 is tossing and turning and waking up more than once, and review the average score with caffeine taken at different times. You may find that while caffeine taken after a certain time is not delaying when you fall asleep, it is nevertheless impairing the quality of your sleep. You will then want to restrict your caffeine intake before that hour of the day in order to avoid sleep disturbances.

3

The Jet Lag Program

WE'VE ALL EXPERIENCED IT. You pack for your two-week vacation in Europe, and get a good night's sleep before you leave. Then you catch a flight that drops you off at dawn local time. Unfortunately, it's nearly midnight back home—and according to your body's clock as well. You end up sleeping through the first day, feeling groggy the second. Eventually, as much as ten days later, you're pretty much adjusted. But by then, you've lost a substantial part of your precious time away, time you could have spent seeing the sights and enjoying all the reasons you took your trip in the first place. You might even be on your way back home again.

As bad as it is to sacrifice some of your vacation to body clock adjustment, it's even worse to fail to close a business deal or perform poorly in an athletic event because your body tells you it's the middle of the night. Ronald Reagan's meetings abroad were scheduled to help him avoid the jet lag problems that used to put him to sleep in the middle of world summits. Secretary of State John Foster Dulles actually blamed some of his questionable decisions on jet lag. When champion diver Greg Louganis hit his head on the 10 meter diving platform at the 1988 Olympics, he blamed jet lag. If you imagine traveling across eight time zones to attend a major meeting or compete in the sporting event of a lifetime, you can see why any successful businessperson or top athlete who flies around the world should look for a way to get jet lag under control.

Jet lag arises because our body has its own regulating mechanism that keeps track of morning and night. When you suddenly find yourself in another time zone, it takes this regulatory mechanism a few days to reset itself. According to scientists at the National Aeronautics and Space

Administration (NASA), for every time zone that you cross, it takes roughly one day to adjust your body's clock and regain normal rhythm and energy. However, it is easier to fly west than east, because it's easier to set your clock back than it is to set it forward.

During the time that it takes you to adjust, you're not yourself. But relax! There's good news. Caffeine can enable you to reset your body's clock, avoid the consequences of jet lag, and effectively give you an extra few days to enjoy your trip when you're on vacation and to perform at your best when you're attending a business conference or athletic competition—if you know how to use it properly.

A Real Malaise

Jet lag syndrome is a recognized medical condition: a disruption of the circadian clock, the brain's timekeeper, which determines the daily individual cycle of sleep and wakefulness, hormone levels, alertness, and body strength. It is experienced by approximately 94 percent of long-distance travelers. According to French researcher Daniel Lagarde, this so-called syndrome is induced by "a transmeridian flight across four time zones," although you can experience milder jet lag problems when crossing just two or three zones. Dr. Maria Simonson, director of the Health, Weight,

A Daily Routine—Fighting the 25-Hour Day

Sleep scientists say that because of the effects of late-night electric lights, your body clock operates on a 25-hour schedule instead of the almost exactly 24-hour schedule that nature intended.[1] If you get up at the same time each morning, you are attempting to conform to a 24-hour schedule. Therefore, each morning, you are trying to reset your body clock back by one hour. This is a constant battle, as if we were each experiencing a little jet lag every day. By giving you a jump-start that helps you to reset your clock, caffeine helps you compensate for the inherent conflict between the biological day and the calendar day. The daily use of caffeine as a morning ritual has more reason behind it than simply giving you a burst of energy. It is a good way of compensating for the discrepancy between your body clock and the 24-hour day.

and Stress Clinic at the Johns Hopkins Medical Institutions in Baltimore, says that jet lag affects everyone differently, but that the most common symptoms are "fatigue, sleep disturbances and insomnia, mild depression or irritability, gastrointestinal distress and headaches."[2] Other symptoms can include dehydration, disorientation, anxiety, and impaired coordination, reaction time, and concentration. Some people even drop off to sleep while waiting for their bags at the airport. In addition, the World Health Organization links jet lag to lowered resistance to infections, such as those causing diarrhea.

Jet lag can seriously impair our abilities to perform mental and physical tasks. A British Airways study made in conjunction with a team of former NASA scientists revealed that jet lag interferes with our ability to make decisions and downgrades our attention span by 75 percent, communications skills by 30 percent, and memory by 20 percent.[3] But the actions of caffeine have been proven to increase attention span and vigilance, improve verbal fluency, and boost short-term memory. So in addition to helping reset your body clock, caffeine acts as a specific antidote that counteracts the most damaging impairments caused by jet lag and helps us to function normally even when we find ourselves in the grip of the condition.

The body clock's principal control center is part of the hypothalamus in the brain. (The superchiasmic nucleus is the subpart that regulates clock function.) To avoid jet lag, we must trick the hypothalamus into shifting to

Symptoms of Jet Lag

- Fatigue
- Disorientation
- Insomnia
- Loss of appetite
- Stomach distress
- Prolonged reaction time
- Decreased short-term memory
- Decreased concentration
- Reduction in muscle power and capacity
- Higher injury rates
- Reduction in dynamic strength

Jet Lag and World-Class Sports Competition

Experiencing the decrements in speed, strength, and reaction time that are caused by jet lag can be fatal to the chances of winning in individual or team athletic events.

a new pattern that fits the time zone of our destination. The devices used to make this phase change are called "*Zeitgebers*," a German term meaning "time giver." *Zeitgebers* are agents such as bright light, melatonin, exercise, and caffeine that regulate or shift the phase of circadian rhythms. In other words, they help realign your body clock to a new schedule.

Strategic Caffeine Use: Knowing When to Stop . . . and When to Start Again

There's a cottage industry of jet lag diets, dietary supplements, and computer-generated jet lag schedule programs, but the truth is that studies have shown that complex eating schedules, which attempt to juggle measured amounts of carbohydrates and proteins, routines of feasting and fasting, or the use of vitamin and mineral supplements contribute little or nothing to solving the jet lag problem.

Many jet lag gurus warn their followers to avoid caffeine during flight in order to avoid the dehydration that caffeine supposedly causes. Because dehydration is thought by some to be a symptom of jet lag, their theory is that caffeine will make the condition worse. Here we encounter one of the most common myths about caffeine: that it causes dehydration. This myth probably originated from the observation that the frequency and amount of urination typically increase after consuming caffeinated beverages. In fact, caffeine does not alter the fluid balance within the organs of the body, and there is no reason to avoid using it to keep from "drying out." (This fact has important implications for the use of caffeine by athletes. See Chapter 8.) And in any case, whether you are traveling or otherwise, if you feel you are becoming dehydrated, drink a glass of water, and your fluid balance will naturally restore itself.

Caffeine Myth: Caffeine Causes Dehydration

People are frequently warned to avoid caffeine when traveling on a plane because it causes dehydration. However, it has been proven in studies of athletes that caffeine does not alter overall hydration levels or the fluid balance within the organs of the body. This myth arose because drinking several cups of hot liquid naturally occasions the need to urinate. Nevertheless, dehydration is a real problem when flying because cabin air is typically extremely dry, with humidity ranging from 1 to 10 percent. Some travel advisers suggest using eye drops to lubricate your eyes (especially if you wear contact lenses) and coating the inside of your nostrils with almond, jojoba, or olive oil to keep them moist.

Despite these groundless warnings against using caffeine, travelers instinctively seem to know that caffeine can help. A survey conducted by Hilton Hotels and the National Sleep Foundation found that many Japanese, German, British, and American international business travelers increase their caffeine consumption when away on business. We might reasonably suspect that these businesspeople are trying to manage sleepiness and fatigue experienced while traveling by upping their dose of caffeine. However, although ad hoc use of caffeine to help cope with jet lag is useful, it is no substitute for a well-thought-out program that will maximize the benefits that caffeine can confer.

Caffeine takes about 15 minutes to achieve 75 percent of its maximum effect and about 1 hour to reach its maximum effect, depending on the contents of the stomach. Its primary stimulant effect lasts 3 to 4 hours. Instead of drinking coffee haphazardly throughout the day, you should plan exactly when you need a lift and maximize the effectiveness of the caffeine you use. For example, you have an important business meeting at 4 P.M., when you know you will probably be sleepy. You might want to start drinking the caffeinated beverage at around 3:30 P.M.

The Caffeine Jet Lag Program

What you do before you leave is just as important as what you do *after* you arrive. You can knock out jet lag with a "one-two" punch:

1. Before you leave, taper off caffeine.
2. After you arrive, follow a program of caffeine use designed to reset your body clock.

The reason you reduce the amount of caffeine you are using is to reduce your tolerance to it. By reducing your tolerance, you multiply the power of caffeine to increase the physical and mental benefits it will confer after you land. In other words, if your system is "caffeine clean," you'll get a much bigger lift from caffeine when you begin using it again.

Kicking Caffeine

It's easy to tell people to stop using caffeine, but it's not so easy to actually do so. Some people recommend that you stop using caffeine by substituting tea or chocolate or something more exotic, like guarana capsules, for coffee. The only problem is that all of these things contain caffeine. You're really just changing the delivery system, not stopping your caffeine intake at all.

If you stop using caffeine, within three to seven days your system will be completely "clean," that is, you will have lost all tolerance to caffeine's effects and you will have lost all trace of withdrawal symptoms. Suddenly stopping the use of caffeine can be uncomfortable. Common complaints include headaches of varying intensity, lack of energy and sleepiness, and moodiness and depression. More severe symptoms, which a very small minority of people experience, include a running nose, nausea, hot and cold spells, aches and pains, and migraine headaches.

In order to minimize these unpleasant symptoms and avoid the worse ones entirely, our program calls for tapering off slowly by stepping down your dose. Begin reducing your caffeine intake by adding the number 2 to the number of cups of coffee you usually have each day. This gives you the number of days you will need to "go off" caffeine. Progressively decrease your caffeine intake by one cup each day. (Three cups of black tea or three 12 ounce servings of caffeinated soda should count as one cup of coffee.) If you generally consume five cups of coffee a day, for example, begin seven days before your trip to decrease your intake by one cup each day. You will then spend the final two days caffeine free.

You should expect to feel some withdrawal symptoms. The nature and seriousness of these symptoms, the intensity of which will vary considerably with each person, are determined by two factors. The first is the degree of your physical dependence on caffeine. If you are used to taking in 600 mg of caffeine a day, your symptoms will tend to be more severe than if you are used to taking in only 200 mg a day. If you take less than 50 to 100 mg a day, you will probably not experience any withdrawal symptoms, because this dose is too low to support a physical dependence. (The average American who uses caffeine consumes more than 300 mg a day, and the average European consumes over 400 mg a day.) The other factor is your genetic makeup. Some people become more readily and deeply dependent on substances that support a physical dependence, and on caffeine in particular, and they experience more intense withdrawal symptoms when they are discontinued. The first time you detoxify from caffeine, or eliminate it from your system, you will learn the degree of your personal sensitivity; however, some people experience variability in withdrawal severity across episodes.

Most people don't have trouble stepping down caffeine use from higher daily doses, such as 500 mg, to a daily dose of 100 mg. The most difficult stage of the stepping-down program is going from 100 mg of caffeine a day to none at all. If you are in the minority of people who experience significant discomfort when doing this, you can alleviate it by taking a very small dose of caffeine, about 15 mg—what is found in a cup of green tea or 4 ounces of caffeinated soda. Because the dose is so small, you won't be greatly interfering with your step-down program, and you may feel a great deal better.

Watch Out for Hidden Sources of Caffeine!

Everyone is aware that coffee and tea contain caffeine. However, when you are following your withdrawal program, be careful you don't get caffeine from hidden sources, such as headache remedies or chocolate, that you don't normally think of as containing caffeine. Many carbonated soft drinks, including Coke, Mountain Dew, and Dr Pepper, also contain caffeine. Using them indiscriminately will sabotage your stepping-down program.

The idea behind decreasing your dosage slowly is to minimize any possible discomforts of withdrawal. Doing this requires discipline and determination. For example, if you are used to using coffee to get yourself over the afternoon slump at work, you will dearly miss the cup that your withdrawal schedule says you can't have. But that's what you must do if you want to enjoy every day of your vacation to the full or to be at the top of your game while you are away.

The Caffeine Cure: Getting the Caffeine Lift After You Land

Staying free from jet lag means having the willpower to overcome your body's tendency to sleep at what for you is bedtime. The most important thing is to stay awake the entire first day and to go to bed around 10 P.M. or 11 P.M. local time. How do you do this? You use caffeine to keep your body awake and your mind alert for your first few days in the new time zone. And at the same time that caffeine is helping you to stay awake, it's also signaling your body to reset your clock to local time.

If you have followed the schedule of caffeine withdrawal, you'll have had two days entirely free of caffeine before you leave for your trip. This isn't usually enough time to completely clear your body of any residual dependence on the drug, but it is enough time to increase your sensitivity to it dramatically. Because of your increased sensitivity to caffeine's effects, taking a jolt on arrival will start to signal your hypothalamus to begin resetting your body's clock.

Take caffeine tablets such as Vivarin with you on the plane so that when the pilot says you will soon be landing, you can take them. Tablets are most widely available in the 200 mg dosage strength. This is a good dose for most people who are looking for the immediate benefits of caffeine, but it might not be the right dose for you. Before implementing the jet lag program described here, you should follow the instructions in Chapter 1 for determining your base sensitivity to caffeine and your personal pickup dose. Take this dose of caffeine about 15 minutes before landing, so that it has time to wake you up and make you alert. You should be able to collect your baggage, go through customs, and get to your hotel on this first dose of caffeine. Once you are comfortably accommodated, sit down and eat a nourishing meal, including both protein and carbohydrates, and take another dose of caffeine, this time probably in the form of a couple of cups of coffee or several cups of tea. In order to reset your clock, get out into the sunshine and get moderate exercise. It's always a good idea to spend your first day strolling around your new city, so do this now. Enjoy your new location, allowing the novel sights and sounds to keep you from napping.

Continue consuming your personal pickup dose of caffeine throughout the day, every 3 to 4 hours. The important thing is to keep to a regular schedule of caffeine administration. Don't simply wait to have a cup of coffee after you suddenly realize you've been "out of it" for an hour. If you are going to reset your clock effectively, you need to keep adding caffeine to your system as soon as your caffeine blood levels decline below an effective amount.

Be careful, though. You must stop drinking coffee or tea or using any caffeine source before you reach your personal caffeine cutoff point—the time in the afternoon or evening after which caffeine consumption interferes with sleep, which you should also have determined prior to embarking on this jet lag cure. This cutoff point is different for different people. Some people cannot sleep at night if they have caffeine after about noon. Others can fall asleep even immediately after drinking a cup of strong coffee. Most are somewhere in between. You will have to determine where your cutoff point occurs by trial and error. If you know from your experience at home that you cannot sleep well if you consume caffeine at dinnertime or after, then you should avoid consuming it after that hour when you arrive at your destination. If you follow this advice, you should be able to fall asleep at around 10 P.M. or 11 P.M. because you have stayed awake all day.

Beaten by Jet Lag

To find out how jet lag affects the performance of professional athletes, researchers in the Department of Neurology at the University of Massachusetts Medical School reviewed the win–loss records of nineteen East Coast and West Coast baseball teams in the 1991–1993 seasons. Home teams won nearly 63 percent of their games if their opponents traveled west to east the day before a game, but they won only 56 percent of their games when their opponents traveled east to west. This suggests that home teams gain an advantage when opponents must travel east—and suffer disruption of their biological clocks by jet lag—the day before a game.[4]

The next morning, begin your breakfast with at least two cups of coffee or four cups of tea and continue consuming your personal pickup dose of caffeine throughout the day, every 3 to 4 hours. Again, be sure to keep to a regular schedule of caffeine administration. Finally, be certain to observe your cutoff point, so you can again get a good night's sleep. Most people are completely adjusted by the third day. If you still have a problem staying awake, continue this routine for as many days as necessary.

Summing It Up

Travel writers who advise you to avoid caffeine on the day of your flight are giving rather questionable advice. Quitting a few days before you start your trip is the way to go. Caffeine creates a physical dependence. If you stop using it suddenly, you may experience the discomforts of withdrawal, the seriousness of which will depend to some extent on your usual intake of the drug and your genetic susceptibility to withdrawal symptoms. These are problems you don't want to deal with when you are carrying heavy bags, waiting in line at customs, or trying to figure out how to get to your hotel.

Studies have found that immediately switching your routine to the new time schedule, which is exactly what our caffeine-based jet lag program enables you to do, aids in decreasing the effects of jet lag. For example, when athletes travel to Sydney from the United States, most of them will arrive in the morning, and they are advised by their trainers to stay up through the day and go to bed that night at local time. They are also told to exercise to help cut down the length of time that jet lag causes impairments. Some athletes report that they were able to decrease the length of time needed for adjustment to a few days by getting back into their training routines the day after arriving in the new time zone. For example, a study conducted by Dr. Shiota in 1996 showed that those who exercised outdoors when they arrived hastened their "resynchronization to the new environment" when compared to a group that stayed indoors and did not exercise.[5] But nothing can solve the problem of jet lag as fast or effectively as caffeine.

If you are going to take advantage of the power of caffeine to give you an edge in overcoming jet lag by resetting your body's clock, you must follow a program such as the one we outline in this chapter. By planning ahead, you can minimize the discomforts of caffeine withdrawal and at the same time greatly multiply its power to help you reset your clock on arrival.

4

Sharpening Your Mind

H ow MUCH WOULD YOU GIVE to have access to a safe substance that
would enable you to perform better on an IQ test, the SAT, or a bar
examination? Or one that would help you to handle problems at work
more successfully, speak and write more fluently, read faster, program a
computer with more acuity, prepare your taxes or balance your checkbook
more accurately, or even play chess more cleverly? This miraculous substance is already within the reach of everyone. We're speaking, of course,
about caffeine.

We saw in Chapter 2 how caffeine dissipates the clouds of fatigue and
makes us energetic and awake when we should otherwise have been tired or
sleepy. In this chapter, we'll explore the ways in which caffeine, when taken
by a well-rested person at the height of his normal mental powers, increases
mental performance in a host of areas, including reasoning ability, reaction
time, memory, computational ability, alertness and attention span, and verbal fluency. It may seem incredible, but decades of research have established that by nearly every objective measure of intelligence and mental
capacity, caffeine actually makes you smarter.

As we shall see, this boost to intelligence is acute, or short term, and
may well be sustained, or long term, as well. That is, people who take a hit
of caffeine find that their cognitive powers increase within the hour. But
most people who use caffeine regularly find that they are sharper and
quicker on an ongoing basis, an improvement that is directly proportional
to the amount of caffeine they use, whether they have just consumed caffeine or not.[1]

Best of all, caffeine's power to increase intelligence does not wear off over time or require us to take larger and larger doses of the drug. Low to moderate amounts of caffeine produce an almost instant improvement in many of the indexes of intelligence, and the same dose will continue to yield the same improvement indefinitely.

The Arousal Theory: How Caffeine Affects Mental Performance

Interesting studies in the 1990s revealed that the way caffeine affects mental performance depends on a variety of personal and environmental factors that contribute to something psychologists call our total arousal level. It turns out that the degree to which caffeine improves our mental functions—or even if it will improve them at all—depends a great deal on the degree to which we are "aroused" when we take it.

"Arousal," in the sense in which the word is being used here, refers to the factors that contribute to excitation and stimulation of the central nervous system, whether these things are pleasant or unpleasant. For example, loud noises are factors that contribute to arousal. Good health also contributes to arousal, while fatigue and illness tend to diminish arousal. In addition, your personality type—whether you tend to be more of an introvert or an extrovert—is important in determining your level of arousal. Finally, caffeine itself increases arousal levels, so the amount of caffeine you take is itself a critical factor in calculating your total arousal.

The key idea for understanding how arousal levels determine the effects of caffeine is found in the Yerkes-Dodson biphasic curve of caffeine's activity—that is, the relationship between the level of stimulus, or arousal, and the level of output, or performance. The Yerkes-Dodson principle states that there is an optimal level of arousal for maximum performance.[2] Low levels of arousal produce low levels of performance, medium to high levels of arousal produce proportionally higher levels of performance, and very high levels of arousal reduce levels of performance. This arousal-performance curve takes the form of an inverted U. (If you want to understand the way high arousal levels can interfere with your activities, remember all the times you've heard people say to a coworker, "Stop playing that radio so loud. I can't hear myself think!" or heard someone complain, after a heated argument, "I'm so upset, I can't concentrate.")

The Up-Then-Down Curve of Caffeine Dosing: The Yerkes-Dodson Biphasic Curve of Caffeine's Effects

1. Small doses of caffeine confer some benefits.
2. Medium to large doses of caffeine confer more pronounced benefits.
3. Very large doses of caffeine do not increase benefits further and may even cause decrements.

What is a "small" dose or a "medium" dose of caffeine depends on your personality type, weight, state of health, the activity or kind of work you intend to be engaging in, and individual sensitivity to caffeine.

Low-arousal people, who tend to be extroverts, don't easily become "riled up," and they tend to be more impulsive and to look for more intense external stimuli to get them and keep them going than high-arousal people do. High-arousal people, who tend to be introverts, are more easily disturbed by external stimuli, and they tend to be less impulsive and to shy away from high levels of external stimulation. Psychologist Hans Eysenck, in his 1998 book entitled *Intelligence: A New Look,* says that introverts are normally closer to an optimal level of performance because they use their central nervous system (CNS) more extensively—at closer to their full potential—and are relatively more resistant to the psychopharmacological effects of caffeine and other drugs than extroverts are.

But there is more to arousal than whether you're an introvert or an extrovert. Many factors contribute to your total arousal at any given moment. For example, if you're tired or sick, your arousal level goes down. If you're in a crowded room, surrounded by distracting conversations while you're trying to work, your arousal level goes up. Caffeine itself increases arousal levels in proportion to the dose taken. The point is that your total state of arousal is what governs how much benefit to your cognitive performance you can expect to get from a given dose of caffeine. And because of the Yerkes-Dodson curve, when your total arousal level is too high, you probably won't get any benefits from larger doses of caffeine—and you might even lose the benefits conferred by lower doses.

Clearing Up the Mental Confusion

Although the case for caffeine's benefits to cognitive performance has been convincingly made, studies over the past few decades have been riddled with some contradictory findings. In fact, in scouring the scientific literature concerning the effects of caffeine on memory, learning, reaction time, attention span, decision making, and sensation and perception, we came across summaries stating that caffeine "increased or improved," "decreased or impaired," or "left unchanged or had no effect" on each of these mental powers!

The mystery was solved to the satisfaction of many in the 1990s when Barry D. Smith, a psychologist at the University of Maryland, revealed the complex ways that the Yerkes-Dodson curve determines caffeine's effects. By dividing people into "introverts" and "extroverts," following the classification system developed by the great psychologist Hans J. Eysenck, and bringing in numerous other factors that contribute to total arousal, Smith proved that improvements were observed in mental function when people are in a low to moderate state of arousal, while no additional improvements and even some decrements are observed when arousal levels become too high.[3]

Researchers Uma and G. S. Gupta extended this theory by using measures of "impulsivity" to understand who benefits the most from caffeine: Low impulsives get little benefit, while high impulsives enjoy the greatest benefit.[4]

Arousal Factors and Performance: Customizing Your Dose

Arousal theory offers a theoretical model of how caffeine affects the mind that enables us to sort through the enormously complex factors that have contributed to the variability in the research findings. Here are the most important factors that contribute to total arousal:

Dose

Caffeine contributes to your total state of arousal in proportion to your dosage. A large amount of caffeine can push a person past the optimum arousal level in the Yerkes-Dodson curve and diminish the benefits conferred by smaller doses. Failure to understand this dynamic is one of the reasons early studies of caffeine seemed to produce contradictory results. For example, researchers were initially confused by the fact that studies of rapid information processing showed that a low dose of 150 mg improved performance, whereas a high dose of 600 mg impaired performance.[5] Similar effects were also apparent on attentional, problem-solving, and memory tasks: Doses of 75 mg and 150 mg significantly improved performance on these tasks, whereas high doses interfered with performance.

Baseline Arousal

Baseline arousal, that is, a person's state of excitation or stimulation on beginning the performance of a task, is an important factor in determining total arousal levels. When baseline arousal is elevated, highly arousing tasks, including those that are complex or involve loud noises or other intense stimuli, can result in overstimulation. This excessive stimulation impairs performance and will actually generate errors in tests of mental abilities.

The following factors contribute to baseline arousal:

• Personality-based factors: Introvert versus extrovert. Introverts (about 25 percent of the population) start with higher arousal levels than extroverts do.
• Gender: Male versus female. Women tend to have higher levels of arousal than men do.[6]
• State of health: Sick versus healthy. People who are ill have lower states of arousal than people in good health.
• State of fatigue and time of day: Tired people and people at lower points in the 24-hour cycle of energy and alertness demonstrate lower arousal levels than well-rested people or people at higher points in this cycle.

Relative Task Complexity

Complex or difficult information-processing tasks increase arousal levels.[7] The more complex a task is, the more likely it is to produce higher arousal levels that contribute to overstimulation and impair performance. Remember, however, that task complexity is relative to each person's capacity and experience. Consider, for example, the task of programming a computer.

This can be a very challenging job, and therefore very arousing, to people without strong abilities or skills in performing it, but it will seem relatively straightforward and simple to talented, experienced programmers. Presumably, caffeine would tend to have opposite effects on the same task, depending on the person who is performing it. That is, caffeine would augment the speed and accuracy of an experienced programmer but might not help a beginner.

The more able you are at a task, the more caffeine tends to improve your performance of it. It's not absolute task complexity that counts. Rather, it is how complex or difficult the task is for you.

Environmental Arousal

Challenging features in the environment, including loud noises, harsh temperature conditions, and other adverse circumstances, raise arousal levels.

Individual Caffeine Sensitivity

Individual sensitivities to caffeine vary enormously. Some people can detect the stimulating power of 1.8 mg, about the amount in an eyedropper full of coffee. Others can't feel 180 mg, more than you'll find in a 6 ounce cup of filtered coffee. All other things being equal, your sensitivity to caffeine will determine how much caffeine is a small dose for you and how much is a large dose.

Body Weight

All other things being equal, the effect a given dose of caffeine will have on you is proportional to your body weight. In other words, 100 mg of caffeine will tend to affect a 100 pound woman to the same degree as 200 mg of caffeine will affect a 200 pound man. So whereas 200 mg to 300 mg might be a good dosage for this man to sharpen his mind, the same dose might push this woman past the peak of her curve of arousal and produce less pronounced benefits than a smaller dose would have.

Additive

These effects—dosage, baseline arousal, relative task complexity, environmental factors, individual sensitivity, and body weight—are additive. Each contributes to total arousal level in a way that can lead to overstimulation and performance decrements.

Because very high arousal levels reduce performance levels, the dosage of caffeine you use must be adjusted to take all of these arousal factors into account. It is wrong to say simply that caffeine impairs performance at high arousal levels. Lower dosages may help more highly aroused people to perform better than they would have without caffeine, even though the regular dosages may be too much for them. The table gives advice on adjusting dosage.

How to Adjust Your Caffeine Dosage for Physical Conditions and Personal Factors

Condition	Adjustment of Caffeine Dosage
Sickness	Increase
Noise	Decrease
Complex, unfamiliar tasks	Decrease
Fatigued	Increase
High levels of stress	Decrease

Personal Factors	Adjustment of Caffeine Dosage
Introvert	Decrease
Extrovert	Increase
Low body weight	Decrease
High body weight	Increase
High sensitivity to caffeine	Decrease
Low sensitivity to caffeine	Increase
High or low regular caffeine use	No change—level of habitual use does not affect arousal levels[8]

The Impulsivity Theory and Caffeine's Cognitive Effects

Introverts tend to be more careful about expressing themselves in action; that is, they tend to be less impulsive. Extroverts tend to be more impulsive. Recent studies show that people who are less impulsive—who are more cautious and less spontaneous—do not necessarily think better and faster when taking caffeine. B. S. Gupta, one of the world's leading caffeine researchers, has found that when impulsive people use caffeine, they show significant improvements—proportional to the dose—on IQ tests, as well as on tests of memory and psychomotor performance, while those who are not impulsive show little or no benefit when they use caffeine.[9] This result is consistent with arousal theory, because less impulsive, introverted people tend to be more highly aroused and are more easily pushed past the optimal point in the Yerkes-Dodson curve of activity. Even a small hit of caffeine can make them so aroused that their mental performance begins to even out or even to suffer decrements. However, more impulsive people tend to be less aroused, so they can benefit increasingly from the stimulation supplied by the drug.

What does all this mean for you? It means that if you are an introvert and tend to be somewhat cautious and withdrawn, "normal" doses of caffeine may be too much for you. So, apparently paradoxically, if you are an introvert and not getting the benefits you expect from caffeine, you should try taking *less*. As an introvert seeking to boost your IQ performance with

How Does Caffeine Do What It Does for Our Minds?

In looking to the actual mechanisms by which caffeine improves mental function, we quickly become lost in complexities of neurotransmitter systems, brain metabolism, and the general stimulation of the central nervous system. The full story of the biophysical processes that underlie caffeine's effects on arousal remains to be discovered.

The latest thinking is that all the actions of caffeine are mediated by its effect on the adenosine neurotransmitter system, changes that affect nearly all of the other neurotransmitter systems, such as the dopamine, the catecholamine, and the adrenaline systems.[10]

With existing knowledge, it is difficult to determine if the benefits of caffeine to mental processes arise at the stage at which perceptual information enters the brain, during the processing of this information, during the decision about what action to take, or in the course of executing this decision—or even, as seems more likely, in all of these stages. All we can say for certain is that caffeine improves the levels of cognitive performance for most people in a host of areas.

caffeine, you should try small doses, perhaps in the range of 50 mg to 100 mg. If you still do not experience a benefit, you might try an even lower dose. If you are an extrovert and you tend to be spontaneous and outgoing, caffeine will raise your IQ and, within a reasonable range, the more you take, the more your IQ will go up.

Using Caffeine to Sharpen Your Mind

No one can say exactly what intelligence is. However, psychometricians, the psychologists who specialize in measuring intelligence, have come up with the concept of *g*, their name for the general intelligence that underlies achievement at school and success in the workplace. Over the past 100 years, these scientists have devised tests—notably, IQ tests—to estimate *g* by measuring performance on a cluster of specific tasks that have been found to correlate highly with each other and with overall attainments. People who do well on any one of these tests tend to do well on all of them, and, perhaps more significant, people who do well on these tests tend to be the ones who achieve the most in academics and on the job. Different components of intelligence tests measure rapid information processing, abstract reasoning, verbal fluency, computational ability, and memory. Caffeine has been shown to improve performance on *all* of these tests, which is to say that caffeine raises IQ and by every objective measure actually makes a person smarter.

Caffeine offers additional benefits to mental function apart from improving our thinking ability. By improving what is called vigilance, the ability to sustain attention over a long time, and divided attention, the ability to pay attention to two things at once, it dramatically increases our capacity to focus on our work and in this way to accomplish more and do it faster and with fewer errors. Adding further to its power as a "brain tonic," caffeine also improves psychomotor performance, enabling us, for example, to use a word processor more adeptly.

We should note again that the mental benefits conferred by caffeine have nothing to do with alleviating caffeine withdrawal symptoms. Countless studies have shown that withdrawal from caffeine does not produce a decline in performance in cognitive functions, and numerous other studies have confirmed that abstinence from caffeine is not a prerequisite for

Caffeine and the Common Cold

In 1992, ninety-nine university students were tested on psychomotor tasks while healthy. They returned to the laboratory when they had colds and were retested after being given regular coffee, decaffeinated coffee, or a fruit juice to drink. Subjects with colds who drank decaffeinated coffee or fruit juice were found to be significantly less alert and to have slower reaction times than when they were healthy. However, "In the caffeinated coffee condition, there was no difference between those with colds and those who were healthy."[11] It didn't take much caffeine to compensate for these upper respiratory infections. The experimenters administered only 1.5 mg of caffeine per kilogram of body weight, or the equivalent of 100 mg for a 150 pound person.

enjoying its benefits. In fact, even when not given caffeine, high caffeine users consistently outperform nonusers and low users on cognitive tests, suggesting that regular use actually confers long-term benefits to the mind. Research proves that caffeine produces a real and significant boost in mental performance and one we can benefit from throughout our lives.[12]

Thinking Fast: Rapid Information Processing and Reaction Time

Scientists have found when comparing people within the same age-group, that the speed of information processing by the brain is one of the strongest indexes of *g*. That is, people who process information faster tend to have a higher general intelligence than people who process it more slowly.[13] Therefore, the proven ability of caffeine to increase virtually every measure of reaction time (RT) is strongly suggestive of its power to augment the overall operations of intelligence and effectively increase the intelligence level of the caffeine user. Even better, in the performance of many mental tasks, caffeine has been shown not only to increase thinking speed, but to decrease the frequency of errors as well.

In an example of an RT test, subjects are asked to press numbered response keys as quickly as they can when a number appears on a screen. In a simple RT test, only the number 1 would appear, and the subjects were required to press the key labeled 1. In a choice RT test, the digits 1, 2, 3, or 4 could appear, and subjects are asked to press the corresponding key. Caffeine has been found to improve performance dramatically on tests of both simple and choice RT.

Driving an automobile is an everyday example of a task that requires good choice RT. As you travel down the road, you are bombarded by many different signals—other cars, traffic lights, pedestrians, road signs, and so on. In response to them, you must make decisions in real time about how to regulate the control of your vehicle. Clearly, improved choice RT will improve your ability to do so successfully. Another real-life example is playing a computer game. As the images move quickly around the screen, you must make quick decisions about how to respond. A quicker choice RT will enable you to get a higher score.

Interestingly, higher caffeine users demonstrate faster reaction times than nonusers or lower caffeine users, even when they have not taken any caffeine before the test.[14] This suggests that regular caffeine consumption has long-term benefits on the ability to make quick responses.[15]

Alertness: Vigilance and Attention

Everyone knows that when we are groggy in the morning or sleepy late at night, caffeine can make us alert and attentive. Perhaps surprisingly, many studies have proven that caffeine greatly improves alertness in people who are fully rested as well.[16]

Attention comes in three types: *vigilance,* or sustained attention; *divided attention,* or paying attention to two things at once; and *focused attention,* that is, paying attention to something in the face of distractions. Caffeine helps improve both vigilance and divided attention, but doesn't do anything to improve focused attention.

Faster Is Smarter

In performing tests of intelligence that required subjects to initiate the test by pressing a button, one scientist noticed that the speed at which the subject was able to press the button correlated as highly with his IQ as his score on the test itself. In consideration of results such as this one, Eysenck, the great personality theorist, argues that reaction time is a strong index of intellectual power.[17] It is interesting to note, therefore, that one of caffeine's most notable effects on cognitive performance is to shorten reaction time dramatically.

Caffeine has a profound ability to improve vigilance, that is, the ability to pay attention to something for a long period of time. In a vigilance task, a subject is asked to maintain attention on one or more information sources, looking out for certain specific, infrequent signals. In an auditory version of a vigilance test, people listened through headphones to a series of half-second tones presented every 2 seconds against a background of white noise for an hour. Occasionally, slightly shorter tones were substituted, and the subjects were instructed to press a button whenever they heard one of these shorter tones. A dose of 200 mg of caffeine (about the amount in 8 ounces of filter drip coffee) significantly improved the number of correct hits. In another sort of vigilance test, the Bakan test (described in more detail in Chapter 2), single digits were presented on a screen at a rate of 100 per minute. The task was to detect, by pressing a button, the occurrence of three successive digits that were all odd or all even. The study used 250 mg and 500 mg of caffeine and showed that either dose significantly improved the detection rate without increasing the number of errors.[18]

The need for high levels of vigilance occurs in many areas of life. For example, when you do research, you are looking through page after page of printed text or web sites in search of certain words or phrases. The ability to sustain vigilance as you do so will ensure that you notice each occurrence of what you are looking for.

Two Ways of Maintaining Vigilance

There are two aspects to maintaining vigilance performance:

1. Combating the decline in overall arousal levels, which represents the difficulty in sustaining attention as you become fatigued.
2. Combating the decline in vigilance performance over time, sometimes called habituation, which represents the failure of attention as tasks are repeated and boredom ensues.

Caffeine improves the first by increasing arousal levels. Caffeine improves the second because moderate doses of caffeine reduce boredom (see Chapter 6). It has been shown that long-duration vigilance tests are particularly sensitive to the use of caffeine.[19]

Not surprisingly, some studies have found that the Yerkes-Dodson effect limits the effects of caffeine on vigilance. If arousal levels are high or if high doses of caffeine are used, performance on vigilance tasks is impaired—at least at first. Interestingly, as blood levels achieved by high doses of caffeine decline over a 2-hour period, the impairment reverses itself, and the lower levels of the caffeine remaining in the body start to improve performance.[20] The same thing is true when arousal levels are increased by annoying sounds. In a vigilance experiment, subjects were asked to spot lines on a computer screen that were either vertical or horizontal, with and without loud white noise, an irritant that increases arousal levels. Their performance improved without the noise but declined when noise was added.[21]

Caffeine can help us when our work requires that we pay attention to two or more things at the same time, a great benefit in an age of multitasking. The benefits of caffeine to divided attention have been demonstrated by researchers in both visual and auditory tasks. For example, in a study requiring subjects to track a moving target across a computer screen with a joystick and detect the sudden appearance of a white circle, 300 mg of caffeine significantly increased the number of correct hits.[22]

This improvement in the ability to be aware of several things at once even applies to so-called self-focused processes. For example, while engaged in other activities, diabetics were better able to notice that they were beginning to experience low blood sugar after 250 mg of caffeine than when they were without it, and as a result, they were alerted to eat something and thereby avert a potential hypoglycemic crisis.[23]

In contrast with divided attention, focused attention, that is, the ability to concentrate on a task while being distracted by external stimuli such as loud noises, is, perhaps surprisingly, not affected by caffeine. In fact, if the distraction is sufficiently annoying and drives your arousal levels up too high, caffeine might actually impair your ability to concentrate under these trying circumstances. So if you're trying to concentrate on your work and there's a chorus of jackhammers going full blast outside your window, perhaps you should lay off the caffeine while the construction is going on.

Thinking Smarter: Abstract Reasoning and Problem Solving

As important as faster responses and more focused attention may be, no improvement of mental powers is as valuable or as universally coveted as an

The Dual System Theory of Wakefulness

Matthew Miller, a pharmacologist researching the effects of drugs on sleep, says that we have evolved two brain systems to manage what we ordinarily lump together as wakefulness and distinguishes what we might call the alertness system from the attentiveness system:

- Alertness system: A vigilance system that developed to keep us alert to opportunities and threats in the environment. The activation of this system, Miller says, reduces reaction time, among other things.
- Attentiveness system: What might be called the calm attention system, which, when activated, enables the mind attentively to carry out cognitive tasks, such as reasoning and remembering.

Because caffeine stimulates all of the neurotransmitter systems, says Miller, it activates all of the neurons that promote wakefulness—in every sense of the word.[24]

improvement in the ability to reason and solve problems. In fact, it is this ability to which we are usually referring when we call a person "intelligent" or "smart," and there is no doubt that this power is a key to achievement at school and in the workplace.

As early as 1933, one researcher analyzed the effects of caffeine on solving more than 250 chess problems, comparing the performance of test subjects with and without caffeine. He observed a consistently remarkable improvement in performance with caffeine.[25] It was only around 1990, however, that scientists began widely studying the effects of caffeine on tests of intelligence and reasoning ability. The results? More than ten years of research suggest that caffeine is the "smart pill" that people have always dreamed of finding.

It is astonishing to consider that according to the most accurate and sensitive tests of abstract reasoning, Raven's Standard Progressive Matrices (SPM), caffeine actually improves our ability to think more cogently. So-called figural analogy or visuospatial reasoning tests like the SPM challenge our underlying powers of thought, not how much we have learned or studied or the amount of experience we have in life. These tests, and others, like the Culture Fair Intelligence Test (CFIT), measure what is called "fluid intelligence," the name psychometricians give to the intrinsic capacity to learn, master new situations, and, in general, use mental abilities, solve problems, and succeed.

Figural analogy and verbal analogy tests are the most accurate indicators of *g*, and these show improvement in speed and correctness when test subjects have taken small to moderate doses of caffeine. Verbal analogy questions take the form "*father* is to *son* as *mother* is to *child, home, sponsor,* or *daughter.*" The correct answer, *daughter,* is supposed to emerge when a person has a correct insight into the abstract relationship between the first two terms. In a test of the effects of low doses of caffeine on cognition, conducted in 1995, David M. Warburton at the Department of Psychology, University of Reading, England, found that caffeine produced improvements in attention, delayed recall, and, most important for our purposes here, verbal problem solving. Warburton tested problem solving using the Baddeley Semantic Verification Task (examples of this test—Who's on First? The Caffeine One-Minute Intelligence Test—are found at the end of this chapter). He found that after taking only 75 mg or 150 mg of caffeine, test takers' number of correct answers increased substantially. We might also mention that none of the participants in Warburton's study reported any adverse effects from using the caffeine—not surprising considering the very low doses he was giving them.[26]

Many scientists have demonstrated that caffeine improves both the speed and accuracy of logical reasoning. A particularly interesting study found that caffeine improved performance on a semantic processing test, in which subjects were shown a series of statements and had to decide, based on general knowledge, which ones were true.[27]

Other studies have shown an improvement in calculation speed and error ratios, and specifically demonstrated benefits in performance on mental arithmetic, perhaps because of improved attention or perhaps because of improved mental processing.

In studies focusing on impulsive personalities, Uma Gupta and B. S. Gupta found that caffeine facilitated high performance in these people on both the SPM and the CFIT. The Guptas were considering experiments that used 1, 2, or 3 mg caffeine per kilogram of body weight, or about 65, 130, or 200 mg for a 150 pound person. Significantly, their test subjects were either noncaffeine users or very low caffeine users, with an intake of fewer than three or four cups of coffee a week.[28] Because people tend to self-select for caffeine use—that is, those who benefit from it tend to use more, and those who don't benefit from it or experience unpleasant side effects tend to use less—we can only assume that an examination of the general population of caffeine users would have produced even better IQ test results.

And, finally, although caffeine sharpens mental performance in all age groups, it improves the performance of older people in reasoning, memory, and reaction time tests more than it does the performance of young people, actually closing the gap in performance between the older and younger group.[29] We'll learn more about caffeine's ability to reverse age-related deficits in cognitive functioning in Chapter 11.

Memory: Short-Term and Long-Term

Scientists measure recall by administering memory tests to volunteers. For example, a typical verbal memory test might consist of reading a list of words immediately after, 15 minutes after, or 60 minutes after taking caffeine. Subjects would then be asked to write, in any order, as many words as they can remember. Memory studies can be complex, distinguishing, for example, between memory for numbers and memory for words or nonsense syllables, and they can include distracting tasks or stimuli designed to confuse the memory.

Most such studies have found that caffeine enhances memory functions such as delayed recall, recognition, semantic and verbal memory, and both short- and long-term memory and that it improves performance on easy and sometimes difficult memory tasks. In fact, the benefits of a moderate dose of caffeine in the morning can improve your memory for the entire day. Caffeine has also been shown to reverse the decline in memory that comes with increasing age and that it is especially effective in preventing the decline in memory that occurs in older people between morning and afternoon.[30]

However, as is the case with many of the other cognitive effects of caffeine, arousal levels are important in determining if caffeine will improve, leave unchanged, or even impair your ability to remember. When arousal levels are normal or low, all memory functions appear to improve significantly. When arousal levels are high, whatever the cause, caffeine in ordinary doses tends not to affect or even diminishes performance. In support of the arousal theory, a 1930s study by R. B. Cattell, one of the pioneering psychologists of the twentieth century, found low doses of 200 mg increased recall, while higher doses of 400 mg decreased recall.[31] A subsequent study demonstrated that memory span increases with lower doses of caffeine (around 150 mg) but not with higher doses (325 mg).[32] Another study showed that after being given a moderate dose (250 mg) of caffeine, subjects demonstrated increased working memory ability. However, at higher doses (500 mg)—and therefore at higher arousal levels—subjects started to show impairments in memory performance.

Similarly, caffeine helps improve accuracy in so-called less demanding memory tasks, while it impairs performance on more demanding ones. The idea is that the arousal level is raised when the subjects confront the more demanding task and that combined with caffeine, this higher relative task difficulty pushed the subjects past the peak of the inverted U-shaped function and resulted in performance deficits.[33] When evaluating the effects of 300 mg of caffeine on a memory task, researchers found that when subjects were exposed to white noise, their memory performance was decreased with caffeine.

The conclusion is clear: You can rely on caffeine to improve your memory in ordinary situations if you use low to moderate doses of the drug. However, higher doses, extremely demanding memory tasks, and adverse conditions will probably erode the benefits you get and may even result in a memory impairment. So if you are comfortably relaxing in your bedroom preparing for a French vocabulary test, you will probably discover that moderate amounts of caffeine give your memory a boost. However, if you are an air traffic controller trying to remember the positions of a dozen flights while overhearing a heated argument between two of your colleagues, caffeine might interfere with the performance of your job.

Hand-Eye Coordination, Motor Skills, and Psychomotor Performance

Psychomotor tasks link our decisions about what action to take with actually executing the action. Driving is a good example of a real-life task that demands good psychomotor skills. When we are on the road, we process information about the movements of the vehicles around us, about traffic signals, and about potential obstacles and hazards. Once we've evaluated the circumstances, we make a decision about what to do and must express this decision through the control of the muscles in our heads, hands, and feet. The ability to execute the required actions is called "psychomotor control." Another everyday task requiring good motor control is word processing, in which you use your brain to direct the motions of your fingers and hands.

Happily for drivers and for people who sit at a computer keyboard all day, caffeine causes a highly significant improvement in most measures of psychomotor performance.[34] This benefit does not decline with long-term caffeine use, nor does it require us to keep increasing the amount of caffeine in order to maintain it. In other words, if 200 mg of caffeine improve your word processing skills today, the same dose will continue to cause the same improvement indefinitely. In fact, overall, the benefits of caffeine to psychomotor performance are even greater in higher caffeine users than in low caffeine users. This may be because people self-select in the amount of caffeine they use, and those who get the greatest benefits tend to use more.

In addition, one leading researcher showed that a strong dose-response relationship exists between habitual caffeine intake and psychomotor performance, one that appeared to be even stronger in subjects ages thirty-five and up, whose overall performance was considerably worse than that of younger subjects, ages sixteen to thirty-four.[35] Because the improvements noted were independent of caffeine consumption levels immediately prior to testing, these provocative findings confirm other studies that suggest that caffeine has long-term beneficial effects on psychomotor performance and that it somehow increases the underlying speed of our responses and control over our psychomotor processes.

And despite skeptics, including some research scientists, the benefits of caffeine to psychomotor performance are not the result of alleviating deficits caused by caffeine withdrawal. The improvement in psychomotor performance is what scientists call "absolute," that is, it is an improvement over and above normal rested levels. In fact, as is true for mental and athletic performance generally, there is no clear evidence that psychomotor performance is impaired by caffeine withdrawal, so there is no deficit in performance to make up for.

Managing Life: Caffeine in Complex, Real-Life Work Settings

The mental challenges arising in real life are far more complex than the demands posed by laboratory experiments in cognition. Typically, laboratory studies employ well-defined tasks that require concentrating on one or

Steady as You Go! Caffeine and Manual Dexterity

It is possible that caffeine can impair hand steadiness and manual dexterity, although this effect, which has been documented in some studies of people who take large amounts of caffeine and do not use caffeine regularly, may disappear in regular caffeine users.[36] In fact, some measures of fine motor control, such as tracing images and pegboard tests, have been found either to improve or be unaffected by caffeine. Nevertheless, if you do fine work with your hands—for example, if you're a watchmaker or an orthodontist—be alert to the possibility that caffeine may impair your performance.

two sources of stimuli or information and providing a relatively simple response. In contrast, the situations in real life often require decision making in which incomplete or uncertain information must be gathered from many sources before reaching a complex decision and making a complex response. Research on caffeine's actual contributions to the cognitive processes in the workplace is very limited. However, provocative studies do exist suggesting that managerial performance is improved when either managers or employees are using caffeine. One study showed that managers who consumed 400 mg of caffeine or more a day reached decisions more quickly than managers who did not.[37] Another study demonstrated that managerial effectiveness was improved when employees were using caffeine.[38] Similarly, other studies revealed that employee performance is improved by caffeine. For example, one scientist found that moderate to large doses of caffeine (6 mg per kilogram, the equivalent of about four cups of filter drip coffee for a 150 pound person) "caused people to work harder because they underestimated how hard they were working." The workers thought that they were working at the same speed as they had without caffeine, but they were actually working considerably faster.[39]

Caffeine contributes other significant workplace benefits in addition to increasing wakefulness and alertness, sharpening reasoning, and improving memory and reaction time. For example, headaches are a common complaint in the workplace, whether caused by job tensions or other problems. One study has shown that workers use caffeine to relieve these headaches—one of the proven therapeutic uses of caffeine—with a resulting improvement in their efficiency.[40]

Another of the contributions of caffeine to workplace performance depends on its power to relieve boredom. "Habituation" is the word psychologists give to the psychological adaptation that takes place when there are many repetitions of the same activity. As habituation takes place, each additional similar stimulus tends to produce less and less of a response. The result is that you become bored. Although this mechanism was apparently designed by nature to help us become more alert to changing circumstances—by helping us to ignore the unchanging ones—it can have a detrimental effect by increasing our psychological discomfort, fatigue, and boredom when we are repeatedly exposed to the same people, questions, and problems, as we often are at work.

For example, part of your job may consist of checking tax records for certain entries and then entering long lists of the data into your computer. As you look at one tax record after another, habituation occurs, and it becomes increasingly difficult to focus on the information contained in each successive record. As a result, you start to overlook and then entirely miss the things you are looking for. When it comes time to enter the data, typing a long list of numbers also causes habituation, causing your attention to drift and increasing the number of errors you make. If you take caffeine before undertaking work like this, the process of habituation is dramatically slowed, which means you don't become bored as quickly. The result is that your work becomes more pleasant, productive, and accurate.[41] (Caffeine's effect on boredom is discussed more fully in Chapter 6.)

It is worth remembering one workplace caveat, however. Because stress increases our total arousal levels, too much caffeine in highly stressful job situations may push us past the optimal point in the Yerkes-Dodson response curve and diminish our mental capacity to complete work assignments.

You Work Better When You Think and Feel Better

Bad moods, boredom, fatigue, and pain decrease the power to concentrate and think clearly. Thus, in addition to its direct actions on cognition, memory, and reaction time, caffeine, by helping to overcome these unpleasant states of mind and body, enables us to think better and be more efficient at our jobs.

The Good Effects Just Keep on Coming!

The increase in brain metabolism is the same after an isolated high dose or daily administration of high doses of caffeine. This would seem to confirm the studies showing that there may not be a tolerance to many of caffeine's cognitive benefits. This means you can take the same dose every day and continue to enjoy the same beneficial effects on your memory and problem-solving abilities.

The English Study: Caffeine Provides Long-Term, Sustained Benefits for Mental Powers

As we've seen from the research discussed, caffeine has been proven to have acute, that is, immediate and short-term, benefits for reaction time, reasoning ability, memory, and attention. Perhaps even more astonishing, in an analysis of the caffeine consumption levels of over 9,000 people undertaken by Martin J. Jarvis at the Institute of Psychiatry of the National Addiction Centre in London in 1992, researchers demonstrated that the more caffeine you use on a daily basis, the higher you will score on tests of reaction time, reasoning, and verbal memory.[42]

The findings were based on information gathered in the massive Health and Lifestyle survey that interviewed randomly selected people over age eighteen who were living in England, Scotland, or Wales. In an initial interview, subjects were asked, "How many cups of coffee do you usually drink a day?" and were given the choice of answering "none," "1 or 2," "3 or 4," "5 or 6," or "more than 6." Similar questions were posed about tea drinking. An estimate of overall caffeine consumption was made based on the rough assumption that a cup of coffee contains about twice as much caffeine as a cup of tea.

The effects of the reported coffee intake, tea intake, and overall caffeine intake on reaction time, reasoning ability, and memory were evaluated by linear multiple regression analysis, a mathematical technique that allowed investigators to correct for confounding variables, that is, factors like social class and education level that might otherwise have confused the results. For instance, higher coffee drinking was found to be correlated with higher social class, educational level, home ownership, and better self-ratings of health. Other confounding variables include the fact that performance tends to decline with age, that men score better on spatial reasoning tests and have slightly faster reaction times, and that women perform better on verbal memory tests. In order to reach a clear conclusion from the data, it is necessary to factor out the statistical contributions made by these variables to performance levels on tests of mental abilities.

The results of the evaluation were as clear and convincing as they were astonishing. In the cognitive areas studied (simple and choice reaction time, visuospatial reasoning, and verbal memory), "a significant improvement was observed for each of the four tasks" among caffeine consumers. The improvement in performance was observed with both coffee and tea but was stronger with coffee, exactly as you would expect from the relative doses of caffeine that each contains. In addition, the performance improvements showed what is called a "dose-response" relationship to increasing levels of caffeine consumption. This means that after correcting for all the factors mentioned above, there were "higher levels of performance with increasing caffeine intake." People who consumed one to two cups of coffee a day tended to do better than people who consumed no coffee, people who consumed three to four cups of coffee a day tended to do better still,

The Tests Used in the English Study

- Reaction time: Subjects were shown a number on a screen and asked to press a button corresponding with that number as fast as possible.

- Verbal memory: Subjects were read a list of ten common foods and asked if each contained dietary fiber. They were not told that they would be tested for their ability to remember the list. A few minutes later, after being distracted by another task, they were asked to name as many as they could of the foods that had appeared on the list.

- Visuospatial reasoning: Subjects were shown drawings of three-dimensional assemblages of cubes and asked how many blocks each assembly contained. In order to reach a correct answer, it was necessary to determine the number of blocks that were hidden, as well as those that could be seen. Therefore, it was necessary to use spatial reasoning about the structures.

all the way on up to people who consumed over six cups of coffee a day, who did the best of all. (The Yerkes-Dodson "less is more" curve of caffeine activity applies only to short-term effects, not to improvements resulting from sustained use.)

Results from this retroactive lifestyle study support the findings of small laboratory studies that larger long-term benefits are found in older subjects than in younger ones. Because age often causes a decline in overall mental and psychomotor performance, we see once more that caffeine helps to close the performance gap between older and younger people.

Equally interesting is the conclusion that tolerance does not develop to caffeine's performance-enhancing effects on cognition. In other words, caffeine retains its beneficial effects on mental function in long-term users, and the same dose will continue to yield the same benefits indefinitely, as the table shows.[43]

Acute and Long-Term Benefits of Caffeine on Cognitive Performance

Type of Cognitive Performance	Benefit of Caffeine	Comment	Type of Benefits
Abstract reasoning (IQ tests, SATs, solving problems at school and in the workplace)	Strong	Improves reasoning power, speed of information processing, and percentages of correct responses	Acute and long-term benefits
Focused attention	None	Doesn't seem to help when you're trying to focus on something and are being distracted	
Divided attention (driving a car, taking care of children)	Strong	Significantly helps when you are trying to do two things at once or to complete a task that requires you to divide your attention between two or more things	Acute benefits

Type of Cognitive Performance	Benefit of Caffeine	Comment	Type of Benefits
Sustained attention, vigilance (typing, adding numbers)	Strong	Reduces errors because it delays the onset of boredom and also keeps your energy up throughout the task	Acute benefits
Short-term memory	Strong	Enables you to remember words and numbers better, whether they are written or spoken; older people benefit more	Acute (all day) and long-term benefits
Long-term memory	Strong (?)	Those who use more caffeine may be growing more brain cells in the areas of the brain responsible for long-term memory	Long-term benefits(?)
Reaction time, psychomotor performance	Strong	Improves speed of information processing and the speed of the response itself; older people benefit more	Acute and long-term benefits

Note: Acute benefits are short-term improvements experienced after you drink coffee or take a caffeine pill. Acute benefits to memory and mood from a moderate dose of caffeine in the morning tend to last all day. Long-term benefits are long-term improvements that are observed in people who use caffeine regularly, whether or not they have recently consumed any caffeine. The "?" indicates that the memory benefits of growing new brain cells have not yet been proven.

Self-Assessments of Cognitive Abilities

The following self-tests of cognitive capacity will enable you to compare your performance before taking caffeine with your performance after taking caffeine in different doses and at different times. Therefore, we don't provide any norms or average scores. These tests compare your performance with and without caffeine; they are not designed to rank you against other people.

We suggest that you try each test when you have not used any caffeine for at least 6 hours. Then experiment with about 100 mg, the amount in 4 ounces of filter drip coffee or half of a Vivarin tablet. Try the same tests on different days, both before taking and after taking 150 mg, 200 mg, and, if you can tolerate it comfortably, 300 mg of caffeine. Make sure that you begin the tests between 15 minutes and 1 hour after taking caffeine. The results should give you some idea of the kind and degree of benefits you can expect to get from a given dose of caffeine in logical and visuospatial reasoning, information processing, reaction time, divided attention, and auditory and visual memory.

Take these tests before and after using caffeine. Compare your results.

Who's on First? The Caffeine One-Minute Intelligence Test

This is a speed test that measures how quickly and correctly you can perform elementary logical operations before and after taking caffeine. We provide no average scores. The point is to see how much improvement, if any, you can achieve with different doses of caffeine.

Use a kitchen timer or have a friend keep track of the second hand on a watch. Your score is your number of correct answers. Record your score when you have not taken caffeine for at least 6 hours and after taking caffeine in different doses. Alternate between test 1 and test 2 in order to avoid learning the correct answers.

Don't be disturbed if you can't answer all of the questions within one minute. Few people can. The idea of the test is not to see how high a score you can achieve, but rather to find out how much improvement you can get by using caffeine.

After each statement, there is a letter pair to which it refers. Circle either *true* or *false* depending on whether the statement is true or false.

Example 1:

B is followed by A　　　AB　　True　　False

In the letter combination AB, B is not followed by A. Therefore the correct answer is *false*.

Example 2:

B is not preceded by A　　BA　　True　　False

In the letter combination BA, B is not preceded by A. Therefore the correct answer is *true*.

Test 1: You have 1 minute to complete the questions in this test. Number the lines on a separate sheet of paper, 1 through 25. Write your answers next to each number, and check them with the answers given at the end of this section.

1.	A follows B	AB	True	False
2.	B does not precede A	AB	True	False
3.	B is followed by A	BA	True	False
4.	A precedes B	AB	True	False
5.	B precedes A	AB	True	False
6.	A is not followed by B	BA	True	False
7.	A is followed by B	AB	True	False
8.	B is followed by A	AB	True	False
9.	B is not preceded by A	BA	True	False
10.	B follows A	AB	True	False
11.	A does not follow B	BA	True	False
12.	B is preceded by A	BA	True	False
13.	A is followed by B	BA	True	False
14.	B does not follow A	AB	True	False
15.	A follows B	AB	True	False
16.	B precedes A	BA	True	False
17.	B is not followed by A	AB	True	False
18.	A is not preceded by B	BA	True	False
19.	A precedes B	BA	True	False
20.	B is followed by A	AB	True	False
21.	A does not precede B	AB	True	False
22.	A is followed by B	BA	True	False

23.	B is not followed by A	BA	True	False
24.	B precedes A	BA	True	False
25.	A is not preceded by B	AB	True	False

Test 2: You have 1 minute to complete the questions in this test.

1.	B follows A	AB	True	False
2.	A does not precede B	AB	True	False
3.	A is followed by B	BA	True	False
4.	B precedes A	AB	True	False
5.	A precedes B	AB	True	False
6.	B is not followed by A	BA	True	False
7.	B is followed by A	AB	True	False
8.	A is followed by B	AB	True	False
9.	A is not preceded by B	BA	True	False
10.	A follows B	AB	True	False
11.	B does not follow A	BA	True	False
12.	A is preceded by B	BA	True	False
13.	B is followed by A	BA	True	False
14.	A does not follow B	AB	True	False
15.	B follows A	AB	True	False
16.	A precedes B	BA	True	False
17.	A is not followed by B	AB	True	False
18.	B is not preceded by A	BA	True	False
19.	B precedes A	BA	True	False
20.	A is followed by B	AB	True	False
21.	B does not precede A	BA	True	False
22.	A does not follow B	BA	True	False
23.	A precedes B	AB	True	False
24.	B is followed by A	AB	True	False
25.	B does not follow A	AB	True	False

Answers:
Test 1

1. F
2. T
3. T

4. T
5. F
6. T
7. T
8. F
9. T
10. T
11. F
12. F
13. F
14. F
15. F
16. T
17. T
18. F
19. F
20. F
21. F
22. F
23. F
24. T
25. T

Test 2

1. T
2. F
3. F
4. F
5. T
6. F
7. F
8. T
9. F
10. F
11. T
12. T
13. T

14. T
15. T
16. F
17. F
18. T
19. T
20. T
21. F
22. F
23. T
24. F
25. F

The Calculating Mind

Perform the calculations indicated. You have 2½ minutes or 150 seconds to complete the questions in this part. This is a speed test, to see how quickly and accurately you can perform elementary calculations.

Use a sheet of paper to copy the problems. Use a kitchen timer or ask a friend to keep track of the time as you answer the questions. Your score is your number of correct answers. Try this test before taking caffeine and after taking different dosages, and see how your score is changed after using the caffeine.

1. $35 \times 24 =$
2. $389 + 723 =$
3. $44 \times 78 =$
4. $912 + 551 =$
5. $27 \times 88 =$
6. $395 + 912 =$
7. $17 \times 53 =$
8. $172 + 366 =$
9. $97 \times 41 =$
10. $825 + 441 =$

Answers:
1. 840
2. 1112

3. 3432
4. 1463
5. 2376
6. 1307
7. 901
8. 538
9. 3977
10. 1266

Reaction Time

For people within the same age-group, the speed of your reactions is a good measure not only of alertness but also of general intelligence. In order to take this test, buy an 18 inch ruler, and ask a friend to hold the ruler suspended vertically from the top. Position your hand so that your thumb and middle finger are 3 inches apart, with the bottom edge of the ruler between them. Your friend should drop the ruler without giving you any advance notice, and you should try to catch it between your thumb and middle finger as quickly as possible. Your score is the inch at which you catch it. Repeat this test four times, and calculate an average score. Try this test before taking caffeine and after taking caffeine in different dosages and see if your average score is higher after using caffeine.[44]

Attention and Vigilance

We use different kinds of concentration to perform different tasks. This typing test, which compares your performance in typing nonsense letter combinations with your performance typing real words, is a way of evaluating how much effect caffeine has on your ability to process two different kinds of information. When you type nonsense combinations, you must identify each letter separately; when you type real words, you can rely on context to determine the letters.

To take this test, prop open this book next to your keyboard. Complete as much typing as you can within 1 minute for the nonsense text. The text in the left-hand column is a transposition of a poem by the Roman poet Horace, "Happy the Man," translated in the right-hand column by John Dryden. If you try typing the original poem, you can see how much easier it is to do than the nonsense version. Use a kitchen timer, or ask a friend to time your performance. Check your results carefully and count the number of "words" you get perfectly correct. See how your before-caffeine and after-caffeine performances compare, on which tests caffeine helps the most, and how much caffeine gives you the greatest performance boost.

Nonsense Poem	Original Poem
Heh apy phe laone mHappy dtan, and,	Happy the man, and happy he alone,
Hwhe, o acn call ay his otodwn:	He, who can call today his own:
Hwho rusece wie, thicn an asy	He, who secure within can say
Toorrodo tmhy wo wstr, fl orhav elvied dtoya.	Tomorrow do thy worst, for I have lived today.
orr ain fiBe ar, ro fulo, ro sehin,	Be fair, or foul, or rain, or shine,
Teh yjos I ssessehave pod, in pties fo tfae, ear nmie.	The joys I have possessed, in spite of fate, are mine.
Nven itot rhesfel pnou tast has phe pwoer;	Not heaven itself upon the past has power;
Btu ween, anhat hsa been, hsa bd hIave hda hroumy.	But what has been, has been, and I have had my hour.

You can try a similar test using any paragraph of prose text. Again, prop open the book next to your keyboard and see how many words you can type correctly within 1 minute. Compare the number of your correctly typed words before and after taking caffeine.

Computer Games

Many computer games are excellent tests of reaction time, logical reasoning, vigilance, divided attention, and memory. Because it's easy to play them over and over again, they make good vehicles for testing many aspects of cognitive performance affected by caffeine. One excellent simple game that tests vigilance and visual and auditory memory was created by Vivarin, manufacturer of the most popular caffeine pill in the United States. You must log on to their web site in order to try it: www.vivarin.com. Once you have done so, you can play the game on-line or download it.

The game consists of a series of notes combined with corresponding flashing lights. As the series increases in length, you are asked to repeat it back without making any mistakes. Each time you do so, another note and flashing light are added. Eventually, you will get one wrong, and the test is over. No average scores are given because the point is to compare your own score before and after using caffeine.

You can also try almost any of the common computer-based games that are available on the web in order to make your own comparisons of performance before and after using caffeine. There are dozens of varieties of the famous Tetris game, a good measure of visuospatial reasoning, reaction time, and vigilance. For people interested in an additional challenge, there are several on-line, interactive versions of the Stroop Test, a fascinating neurobehavioral test of information processing and reaction time. You can find entertaining versions of this test at the following web sites: www.pbs. org/wgbh/nova/everest/exposure/stroopintro and www.faculty.washington. edu/chudler.

5

Enhancing Your Creativity

WHAT TWO THINGS do Dr. William Harvey (1578–1657), the English medical pioneer, Sir Robert Boyle (1627–1691), the English founder of modern chemical theory, Henri Poincaré (1854–1912), the French mathematician, Honoré de Balzac (1799–1850), the French novelist, Ludwig van Beethoven (1770–1827), the German composer, and Dr. Samuel Johnson (1709–1784), the English man of letters, have in common? For one thing, each was a great creator in his field. For another, each relied on the caffeine advantage to stimulate and sustain a prodigious creative output.

Genius is supposed to be self-sufficient, but quite a number of geniuses have used caffeine to spark their imaginations and as a result have made many discoveries and created many works of art that the world still celebrates after hundreds of years. Creativity is hard to quantify and measure. It's impossible to point to double-blind research studies proving that caffeine can boost creative output. However, when we consider the evidence of history and the testimony of artists and scientists, it makes an interesting speculation that if caffeine has given a creative boost to some of the most creative minds in history, perhaps it could also give average people the edge they need to maximize creative output in their own work and recreational lives. (It is true that some creative people have claimed that alcohol, absinthe, or even cigarettes boosted their creative output. However, whatever the benefits these substances might have had for a few people, it can be proven that alcohol, for example, generally impairs reasoning and working ability. And obviously cigarettes are very bad for your health. In contrast, caffeine has been shown to improve most mental functions in ways that facilitate productive mental activity and do so safely.)

We take caffeine for granted today. But in sixteenth-century England, coffee, tea, chocolate, and the other natural sources of caffeine were unknown. Harvey, a promising young Cambridge graduate, traveled to Italy in 1599 to enroll in medical school at the cosmopolitan University of Padua, one of the leading centers of international culture of its day. While there, he fell under coffee's magic spell, after learning about the drink from pioneering botanists who had just returned from expeditions to the Middle East or from Arab students (there were many at the university). This was fifty years before the first coffeehouse opened in England, and coffee had not yet appeared in his native country.

When Harvey returned to England, he began importing the beans for his private use. Evidently finding in coffee a valuable aid to his medical experiments, he continued to be an avid coffee drinker until his death at age seventy-nine. He is said to have died holding a coffee bean aloft between his thumb and index finger, proclaiming, "This little bean is the source of all happiness and wit!" In his will, he left fifty pounds of coffee, his entire stock, to his colleagues in the Royal College of Physicians, with the instruction that they toast him each month with coffee until the supply was exhausted. Legend has it that his most important discovery, the quantification of the circulation of the blood in the human body, was suggested to him when, after drinking too much strong coffee, he heard his pulse pounding in his ears.

Coffee made its big splash in England in Oxford in 1655. In that year, a group of leading scholars and intellectuals prevailed on Arthur Tillyard, a local pharmacist, to prepare and serve coffee to them weekly. The members of this circle included some of the leading luminaries of the time, among them scientists, mathematicians, architects, and men of letters. The group moved to London and was granted a charter in 1662 by King Charles II as the Royal Society of London for the Improvement of Natural Knowledge.

The thousand-year lapse of European science in the Middle Ages, during which naturalism mingled promiscuously with magic, ended at the same time that the first coffeehouses opened in England and that coffee, fresh from the Near East, became suddenly popular with the intellectual and social avant-garde in Oxford and London. The aristocratic Anglo-Irishman Sir Robert Boyle, the father of modern chemistry, regarded in his time as the leading scientist in England, was a founding member of the original Oxford Coffee Club. Credited with drawing the first clear line between alchemy and chemistry, Boyle formulated the precursor to the modern theory of the elements, achieving the first significant advance in chemical theory in more than two thousand years.

Within a few years after the English craze for coffee began, the modern revolutions in science and mathematics were well under way. Twentieth-century scientific studies prove that caffeine increases reasoning power and vigilance, and increases stamina for both mental and physical work. As a result of Boyle's caffeine-inspired investigations, Friedlieb Ferdinand Runge, a promising young German medical student (at the request of the great poet Wolfgang von Goethe), was able to isolate the chemical caffeine at the beginning of the nineteenth century. Because of its avid use by the most creative early scientists, caffeine may well have expedited the inauguration of both modern chemistry and physics and, in this sense, have been the only drug in history with some responsibility for stimulating the formulation of the theoretical foundations of its own discovery.[1]

No account of caffeine's historical connection with creativity would be complete without mentioning the literary and artistic revival that occurred in the coffeehouses of London at the turn of the seventeenth century. During this age, the coffeehouses were places where people of all kinds met and mingled for the first time, and intellectual leaders saw the coffeehouses as places in which people could broaden their minds. "I shall be ambitious to have it said of me," wrote Joseph Addison (1672–1719), a towering figure of early London journalism, "that I brought philosophy out of the closets and libraries, schools and colleges, to dwell in clubs and assemblies, at tea-tables and coffeehouses." The art of conversation became the basis of a new literary style, which was more natural, engaging, and persuasive and less academic and preachy. Under the leadership of pioneers such as Daniel Defoe, the author of *Robinson Crusoe,* the first newspapers in the world were written and published in London's coffeehouses. At coffeehouses such as Button's, the Bedford, and Garraway's, famous essayists, playwrights, and poets congregated. Painters, actors, and scientists each had their own favorite coffeehouse haunts.

The nineteenth-century French writer Honoré de Balzac, one of the most prolific novelists in history, was a hardened caffeine user. While we don't recommend his approach, it was a fascinating one. Locking himself

Confirming the Tradition:
Caffeine as an Agent of Cultural Development

From the old Chinese Taoist lore, the decorous and mysterious Japanese tea ceremony, the ecstatic Sufi prayer vigils, ancient military expeditions in Africa and South America, to the desks of poets and novelists and journalists, the laboratories of scientists, and the dens of revolutionaries, caffeine has played a vital role in sparking cultural and intellectual development the world over.

Two hundred years ago, when the great German poet Johann Wolfgang von Goethe asked a promising medical student to find out what gave coffee its remarkable powers, a request that prompted the discovery of pure caffeine, he had no idea how far the quest for the truth about caffeine would ultimately lead. Today, scientific studies have not only confirmed these traditional uses of caffeine, but revealed that caffeine, properly used, has even more benefits for releasing creative potential than had ever been recognized before.

in his tiny room, he began his career by drinking strong coffee to stay awake all night and work. As time went on, he progressed to making stronger and stronger coffee and, finally, to eating coffee beans in order to get a bigger caffeine rush. Possibly as a result of such excesses, he died at the age of fifty-one, leaving behind one of the largest and most outstanding collections of novels ever written by one person. Balzac even wrote a treatise about the marvelous powers of stimulants to enhance creativity. In it, he says that, after consuming a large amount of strong coffee, "Ideas quick-march into motion like battalions of a grand army to its legendary fighting ground, and the battle rages. Memories charge in, bright flags on high; the cavalry of metaphor deploys with a magnificent gallop, the artillery of logic rushes up with clattering wagons and cartridges; on imagination's orders, sharpshooters sight and fire; forms and shapes and characters rear up; the paper is spread with ink—for the nightly labor begins and ends with torrents of this black water." [2]

Balzac's exuberant use of caffeine to augment his creative powers was shared by Gioacchino Antonio Rossini (1792–1868), the Italian composer, who wrote to Balzac, "Coffee is an affair of fifteen or twenty days, just the right amount of time to write an opera."

Henri Poincaré, who created the theory of chaos and almost anticipated Einstein's theory of special relativity, was one of the most brilliant mathematicians of the nineteenth century. He records how he was able to solve a baffling problem and make one of his most important discoveries only after consuming caffeine:

> For fifteen days I struggled to prove that no functions analogous to those I have since called Fuchsian functions could exist; I was then very ignorant. Every day I sat down at my work table where I spent an hour or two; I tried a great number of combinations and arrived at no result. One evening, contrary to my custom, I took black coffee; I could not go to sleep; ideas swarmed up in clouds; I sensed them clashing until, to put it so, a pair would hook together to form a stable combination. By morning I had established the existence of a class of Fuchsian functions, those derived from the hypergeometric series. I had only to write up the results which took me a few hours.[3]

Paul Erdos, one of the most prolific mathematicians of the twentieth century, who authored nearly 1,500 treatises, was an avid espresso drinker and often spoke of depending on it to sustain his creative mathematical work. He offered compelling testimony to caffeine's ability to augment the creative process when he commented, "A mathematician is a machine for turning coffee into theorems."[4]

Creativity and the Great Leap Forward

There have been no controlled studies that we know of to determine the power of caffeine to increase creative output. Such studies would be difficult to design because of the problems of evaluating the merits of the creative material produced. Some researchers, reasoning that caffeine can impair performance levels on complex and novel tasks, have speculated that caffeine can actually interfere with the creative process. But it is not the absolute complexity of a task that determines whether caffeine will help or hurt your performance. Rather, it is the degree to which the person

A Buzzword for Creative Energies

In reviewing an album cut by a band called Caffeine, Amazon.com writes, " 'Caffeine' is the name of an American techno record label. It's also a weekly rave party on the East Coast, a clothing line, and finally, a banging compilation disk featuring DJ Micro and his funky friends."

doing it finds it baffling or difficult. And it is also true that when you write or paint regularly, caffeine may help to freshen artistic insight by breaking up the habituation—a deadness of sensibilities—that might otherwise cloud your mind.

Poincaré's story is an excellent example. For most of us, the mathematical problems he was tackling would seem overwhelmingly abstruse and confoundingly difficult. Perhaps we would find that caffeine even impaired our limited ability to comprehend them. However, Poincaré was a mathematical genius. And it seems that because of his gifts, he was able to make use of caffeine to increase his insight. Similarly, it makes sense that a man like Balzac, with exceptionally fluid verbal gifts, would experience a surge of creative energy and output on caffeine, whereas people of less than average verbal ability might well find their production reduced in quality and quantity by the operations of the drug. In addition, both Poincaré and Balzac might have found their outlooks freshened by caffeine's power to keep things interesting. Whatever the underlying dynamics, however, it is clear that in order to find out what, if anything, caffeine will do for your creative output, you have to try it out for yourself.

There is another factor that enables caffeine to contribute to creativity. Caffeine is known to increase impulsivity. This can be a double-edged sword when it comes to performance. Impulsive people tend to rush ahead and make more mistakes when trying to complete logical tasks such as solving arithmetic problems, and too much caffeine, as we have seen, can impair your performance on such tasks in states of high arousal. However, impulsivity also helps people generate new ideas more freely and fluently. And there is a sense in which impulsivity and the ideational jumps of intuition, so greatly prized by creative thinkers, are closely related. Perhaps this is another reason that talented artists and scientists are able to benefit from

Off the Cuff with Caffeine

As your dose of caffeine increases, alertness increases, but so does impulsivity. If you want this increased level of alertness, you have to learn to manage the impulsivity, which can range, at extreme levels, into a kind of intoxication. But increasing impulsivity with caffeine can be a way of increasing creativity, as many novelist, poets, and painters have discovered.

caffeine, sometimes even from high doses that would reduce the performance levels of most other people.

Feeling Deeply: Becoming More Sensuous with Caffeine

The intensity and aptness of our interactions with the things we encounter in the world are determined by three things: (1) central processing mechanisms, that is, the underlying cogency and speed of our thinking, including visuospatial reasoning, and memory; (2) response mechanisms, including reaction time and accuracy; and (3) the perceptual mechanisms, that is, the acuteness, vividness, accuracy, and speed, with which we are able to perceive things. We have discussed improvements in central processing mechanisms and response mechanisms. Now we turn our attention to caffeine's effects on perceptual mechanisms, effects that can add to the depth and quality with which we apprehend the world and the ways we can enhance our ability to reshape it creatively.

Caffeine has the power, in the words of one scientist, "to produce a more perfect sensory association of ideas, and to produce a keener appreciation of sensory stimuli."[5] In simpler language, this means that caffeine enables us to judge the contents of what we see, hear, touch, taste, and smell more accurately and also to feel what comes to us through our senses more intensely.[6] For example, caffeine has been shown to reduce the "visual threshold," that is, to improve our ability to see both color and light. In many ways, caffeine actually makes you more sensuous.

How does caffeine make the world more alive to our senses? Scientists speculate that this power may depend in part on the way caffeine affects the function of the thalamus, a mass of nerve cells centrally located in the brain just below the cerebrum and resembling a large egg in size and shape. The thalamus relays the sensory impulses of sight, hearing, touch, and taste to the higher center of the brain, the cerebral cortex. It is an important center of integration, allowing sensory information to evoke physical reactions and affect emotions. Caffeine may profoundly affect this primitive part of the brain that controls both what we perceive and how we feel about what we perceive.

Some research suggests that caffeine works to heighten our perceptions by improving the signal-to-noise ratio in what we see and hear.[7] When we improve the signal-to-noise ratio in a video- or audiotape, the picture or sound jumps out at us more vividly. By helping us to focus or zoom in on an object of interest and ignore other stimuli, caffeine makes the things we pay attention to more vivid.

Everyone has heard that eating carrots is supposed to improve your vision. Using caffeine actually does. After taking caffeine, you can see greater numbers of faint twinkling stars, and you will also be able to see finer gradations in the colors of flowers. You can see more because caffeine decreases the level of brightness or intensity of illumination that the eye needs to recognize the things we see and discriminate between them. Two researchers showed that a relatively small dose of caffeine significantly lowers the luminance threshold, that is, the smallest amount of light a person can detect. In their experiments, the luminance threshold decreased by 20 percent in people who had taken 90 mg of caffeine and by nearly 40 percent in those who had taken 180 mg of caffeine.[8] These effects were observed to continue throughout the entire 90-minute test session.[9] This would mean that a single cup of filter drip coffee should dramatically improve your ability to see details of objects in dim light and enable you to note greater detail in ordinary light.

But caffeine has an even more magical effect on the way we see the world. Not only does it "turn up the light," it actually increases the intensity with which we perceive colors. In one study, participants were asked to place twenty-two disordered hues in consecutive color order. After taking either 100 mg or 200 mg of caffeine, both men and women were better able to discriminate colors in yellow to red hues, and women were also better able to distinguish gradations in blue and green hues.[10] Even more astonishing, it has been shown that people who consume at least one caf-

Opening the Painter's Eye

Caffeine can be a real eye opener for painters in more ways than one. For one thing, caffeine improves visuospatial reasoning, which means that it can help painters create more interesting and complex compositions. Perhaps even more significant, research proves that after taking caffeine or if you use caffeine regularly, color discrimination increases significantly, which means you can see finer gradations in the color rainbow.[11] Who knows what Leonardo might have done if he had known about caffeine! Is it possible that the impressionists' love of subtle pastels originated partly from their many hours in the Paris cafés?

feinated drink a day, whether they had taken caffeine before the test or not, made nearly 60 percent fewer errors in distinguishing colors than people who rarely or never use caffeine.[12]

Even the smell of coffee may induce an "earlier and more intense perception of visual stimuli."[13] So when you drink coffee, there are many reasons that your sense of sight is really raised to its maximum potential.

If there is one faculty that is identified more than any other with sensuousness, it is the sense of touch. In one study of perceptual judgment by Uma and B. S. Gupta, the size of test blocks was compared using 4 cm blocks that were adjustable in size 1 mm at a time. Blindfolded subjects were required to hold the test blocks between the thumb and index fingers and to report when the width of the comparison block equaled the width of the test block. The researchers found that in high impulsives, 1 mg to 3 mg of caffeine per kilogram of body weight (a 3 ounce to about an 8 ounce serving of filter drip coffee for a 150 pound person) significantly reduced the errors in judgment. The accuracy of their responses was proportional to the dose of caffeine consumed. They also found that these doses had no effect on the performance of low impulsives,[14] which is not surprising, because low impulsives are already functioning closer to their full potential. These findings demonstrate that caffeine can refine our sense of touch so that we become aware of very small features and alterations in what we are feeling.

Just like vision and touch, smell and taste are windows on the world.

Smell is important for determining what you understand and feel about the world. To a more limited extent, the same thing is true for taste.

In two well-conducted studies, S. S. Schiffman and his colleagues found that "caffeine presented on the tongue" increased ratings of taste intensity, with the largest increases in bitter tastes with sweet components.[15] The explanation of the authors is that "methylxanthines potentiate taste by competing with adenosine for receptor occupancy via a local mechanism at the level of the taste receptors in the tongue." This means that caffeine is blocking the actions of adenosine, this time in the cells of the tongue, thereby intensifying bitter flavors and the combination of bitter and sweet flavors. Caffeine's actions on the central nervous system seem to have nothing to do with this flavor intensification, because when it is given in pill form, as opposed to being put directly on the tongue, it fails to demonstrate any effect on taste.[16] So when you drink coffee or tea and expose your tongue to caffeine, you are not only experiencing the flavor of caffeine as a small, bitter component of the flavor of these drinks (called "point"), you are altering the function of your taste buds so that you will sense a whole range of flavors more intensely.

6

Getting in a Good Mood

THERE'S AN OLD SAYING, "There's nothing either good or bad, but think-ing makes it so." This may not be a very good guide to morality, but it does aptly express the sovereign power of moods over the quality, character, and enjoyment of life.

Of all of caffeine's remarkable effects, probably no other is so astonish-ing, and certainly none is more precious, than the power to lift our spirits. Scientists have proven that even low doses of caffeine are often enough to create significant increases in feelings of clear-headedness, happiness, opti-mism, tranquility, and motivation for work.

Caffeine's mood effects seem to tailor themselves to our immediate needs. When we are feeling okay, caffeine helps us to feel even happier and to keep us from becoming bored and enervated. When we are edgy, caf-feine relaxes us, helping to smooth out tension and make us calm (see Chapter 7 for a full discussion of these effects). When we are depressed, or vulnerable to depression, caffeine can be the secret of our liberation, increasing our feelings of optimism and brightening our outlook on life. And, when we are facing the challenges of the workplace, caffeine boosts our self-confidence, drive, and motivation and gives us the attitude of suc-cess we need to achieve our goals. In short, when it comes to mood, caf-feine is good for what ails us.

Even more astonishing, perhaps, is the fact that regular caffeine use, even as little as 100 mg a day, seems to result in sustained enhancements of mood. People who are not depressed find that such small amounts of caffeine can significantly increase self-assessments of happiness and friend-liness and reduce tension on an ongoing basis.[1] And people who had been fighting depression and start taking a caffeine pill every morning frequently report waking up with a smile and full of bounce and feel fine even before taking their daily dose. What is perhaps more surprising is that caffeine has such a profound effect on serious depression that it even reduces the rate of suicide. In fact, caffeine's power to enhance moods is so significant and well documented that many scientists have suggested that it be studied as a first-line treatment for clinical depression. (Don't expect these studies to be conducted any time soon. As we explained in the Introduction, there isn't much financial incentive for pharmaceutical companies to invest millions in proving to the FDA that a generic product has new benefits.)

Does caffeine have any bad effects on mood? It can if you take too much. High doses are associated with increases in negative mood self-assessments or what scientists call "dysphoric reactions." One researcher, for example, reported increases in anxiety and tenseness following doses larger than 400 mg.[2] Another reported increases in anxiety and tension after doses of 600 mg, or the amount in four cups of filtered coffee.[3] However, although these findings suggest that high doses can sometimes raise anxiety levels, a large-scale study of over 9,000 long-term caffeine users in England showed no relationship between caffeine use and anxiety.[4] One reason for the discrepancy in these results may be that in real life, people rarely take as much as 600 mg of caffeine all at once (this would be the equivalent of downing four cups of filter drip coffee in a few gulps), and so they don't attain the blood levels that might be anxiety producing. Another reason may be that people adjust their caffeine dose to avoid anxiety reactions and choose to drink only one cup of coffee after finding that two cups puts them on edge, or simply to stop drinking more coffee as soon as the first sensations of tension begin to assert themselves.

As we will see in Chapter 8, researcher Terry Graham has recently proven that caffeine pills do much more to improve athletic performance than coffee. One little-known speculation about caffeine's power to enhance our mood is that caffeine pills may deliver an enormously greater punch in this area than caffeine in coffee. According to Andrew Smith, one of the world's leading researchers into caffeine's mood effects, "It is quite plausible that the effects described by Terry Graham may generalize to some aspects of mood and performance, but there have been no convincing demonstrations of this yet."[5] And although there is no scientific demonstration, anecdotal evidence is growing, and the mood effect of caffeine pills such as Vivarin is something you can easily test for yourself.

As with its effects on cognition and athletic performance, caffeine's power to significantly increase clear-headedness, happiness, and calmness and to decrease tenseness cannot be ascribed to alleviating the deficits caused by caffeine withdrawal.[6] The reason is that all of these mood improvements are observed in people who do not regularly use caffeine, and therefore cannot be withdrawing from it, and are also observed in people who have not been deprived of caffeine prior to the initiation of testing. The conclusion is inescapable: Caffeine produces an absolute improvement in mood. It makes you feel better.

Improving Your Mood

Psychologists have proven that caffeine enhances mood,[7] significantly increasing how happy and contented people say that they feel, in both regular caffeine users and people who rarely or never use caffeine.[8] Doses as low as 65 mg, less than half of what you'll get from a single cup of filtered coffee, generally exert beneficial effects on certain aspects of mood.[9] And many studies have demonstrated that doses of 100 mg to 300 mg of caffeine are associated with improved or positive mood changes that last the entire day, especially in regular caffeine users.[10] These effects do not seem to wear off with time or require increasing our caffeine dose in order to stay happy. In fact, there is strong evidence that caffeine helps enhance the moods of regular caffeine users more than it does nonusers[11] and that in the long run, caffeine use will cause a long term, dose-dependent improvement in overall mood.[12] In other words, people who drink one to two cups of coffee a day tend to be in a better mood throughout the day than people who don't drink any, and people who drink three to four cups are in a better mood still. Caffeine has also been shown to improve the bad moods people often have early in the morning.[13] We also saw, in Chapter 2, how caffeine has the power to counteract the feeling of being down that attends fatigue and that it can even prevent these bad mood slumps as effectively as a nap can.[14]

What gives caffeine the power to shape our moods? Once again, it works to regulate and balance a number of neurotransmitter systems, including the serotonin, the dopamine, and the norepinephrine (adrenaline) systems, that work in our brains to shape the way we feel. To clarify, caffeine combats depression by helping to restore the balance of the serotonin system, the same system that the antidepressants Prozac and Zoloft (and also carbohydrate binges) regulate in order to overcome gloom. Caffeine gives our moods an extra sparkle by stimulating the norepinephrine system, a system regulated by such antidepressants as Effexor and Welbutrin. And here is the secret of why people use caffeine not only for its practical benefits, but also find it delightful. It is probable that all habit-forming drugs, including dangerous drugs like heroin and morphine, cocaine, barbiturates, and even alcohol, nicotine, PCP, and marijuana, finally trace their reinforcing activity to the activation of the dopamine system.[15] Because caffeine also activates the dopamine system, it delivers the same sort of pleasure as these inestimably more dangerous substances, but it does so in a healthy, safe way.

Caffeine augments the mood alterations induced by other drugs, such as alcohol, nicotine, and even cocaine, although we do not recommend these combinations.[16] It has been shown that people who have taken moderate amounts of both alcohol and caffeine achieve a better mood than those who have consumed alcohol alone.[17] This may be one reason that Red Bull, a high-caffeine carbonated soft drink from Austria, has become so popular as a mixer. (Another reason for its popularity may be that caffeine reduces some of the cognitive impairments caused by alcohol, increasing clear-headedness and helping people to perform at more nearly normal levels despite drinking alcohol.[18] But remember that blood alcohol levels are not lowered by caffeine, so it won't improve your score on a breathalyzer test.)

Real mood effects from caffeine emerge more slowly than effects on cognitive performance. Effects on attention span, for example, are seen between 30 minutes and 1 hour after taking caffeine, while mood effects have taken 1 to 2 hours to develop.[19]

The mood effects of caffeine can be profound, even bringing about life-altering changes that amaze the people in which they occur. For example, women who experience depression as a component of premenstrual syndrome can sometimes completely throw off the dark clouds of unhappiness and recover their normal, cheerful state all day by taking as little as 100 mg to 200 mg of caffeine in the morning. As we learned in Chapter 1, caffeine

The *Marquaha:* High on Caffeine?

When coffee was discovered by Arab mystics at the end of the fifteenth century, it quickly became popular among people from all walks of life. Some conservative clerics tried to ban it, on pain of death, because it created what they called a *"marquaha,"* or coffee high, and therefore violated the Koran's injunction against intoxicants. (They lost the fight.) What the clerics were objecting to was the euphoria—the good feelings of happiness, contentment, and relaxation—we enjoy when we use caffeine.

Some scientists claim that caffeine's power as a mood modulator and the way it is "functionally utilized by the majority of consumers to regulate the circadian variations in affective states" is the primary reason people choose to use caffeine regularly.[20]

helps regulate the serotonin system. Whether this accounts for all of its effects on depression is still unknown. In any case, caffeine does much more for your mood than help regulate the serotonin system. It gives you the energy you need to perk up and be active, and keeping busy is one of the best ways to overcome depression. It also relieves the boredom of routine tasks—tasks that are required of almost everyone and can help to keep our spirits low. Finally, caffeine can help relax us in periods of stress, helping to relieve anxiety and in turn helping to give us the break we need to overcome depression.

There can be no more dramatic evidence that caffeine exerts life-altering effects on mood than its ability to combat the worst kind of depression: the depression that leads to suicide. There are over 30,000 suicides every year in the United States—more than one every 20 minutes. Two large-scale studies proved that coffee drinkers have dramatically lower rates of suicide, strongly suggesting that caffeine can significantly ameliorate long-term depression and even make life worth living for some people. A decade-long study of women nurses, completed in 1996, demonstrated that the suicide rate was inversely related to the amount of caffeine the women consumed.[21] In other words, the more caffeine people use, the less likely they are to kill themselves, prompting scientists to conclude that this result stemmed from the mood-enhancing power of the drug. A 1993

Kaiser Permanente Medical Care Program study of nearly 130,000 men and women, reported in the *Annals of Epidemiology*, examined the effects of coffee and tea on mortality and also found that the risk of suicide decreased as caffeine consumption increased. Under the direction of Arthur Klatsky, a cardiologist, the study tracked northern California residents, including the records of 4,500 who died during the research, and found a statistically significant lower rate of suicide among coffee drinkers than among coffee abstainers. Klatsky asserted that this was not a fluke finding; the study was very large, involved a multiracial population of men and women, and examined many factors related to mortality, such as alcohol consumption and smoking.[22]

The Extra Power of Caffeine Pills

Scientists have discovered that caffeine pills such as Vivarin exert a far more powerful beneficial effect on athletic performance than the caffeine we get from coffee. Although no studies have yet been completed making the same comparisons for mood effects, anecdotal evidence is growing that the mood-enhancing power of pills is more profound and sustained than anything coffee can deliver.

If you are interested in using caffeine to improve your mood, we recommend that you skip your coffee and try a 100 mg pill first thing in the morning. If that doesn't seem to do the trick, up the dose to 200 mg. You may find pervasive and sustained improvements in your mood, including increased energy, optimism, and self-confidence, as well as deepened relaxation. After trying this regimen for a few days, some people report transformational changes.

Why skip the coffee? The theory is that something in coffee dampens the effects of caffeine, clouding and limiting its ability to improve your mood. So if you want to test out "pill power," postpone your coffee until the afternoon—or maybe even avoid it altogether. These pills are perfectly safe and will not upset your stomach the way coffee sometimes can. They present no problem for Olympic drug testing, because the blood levels produced by a pill and by a cup of coffee that contains the same amount of caffeine as the pill are identical. The pattern of metabolites, that is, the substances into which the caffeine is converted by the body, is also identical.

If caffeine has such an amazing positive effect on moods, why isn't it prescribed by doctors to treat clinical depression? A growing number of scientists think that caffeine should be evaluated for just this purpose.[23] Depressed patients often self-medicate with caffeine.[24] And with good reason: Caffeine's mood-enhancing power is global and profound, and it is effective at such low doses that adverse side effects, never much of a problem with caffeine, are nearly nonexistent. And it is certainly cost-effective compared with standard pharmaceutical therapies for depression. Perhaps ten years from now, physicians will routinely put their patients on a daily 100 mg caffeine pill as a first-line treatment for depression. (See Appendix B for a discussion of caffeine's interactions with antidepressant medications.)

One woman we spoke with had encountered the trials of approaching menopause. She began to suffer from a chronic depression. In the mornings, she was groggy, fatigued, and lethargic, without any of the bounce and spirit that she had known all of her adult life. In the afternoons, she became edgy and overly excitable. She sometimes found herself literally flinching when hearing a sudden noise, such as someone entering the room unexpectedly. This alternation between lethargy and edginess continued for some weeks, until she felt she'd have to give up any hope of enjoying life or accomplishing more than simply making it through the day. Apparently gone were the carefree, productive days of her youth.

Once-a-Day Caffeine

Many drugs of different kinds, including alcohol, nicotine, cocaine, and morphine, have a short-acting effect on mood, imbuing the user with euphoria that ranges from mild to intoxicating. However, caffeine is unique in its ability to engender sustained improvements that apparently outlast the initial stimulating and energizing effects of the drug. Researcher I. Kawachi says that a 100 mg dose of caffeine, taken once a day, has a profound effect on mood for the entire day, increasing feelings of "well-being, social disposition, self-confidence, energy, and motivation for work." [25] We may speculate that caffeine's ability to restore the regulatory balance of serotonin and other neurotransmitters is responsible for such pervasive and stable responses, but no one knows for sure.

She tried exercise. She tried vitamins. She tried meditation. She tried talking herself out of it. She even tried Prozac. Most of these things helped, but only a little. She found herself slipping into a darker and darker state.

Like many other people, she tried caffeine pills when, one morning, she didn't have time to prepare and drink her usual cup of coffee. The effects were nothing short of amazing: Her depression lifted, and her fatigue dissipated. She had never experienced such benefits from coffee, so she continued experimenting with caffeine pills. Each morning when she got up, she would take a 200 mg dose of caffeine in pill form. As afternoon approached, she would take another 100 mg. The results were awe-inspiring changes in her quality of life. It was as if her body and mind had been off-kilter and all her mood-regulating mechanisms had gone awry. Caffeine seemed to restore the balance, "leveling it all out," as she put it. In the mornings, she was once again cheerful and energetic. In the afternoons, she retained her energy but felt calm and relaxed, no longer jumping out her chair when someone down the hall dropped a stack of file folders. Caffeine turned her life around, giving her energy, optimism, and joy. She summed it up vividly when she told us, "I feel like I'm twenty years younger!"

What was going on here? It's hard to say for certain. In part, the Yerkes-Dodson curve of caffeine's effects might help to explain things. When she was at a low level of arousal in the mornings, caffeine contributed to her energy output, waking her up and helping to get her going. When she was at a high level of alertness during the height of the workday, caffeine took her past the peak of the arousal curve and helped her feel more relaxed and calmer. Another mechanism might be caffeine's ability to shape the operations of various neurotransmitter systems that affect mood. For example, in people with migraines, caffeine restores the balanced functioning of the serotonin system and thereby relieves the headache. Perhaps caffeine's balancing effects were helping to smooth out the mood-wrecking consequences of neurotransmitter systems that were going haywire because of hormonal changes.

We don't completely understand how caffeine helped this woman, but her experience is a perfect example of the remarkable adaptogenic powers of caffeine. (See the next section for a discussion of adaptogens.) If you have a mood problem, you might want to experiment with small doses of caffeine pills for yourself. You could find they give you a whole new outlook.

Getting What You Need: Caffeine as an Adaptogen

"Adaptogen" is a term from alternative medicine that is used to describe substances like ginseng that are supposed to exert a variety of different effects that mysteriously adapt themselves to whatever your body needs to return to its normal, healthy condition. Caffeine, in its effects on mood, acts as an adaptogen. When you need to be brought to life, it enlivens you; when you need to dispel depression, it cheers you up; when you need to relax, it calms you down.

We all associate caffeine with perking up, getting into gear, and sharpening our mental faculties. However, by exerting so-called paradoxical effects, especially in women and men who are introverts or are in high states of arousal, caffeine acts to calm us and help us relax when we're unusually agitated. In general, when you are in a high state of arousal, caffeine tends to calm you down. These same paradoxical effects can be reproduced by scientists in laboratories by pushing people into high states of arousal with high doses of caffeine. Rather than becoming increasingly stimulated as their dosage increases, most people find that they feel more tranquil.

There may be a trade-off between caffeine's power to stimulate you, on the one hand, and to help you become calm when you're upset, on the other. In other words, when you are agitated, some of caffeine's power to give you a lift may be exchanged for its power to relax. In fact, larger doses can put you through a cycle of changes over a period of time, first making you perk up and then, as you metabolize the drug and attain higher blood levels, helping you to slow down and take it easy. This is a powerful one-two punch of mood elevation.

The Friendliness Factor: Caffeine and Conviviality

The atmosphere of the typical coffeehouse, populated with people sitting in lounge chairs, reading or talking quietly, is tranquil and domestic. The goal of many café proprietors is to create a home away from home, a haven in which people can sit alone, congregate with friends, or even chat with strangers to recover from the stress of everyday life.

However, it cannot be denied that on some occasions when people assemble in coffeehouses, they become more vehement, forceful, and garrulous, so, whatever their concerns are, they try to engage these same feelings in others. Although there are no scientific studies to prove this, kings and sultans recognized that caffeine can have a tendency to incite people, and this thought was behind their desire to close down coffeehouses. It was said of King Charles II of England that he would never have taken the throne if not for the many coffeehouse conversations in which dissatisfaction with Cromwell was voiced and the means of his ouster plotted. After his accession to the monarchy, one of Charles's first edicts was an order closing all the coffeehouses in the country—ostensibly to prevent a fire hazard, but actually to stop the political talk that now often leveled criticism at him. Daniel Webster called the Green Dragon coffeehouse in Boston "the unofficial headquarters of the American Revolution," and it was the site of many secret meetings in which political upheaval was plotted. Like its English and American counterparts, the Café Procope, in Paris, became a center for political discussions. Robespierre, Marat, and Danton convened there to debate the dangerous issues of the day and were supposed to have charted the course that led to the French Revolution of 1789 from the café's tables. Caffeine's revolutionary history is not confined to coffeehouses. Teahouses in China, which date from the thirteenth century, like coffeehouses in the Islamic world and Europe, played a large part in the political life of the country. For example, the 1911 revolution was plotted in the back room of a Shanghai teahouse.

In the 1950s and 1960s, social rebels from Lenny Bruce to Bob Dylan used the coffeehouse as a platform from which to protest the establishment. The message delivered there by people like songwriters Phil Ochs and Joan Baez helped to change history by convincing the American people that the Vietnam War had to be brought to an end.

People can become more animated, talkative, even more passionate and outspoken after taking caffeine. Yet scientific studies prove that this increased arousal does *not* translate into increased aggressiveness. In fact, caffeine has what scientists call "selective suppressing effects" on human aggression. Although their sharpness, energy, and forcefulness are not impaired—and are probably increased—hostility is dampened, and people become more tolerant and more easygoing when using caffeine. (Perhaps caffeinated beverages, usually served at peace conferences or when making up after a lover's quarrel, lead to beneficial outcomes.)

Eliminating Hostility and Aggression

Scientific research supports the idea that caffeine operates to decrease aggression in most people. Studies in 1983 and 1984 by D. R. Cherek examining the effects of caffeine administration on aggressive behavior confirmed this. Mindful of the aggressive response normally elicited when someone has money snatched away, this researcher designed an experiment in which participants were promised certain immediate financial rewards for their performance. He then pretended to renege on his promises, giving the participants, who had received either caffeine tablets, coffee, decaffeinated coffee, or a placebo, the impression that they had been cheated. He found that those who had ingested either coffee or caffeine were more tolerant of being cheated. Among those given caffeine, subjects who regularly consumed more than 200 mg of caffeine a day, the amount in an 8 ounce cup of filtered coffee, averaged nearly 60 percent fewer aggressive responses than those in the group who were not given caffeine; those who usually consumed less than 100 mg a day averaged only about 33 percent fewer aggressive responses than the group not given caffeine. In some way, regular caffeine use seems to increase our ability to forgive and forget the small irritations in life.[26] Regular caffeine use increases caffeine's "friendliness factor."

Caffeine helps you relax and feel less hostile when confronted by hostile persons or conditions. Scientists who administered mental arithmetic and anagram tests while harassing their subjects ("Come on, you can do better than that!") found that the combination of caffeine and stress pushed participants past the peak of the Yerkes-Dodson curve of arousal, causing them to relax and their blood pressure to fall. Similar results—a decline in arousal responses—have been found when participants were exposed to adverse conditions, such as loud white noise, as well.[27]

Is there no foundation for a common belief that coffee can increase hostility? Some researchers think that added aggression is in fact produced by caffeine only in certain subgroups of the general population. Some studies show that in psychiatric patients suffering from anxiety disorders, switching from regular coffee to decaffeinated coffee decreases irritability and hostility.[28] It could be also be true that caffeine was interfering with the medications that the patients were taking (see Appendix B). Other people, who are unusually sensitive to caffeine's effects, may experience something similar. Perhaps (despite caffeine's generally adaptogenic properties) the guideline is found in the work of two leading researchers, who found that caffeine makes a person's personality tendencies, whatever they are, more pronounced.[29] In effect, they are saying that caffeine makes you more like yourself. So consider this before downing a few double café lattes if you're the type gets involved in heated altercations.

Overcoming Boredom

Boredom, the unpleasant sense of stagnation that occurs when we feel trapped in a repetitive activity or unchanging situation, is one of the nearly unavoidable banes of life. One of the subtle and mysterious powers of caffeine is its ability to enhance our mood and the quality of our lives by keeping us from becoming bored.

Caffeine helps to reduce boredom in two distinct ways. As activities are repeated, each additional repetition tends to become less interesting, until we reach a point where further repetitions become disagreeable indeed. Caffeine slows this process and makes the things we are doing seem somehow more interesting for a longer time.[30] In addition, psychologists have found that the process of becoming accustomed to a repetitive activity is a bumpy one. As we repeat an action, it sometimes seems less and sometimes seems more familiar, in a random alternation that becomes disconcerting over time. Caffeine smooths this process, stabilizing what psychologists call habituation, and in this way it makes repetitive activities pleasanter to undertake and less subject to fits of exasperation. For example, if you have a room filled with dusty objects that you would like to clean but dusting bores you, have a cup of coffee before you start your work. If you do this, you'll find the task seems more interesting for a longer time, and you'll experience fewer bouts of frustration as you go about your job. You may still not get the job done, but at least you'll have made a good start and have felt less discomfort along the way.

Putting It All Together: The Attitude of Success

As we've just seen, caffeine increases feelings of optimism and self-confidence and dispels boredom and fatigue. It also increases mental and physical capacities and allows you to release your hidden potential. Can there be any doubt that this lineup of benefits adds up to creating an attitude of success in the caffeine user, a person who is ready, willing, and able to succeed?

Caffeine can be the secret ingredient we need to give us the edge to succeed. By inducing feelings of self-confidence and optimism, while at the same time sharpening our abilities and increasing our energy, caffeine fosters a positive attitude that can become the driving force that carries us through difficult times and past obstacles, enabling us to persist in our efforts until we achieve our goals. Caffeine also makes us more tolerant of adversity and adverse conditions and can help us to get along with others and to persevere. If there is one substance in the world that can actually contribute to success, it certainly is caffeine.

The cumulative effect of caffeine's benefits on success should not be underestimated. Most jobs require a combination of the ability to undertake new tasks boldly and resourcefully while at the same time continuing to perform dull, routine tasks with consistency. Caffeine helps us to do both. By leveling out stress, increasing your confidence, and increasing your vitality and mental ability, it contributes to your success in beginning

Beth's Tale

Beth had a challenging job in computer programming. After ten years, she found the work, which required great mental clarity and alertness, to be dull and tedious. She always enjoyed the boost she received from a cup of freshly brewed coffee during the morning or afternoon, which seemed to make her work more interesting and easier to complete.

She thought she had to give up caffeine because of concern that it caused high blood pressure, so she did. She quickly discovered that without caffeine, she couldn't work efficiently or think as clearly, and her job now seemed intolerably boring. She thought it might be caffeine withdrawal, but after a few weeks of boredom and lassitude, she realized she was missing the mood-enhancing effects of caffeine. When she learned that caffeine doesn't increase the likelihood of developing any cardiovascular problems, she immediately began enjoying her coffee once more, and her good mood and positive work attitude returned immediately.

new ventures. By keeping you interested, it helps keep you on an even keel and helps you to persevere in your established routines.

Scientific proof of caffeine's power to boost workplace performance is ample. A good example is a massive study of 85,000 female nurses conducted by a Harvard University researcher in 1996 demonstrating that only 100 mg of caffeine a day, about one 4 ounce cup of coffee, produced increased feelings of "well-being, social disposition, self-confidence, energy, and motivation for work."[31] Another study, based on several hundred interviews, found that about one-third of women questioned said that they were aware of working more efficiently and being more active after using caffeine.[32]

Thomas Edison's famous maxim, "Success is 1% inspiration and 99% perspiration," is still true today. And there is no substitute for perseverance when you are trying to achieve success. One scientist found that moderate to large doses of caffeine (6 mg per kilogram, the equivalent of about four cups of filter drip coffee for a 150 pound person) "caused people to work harder because they underestimated how hard they were working." Without being aware of the increase in pace, they were actually working considerably faster.[33]

We should not forget that, as we saw in Chapter 4, caffeine not only gives you the confidence that you can do more and succeed, it actually gives your abilities a boost so that you have a better chance of more successfully putting your plans into action. This increase in capacities itself results in an extra lift that can pay off handsomely in enabling us to realize our ambitions.

Self-Assessment of Mood

Moods can't be measured with a yardstick; however, it is possible to use simple tests to gauge roughly the way you are feeling at any time. In order to make your comparisons as meaningful as possible, take the following test at the same time of day and in the same environment both before using and after taking caffeine. This test includes all the mood factors discussed in this chapter and also incorporates tests of relaxation and tension, discussed in the next chapter.[34]

In each category, rate your own mood on a scale of 1 through 10. Write

Summary of Caffeine's Mood-Enhancing Powers

Increases

- Motivation, drive
- Self-confidence, assertiveness
- Sense of well-being
- Optimism
- Relaxation
- Friendliness

Decreases

- Boredom
- Depression
- Tension

your numbers on a separate sheet of paper. Add the numbers, and calculate the average. The higher the average score, the better your mood.

1.	Happy	10 9 8 7 6 5 4 3 2 1	Sad
2.	Interested	10 9 8 7 6 5 4 3 2 1	Bored
3.	Gregarious	10 9 8 7 6 5 4 3 2 1	Withdrawn
4.	Amicable	10 9 8 7 6 5 4 3 2 1	Antagonistic
5.	Alert	10 9 8 7 6 5 4 3 2 1	Drowsy
6.	Clear-headed	10 9 8 7 6 5 4 3 2 1	Muzzy
7.	Quick-witted	10 9 8 7 6 5 4 3 2 1	Mentally sluggish
8.	Attentive	10 9 8 7 6 5 4 3 2 1	Dreamy
9.	Strong	10 9 8 7 6 5 4 3 2 1	Feeble
10.	Well coordinated	10 9 8 7 6 5 4 3 2 1	Clumsy
11.	Energetic	10 9 8 7 6 5 4 3 2 1	Lethargic
12.	Proficient	10 9 8 7 6 5 4 3 2 1	Incompetent
13.	Calm	10 9 8 7 6 5 4 3 2 1	Tense
14.	Contented	10 9 8 7 6 5 4 3 2 1	Discontented
15.	Tranquil	10 9 8 7 6 5 4 3 2 1	Troubled
16.	Relaxed	10 9 8 7 6 5 4 3 2 1	Tense

17.	Secure	10 9 8 7 6 5 4 3 2 1	Fearful
18.	Confident	10 9 8 7 6 5 4 3 2 1	Nervous
19.	Industrious	10 9 8 7 6 5 4 3 2 1	Sluggish
20.	Optimistic	10 9 8 7 6 5 4 3 2 1	Pessimistic
21.	Cheerful	10 9 8 7 6 5 4 3 2 1	Grouchy

7

Relaxation and Meditation

IT MAY SEEM PARADOXICAL, but the same drug that energizes us and keeps us on our toes can also help to relax us. Although too much caffeine is associated with higher levels of tension and even anxiety, low to moderate doses of caffeine induce feelings of relaxation, peace, and tranquility. A leading study published in 1997 found that doses as small as 100 mg of caffeine in coffee or tea significantly reduced anxiety 30 minutes or so after consumption.[1] Many other studies have confirmed the same phenomenon. A good example is a study of several hundred women conducted in the late 1960s. The researcher found that especially among those who drank coffee frequently, caffeine was often found to calm their nerves and relax them, at the same time as it increased their sense of well-being.[2]

The Truth Behind the Coffee Break

Because most people think of caffeine as a wake-up drug that revs us up and keeps us going, they are often surprised to learn that caffeine has powerful tranquilizing effects. After all, it seems reasonable that an increase in alertness and a faster reaction time should go hand in hand with an increase in edginess. One reason for this belief is that the body's primary natural alerting mechanism, the release of adrenaline into the bloodstream, *does* cause a distinct increase in tension, jitteriness, and anxiety. As it turns out, some studies suggest that high doses of caffeine, over 600 mg or more, can increase tension, which makes sense when we consider that these high doses probably are increasing adrenaline production. In fact, the American Psychiatric Association now recognizes a distinct anxiety disorder related to excessive caffeine intake.

A 1997 study led by Dr. G. B. Kaplan confirmed the difference between low and high doses in mood effects. He gave doses of 250 mg (a little more than you'd find in one and a half 6 ounce cups of filter drip coffee), 500 mg (about what you'd find in three and a half cups of coffee), and a placebo to twelve healthy volunteers. Those receiving 250 mg reported more favorable subjective effects—including increased elation, peacefulness, and pleasantness—than those receiving 500 mg. In addition, those receiving 500 mg reported a higher incidence of unpleasant effects, including an increase in tension and anxiety.[3]

So how can a low to moderate dose of caffeine, such as we take in during a typical coffee break, make us feel laid-back and tranquil at the same time as it is sparking our minds and bodies into higher levels of activation? Curiously, it seems as if the effects of low and high doses of caffeine on mood are not the results of identical mechanisms. Different neurotransmitter systems appear to have primary roles depending on the size of the caffeine dose. Therefore, although large doses of caffeine, especially when consumed all at once—by affecting adrenaline release—probably can increase tension and anxiety in a minority of people, it is not difficult to imagine how low or moderate doses—by affecting only the serotonin, dopamine, and other neurotransmitters instead—not only fail to increase jitteriness, but actually bring about increased relaxation and tranquility.[4] So when it comes to using moderate doses of caffeine, you can sit back, relax, and enjoy the charge it gives you without feeling any increase in tension or anxiety.

There really is no contradiction between feeling buoyant energy and deepened relaxation at the same time. Scientists have noted this happy combination in studies of caffeine going back over thirty years. A leading caffeine researcher explained that "a certain feeling of well being, relaxation, or 'calming of the nerves' is seen as something clearly different from 'slowing down.'"[5] In other words, feeling tranquil does not mean feeling tranquilized. It is perfectly possible to feel more tranquil and also to feel increased drive, alertness, and energy. Caffeine enables us to achieve this happy combination.

Taking the Edge Off Caffeine

Despite these facts, and the experience most of us have of relaxing over a cup of coffee—enjoyed during coffee breaks that are observed throughout the world—we are all familiar with the stereotype of the high caffeine user: tense, jumpy, and nervous. What precisely is the justification for the idea that caffeine *routinely* increases levels of tension and anxiety? The question is of more than academic interest. Anxiety, including such symptoms as unwarranted apprehension, agitation, and uneasiness, is the most common psychological disorder in the United States. In severe cases, it erupts into panic attacks, characterized by increased heart rate, palpitations, jitters, irritability, perspiration, and rapid breathing.

It turns out that the idea that most caffeine users are a nervous group of people is a myth, and scientific research dispels the image of the edgy coffee drinker. If a correlation with normal caffeine use can be stated, it is that the people who do not consume caffeine are more likely to have problems with their nerves than those who do. The members of the population who consume caffeine are dispositionally more relaxed than the general population, and, conversely, those who do not consume caffeine are more jittery than most.

As we have seen, however, although caffeine use at ordinary levels is not correlated with increased anxiety, very large doses may tend to increase your levels of tension. How large is "very large"? Some studies show increases in tension at doses of 600 mg[6] or 800 mg,[7] or about as much as is found in four to five cups of filter drip coffee. Other studies show that tension may begin to increase with doses of only 400 mg.[8] As is true with the other effects of caffeine, the only way to know how caffeine will affect you is to do a little experimenting on your reactions to it.

How much does a large caffeine dose increase anxiety, tension, and jitteriness? A major study of caffeine's ability to reverse the effects of sleep deprivation on mood found that doses equivalent to 600 mg in a 150 pound person increased anxiety by 15 percent and increased jitteriness and nervousness by 25 percent.[9] Although these increases are not entirely inconsequential, they are not earth shattering. In fact, the same study found that improvements in the mood of the participants—in clear-headedness and vitality, for example—more than compensated for their added edginess. We should also remember that the large caffeine doses used in this and most other experiments on anxiety are administered all at once, giving the participants in the study the equivalent of downing several cups of coffee in one gulp. Few people use caffeine in this way. If you drink several cups of coffee over a period of a couple of hours, your blood levels of caffeine would never quite attain those achieved in the laboratory, and your liability of experiencing increased anxiety would be correspondingly lower. Furthermore, because you take in your caffeine a little at a time when drinking coffee, you are likely to stop increasing your dose at the first sign of increased tension.

What happens if you take caffeine when you are already in a heightened state of arousal? In other words, if you are already feeling very agitated, will caffeine make your condition worse? Strangely enough, the answer is that it not only will not increase your tension, it will actually help make you feel more tranquil. How can this be? Perhaps the answer lies in the Yerkes-Dobson arousal model. Remember that as total arousal levels increase, the effects of caffeine begin to reverse themselves. For example, although small doses of caffeine may slightly increase blood pressure in people who don't use it regularly, large doses cause blood pressure to drop.[10] Similarly, when caffeine is given to a person who is under a great deal of stress, that person's total arousal levels are likely to be pushed past the high

Fighting "Parents' Syndrome"

Harried by caring for several children at once, parents value relaxation. And surveys prove that they often use coffee as a way of achieving tranquility.

Keeping track of the quickly changing behavior of small children and monitoring sudden arguments and tears puts parents into a high state of arousal. As we have seen, when a person is wound up, moderate doses of caffeine reduce what scientists call arousal output, lowering blood pressure and causing a person to relax. At these levels of arousal, the caffeine may fail to contribute any benefits to cognitive functions—for example, the ability to do mental arithmetic might not pick up—but a leveling off of certain mental functions is a worthwhile trade-off for precious relaxation when we are very stressed. So don't be surprised if you find yourself sitting back in your chair and breathing easily after having a couple of cups of strong coffee. Caffeine may actually be providing you with the relaxation break you need.

Caffeine: Relaxation versus Tension

- Doses as high as 300 mg have been shown to produce pleasant mood states of mental sedation.
- Doses over 300 mg may tend to increase tension and anxiety in a minority of people.

point of the Yerkes-Dobson response curve, which means that its initial stimulating effects are reversed. The result is that the tense person actually begins to relax.

A few caveats should be kept in mind. People subject to panic attacks or suffering from other anxiety disorders find that in some cases, drinking coffee or tea can provoke an attack. And although the effect of large doses on anxiety is usually modest, panic attacks have been induced in the laboratory in normal people challenged with very high doses of caffeine.[11]

Also, some people have a heightened sensitivity to caffeine that is usually genetically determined and may have increased anxiety after using small amounts of the drug. In assessing the possibility of unpleasant mood effects, we have to consider that genetic factors affect both the predisposition to anxiety and the general biophysical response to caffeine.[12] In other words, a relatively small minority of people, because of their genetic makeup, may find that caffeine does not agree with them in terms of its effects on their mood.[13] They should limit or even eliminate their use of caffeine.

"It Relaxes Me!"

Karen drinks coffee morning, noon, and night: a pot of coffee on awakening, coffee throughout the day, accompanied by cigarettes, and coffee before retiring. "It's like Ritalin to an ADD kid. It relaxes me," she said.

Karen may be right on target with this comparison: If she is a "hyper" person, caffeine will act to push her past the peak of her personal Yerkes-Dodson curve, in exactly the same way as a stimulant like Ritalin calms a hyperactive child. (In fact, caffeine has been used to treat ADD in children.)

Meditating on Caffeine

When you think of meditation and serenity, you think of the peace and relaxed energy of the Zen tea ceremony. What you don't usually think of is taking drugs. But the tranquility and mind-expanding power of Zen meditation owes a great deal to the actions of caffeine. If you want to bring the benefits of meditation into your life, this section will explain why you would be well advised to see if caffeine can help speed you on your own personal road to enlightenment.

Most people associate increased alertness with heightened tension. Increased adrenaline in your bloodstream puts you on edge and at the same time increases your awareness of potential danger in your environment. The increase in alertness produced by caffeine is not the result of higher adrenaline output. In fact, increased alertness can also come with deepened relaxation. This is the kind of alertness and mental clarity that you experience when meditating and, as it happens, that is fostered by caffeine.

Ma-cha, the bright green whipped tea served at formal tea ceremonies, is strong and bitter and is a completely different drink from the weak green tea Americans usually encounter. It is brewed from the cured tips of the just-budding tea plant, which Japanese laboratory analysis reveals contain over 4½ percent caffeine by weight, over two and a half times the amount contained in ordinary tea. Ounce for ounce, it is the strongest caffeinated botanical on earth, providing more caffeine than any other vegetable source. There is no question that especially in the austere setting of the tea ceremony, in which the mind, freed from distractions, is more susceptible and more sensitive to the effects of any psychoactive substance, caffeine plays an important part in creating the huge rush associated with the mystical state that is celebrated by its participants. In a sense, all of Zen is an exploration of meditating while under the influence of caffeine.

It is perhaps ironic that the meditation establishment, including Western and Eastern schools of yoga, psychic institutes, theosophists, transcendental meditation advocates, holistic health advisers, and health food gurus, consistently warn against the ways in which caffeine interferes with meditation and cautions would-be adepts to avoid using caffeine if they want to get the benefits of meditation. In fact, the use of tea in Eastern meditation goes back even before Zen, to Zen's Chinese antecedents, Taoism, Confucianism, and Chan Buddhism, among whose practitioners the

Teahouse in Outer Space

There isn't much room to spare on board the $95 billion international space station (ISS) being planned by a group of nations led by Russia and the United States and scheduled for launch in 2004. But that won't stop Japanese astronauts from practicing the art of meditation in a Zen tea ceremony while circling high above the earth. Japan's National Space Development Agency (NASDA) is planning to include a tearoom in Japan's section of the ISS.

"Space travel is psychologically difficult, so the idea is to provide a calm place where astronauts can relax," NASDA spokesman Yoshihiro Nakamura said. By reducing tension, a tea ceremony, NASDA believes, will help the astronauts maintain a good working relationship. It is true that the tea ceremony cannot be conducted in the typical manner. In fact, they still haven't figured out how to keep the tea in cups. "We can't have it floating around," adds Nakamura. "This is one of the problems we are working on." [14]

psychoactive properties of tea were equally celebrated. Lao Tzu, the legendary founder of Taoism, was said to have started his *Book of Tao* while pondering the universe over a cup of tea.

The Mystery of Tea vs. Coffee

Some scientists think that one or more of the hundreds of physiologically active chemicals in coffee interfere with the actions of caffeine and dampen many of its effects. If this is true, it is almost certain that one or more of the hundreds of active chemicals in tea would also dampen caffeine's effects; otherwise, tea would have become famous as the source for a caffeine supercharge. However, it is highly unlikely that the profile of the interactions of coffee's chemicals with caffeine is identical with the profile of tea's interactions. In other words, it is nearly certain that the contents of tea modify the effects of caffeine in a different way from the ways in which the contents of coffee modify these effects. If this is true, then it may account for the great duality in the cultures of coffee and tea and may also account specifically for the uses of caffeine in meditation. The components of tea

Meditation and the Creation of Tea

A charming story teaches that the creation of tea was a miracle worked by a holy man, born of his self-disgust at his inability to forestall sleep during prayer. The legend tells of the monk Bodhidharma, famous for founding the school of Buddhism based on meditation, called Chan, which later became Zen Buddhism, and for bringing this religion from India to China around A.D. 525. Supposedly, the emperor of China had furnished the monk with his own cave near the capital, Nanjing, where he would be at leisure to practice the precursor of Zen meditation. There the Bodhidharma sat unmoving, year after year. From the example of his heroic endurance, it is easy to understand how his school of Buddhism evolved into *za-zen,* or "sitting meditation," for certainly *sitzfleisch,* or "staying power," was among his outstanding capacities. The tale is that after meditating seated before a wall for nine years, he finally fell asleep. When he awoke and discovered his lapse, he disgustedly cut off his eyelids. They fell to the ground and took root, growing into tea bushes containing a stimulant that was to sustain meditations forever after.

may selectively interfere with caffeine's actions in such a way that caffeine's ability to relax, focus, and energize the mind is at a peak, while some of its ergogenic and metabolic effects are nearly absent. This might make tea better for meditation than coffee.

Review the "Great Duality" table and determine for yourself whether the traditional distinctions between the cultures of coffee and tea ring true to your experience.

The Great Duality Between the Cultures of Coffee and Tea

Coffee Aspect	Tea Aspect
Male	Female
Boisterous	Decorous
Bohemian	Conventional
Obvious	Subtle
Sordid	Beautiful

(continued on next page)

Coffee Aspect	Tea Aspect
Discord	Harmony
Common	Refined
Indulgence	Temperance
Vice	Virtue
Excess	Moderation
Passion, earthiness	Spirituality, mysticism
Down-to-earth	Elevated
Mornings, late nights	Afternoons
American	English
Occidental	Oriental
Casual	Formal, ceremonial
Demimonde	Society
Full-blooded	Effete
Vivacious, extroverted	Shy, introverted
Yang	Yin
Work	Contemplation
Individualism	Conformity
Excitement	Tranquility
Tension	Relaxation
Spontaneity	Deliberation

Source: Adapted from B. A. Weinberg and B. K. Bealer, *The World of Caffeine: The Science and Culture of the World's Most Popular Drug,* New York: Routledge, 2001, pp. 130–131.

It is not only tea, but coffee as well, that has a place in the history of mysticism and meditation. It cannot be a coincidence that the Sufis, ecstatic Islamic religious practitioners and some of the greatest mystics of the world, also relied on caffeine to sustain their nightly meditations, consuming substantial amounts of extremely potent thick black coffee in order to do so. In contrast to the Zen practitioners, who usually meditated while sitting as still as possible, the Sufi "whirling dervishes" achieved their meditative transport by frenetic dancing and spinning about. Despite the difference in their approaches, both of these groups of mystics found in caffeine the transformational power to advance their ecstatic quest. And during the 1600s in the Middle East, Jewish scholars decided that it was permissible to drink coffee before morning prayers, despite the Talmudic

Caffeine's Cousins

Coffee, tea, and chocolate all contain caffeine. Caffeine is one of a family of drugs called "methylxanthines." Other methylxanthines are theophylline, which is found in tea, and theobromine, which is found in cocoa. Coffee contains pharmacologically active amounts of only one methylxanthine: caffeine. It is possible that some of the differences in effects associated with coffee, tea, and chocolate may be owing to the presence of these related compounds.

prohibition against consuming food and beverages until prayers were complete, in order to help focus their thoughts, "especially in Egypt where nobody's thoughts are focused without coffee." [15]

Contemporary "experts" on meditation who pooh-pooh the value of caffeine must be reckoned as rank amateurs compared with the masters of Zen, whose traditions of sitting meditation date back nearly a thousand years. Those who speak out against mixing caffeine and meditation make the mistake of lumping caffeine in with other drugs, like alcohol, that cloud the mind. This is an error. In some way, caffeine, even though a stimulant and psychoactive substance, is capable of fostering a state of meditative clarity and tranquility under the right circumstances. Science, which does not yet understand the nature of brain activity during meditation, does not understand the mechanism of action by which this is accomplished. Perhaps it has something to do with caffeine's ability to increase the powers of concentration, or perhaps it is connected to the fact that caffeine causes the release of dopamine in the brain, or perhaps it is owing to some other mechanism of action entirely.

Will caffeine help you achieve the peace and tranquility and even the enlightenment that comes from meditation? It is difficult to answer such a question scientifically. So far as we know, no controlled laboratory experiments have been done to investigate or evaluate caffeine's contributions to meditation. But because it is difficult to quantify achievements in meditation—can you say you were twice as peaceful today as yesterday?—it is even hard to evaluate the effects that caffeine may be having on your own attempts to meditate. If you find that it helps, you'll be joining the tradi-

Caffeine and Zen

Caffeine produces both increased mental focus and increased impulsivity. You could say that these were the defining characteristics of the Zen state of mind. This may be why so many Zen stories begin and end with sharing a cup of tea. An exchange between the two Zen masters Chokei (853–932), also called Ch'ang-ch'ing Hui-ling, and Hofuku (d. 928), also called Pao-ful Ts'chan, adapted from Suzuki's translation of a passage from the Dentoroku, or *Transmission of the Lamp,* illustrates this point:

"As to the Buddha, he never makes an equivocal statement. Whatever he asserts is absolute truth."

"What, then, is the Buddha's statement?" asked Hofuku.

"Have a cup of tea, my brother monk." [16]

tion of using caffeine as an aid to meditation that dates back over a thousand years. Experiment with meditating on caffeine and determine for yourself if your mind seems clearer, more imbued with relaxed energy, better able to concentrate, and better able to let go of your distracting thoughts. Perhaps, like the ancient Zen masters, you may just "know."

8

Improving Your Athletic Performance

CAFFEINE HAS ALWAYS BEEN RECOGNIZED as an agent that stimulates the release of energy in the body. Among the Aztecs, the energy-giving power of cacao was so jealously prized that apart from the nobility, only soldiers on campaign and the *pochta,* a hereditary class of merchant-adventurers, were permitted to use it.[1] (Montezuma I even promulgated a law that no one who had not participated in armed conflict, not even the king's son, could enjoy the privilege of consuming it.) Similarly, American soldiers in World War II carried ration packs that included caffeine pills to keep them going strong in combat. And for many years, athletes, especially weight lifters and long-distance runners, swimmers, and cyclists, have relied on caffeine's energy-giving powers to boost their performance in training and competition.[2]

In confirmation of this massive experience, scientists have demonstrated caffeine's benefits to muscle activity, physical training, competitive sports events, endurance and, more recently, short-term physical activity as well.[3] Despite extensive research, however, the landscape of studies has been bedeviled by some ambiguous and apparently contradictory findings, confusions resulting largely from mistaken notions about the mechanisms that underlie caffeine's ergogenic, or energy-producing, effects—and, as it turns out, by some surprising differences between the effects of coffee and caffeine pills.

In 2001, T. E. Graham, Ph.D., professor in the School of Human Biology and Nutritional Sciences at the University of Guelph in Ontario, a leading sports researcher and sports physiologist, published an ambitious metastudy in *Sports Medicine* on caffeine and exercise. In this study,

Graham gathers the latest results from the best research worldwide in order to answer many of the questions about the ergogenic benefits of caffeine.

After exhaustively examining what is currently known about caffeine and exercise, Graham concludes that caffeine improves performance in most, if not all, sports activities and has no detrimental side effects on athletes. Based on his review of work undertaken by dozens of scientists, Graham states that caffeine is a "powerful ergogenic aid," which means it boosts the output of energy by the body, at blood levels markedly below the permissible limit of the International Olympic Committee (IOC), and that it is beneficial in both training and competition.

Caffeine enables athletes to train at a greater power output, with greater speed, and for a longer time. It has also been proven to increase power, speed, and endurance in simulated and actual race conditions. Although old theories held that caffeine benefited only endurance athletics, we know now that caffeine's beneficial effects are operative in activities that last as little as 60 seconds or as long as several hours. And although it is still not clear if it can improve maximal strength, caffeine makes a valuable contribution to strength training and performance by imparting enhanced endurance or resistance to fatigue and also by relieving pain. Caffeine is also a powerful antioxidant—much stronger than vitamin C—and can help combat the muscle damage caused by exercise. (See "Caffeine as an Antioxidant" for a discussion of this damage.) There is no evidence that caffeine ingestion before exercise leads to dehydration, ion imbalance, upset stomach, or other adverse effects. Men and women metabolize caffeine in the same way and, given the same dose of caffeine in proportion to their body weight, will exhibit the same blood levels and concentrations of metabolites, the substances into which caffeine is transformed by the body. Tolerance to caffeine does not seem to affect its ergogenic benefits, which means that both nonusers and long-term users of caffeine will respond to it in same way and to the same degree.

It is unknown how caffeine produces its ergogenic and other athletic benefits, but they may be the result of a happy combination of its systemic central nervous system effects and its local effects on muscle tissue.[4] One thing is sure, however: When it comes to enhancing sports performance, a little caffeine helps you go a long way.

Coffee vs. Caffeine in Athletic Performance

Does the form in which caffeine is ingested influence its ergogenic effects? In other words, do the energy-boosting effects of caffeine vary depending on whether the caffeine is delivered in a cup of coffee, a caffeine "alertness aid," a headache remedy, or even a suppository or an intramuscular or intravenous injection? Are tablets of synthesized caffeine somehow different from the same amount of caffeine in tablets made from extracts of coffee, tea, guarana, cola, or other botanicals?

"It couldn't possibly matter," you might answer. "Caffeine is caffeine." However, to the astonishment of many, a recent ground-breaking study found that there are major differences in the ergogenic effects produced by caffeine in coffee and caffeine pills.[5] In this study, high-performance runners ran to exhaustion at a pace approximating their best time on a 10 km (6 mile) run. Caffeine, about 4.5 mg per kilogram (or about 300 mg for a 150 pound person, about as much as is found in two cups of filtered coffee) mixed with water, when taken an hour before the run, produced a remarkable improvement in endurance of nearly 33 percent, an increase in running time from 32 minutes to 41 minutes. But the same amount of caffeine delivered in coffee (or in decaffeinated coffee mixed with powdered caffeine) produced no improvement at all.

The differences in outcome could not be explained by differences in caffeine absorption, because blood tests proved that the time of peak plasma caffeine concentration (highest blood levels) and the overall actual caffeine concentrations achieved were identical in both groups. The differences could not be explained by differences in caffeine metabolism, because the pattern of its metabolites was also identical in both groups. In fact, no precise explanation for these differences has yet come to light. Nevertheless, the absence of an ergogenic response to regular coffee is proof that coffee does not have the same pharmacodynamic actions as caffeine alone. The conclusion must be that one or more of the hundreds of active components of coffee counteract some of the primary benefits of caffeine for athletic performance. Perhaps coffee actually has ergolytic (as opposed to ergogenic) effects—that is, something in coffee is detrimental to energy output.

Peter R. Martin, M.D., professor of psychiatry and pharmacology at

Vanderbilt University, has shown that the stimulating effects of caffeine are offset by other chemicals in coffee called "chlorogenic acids." Chlorogenic acids, which are dietary phenols, kinds of aromatic organic compounds, aren't all bad. In fact, like caffeine, they are antioxidants. And Martin is also studying possible therapeutic uses of a synthetic form of the chemicals. However, if Martin is right, they may be the culprits that work to limit the power of caffeine when it is delivered by coffee. Tea also contains chlorogenic acids, so it may interfere with caffeine as well.

Has it been conclusively established that coffee has no ergogenic benefits? Not really. Coffee *may* help improve your athletic performance, but caffeine in the absence of coffee *definitely* produces significant improvements in almost any athletic activity.[6] If you want to use caffeine strategically to boost your attainments in sports, you should consider skipping the coffee and getting your caffeine from caffeine pills.

Is Caffeine Good Only for Endurance Exercise?

A theory first enunciated in 1980 explaining the source of caffeine's ergogenic effects—and one that you will still encounter in almost all health and fitness books and magazines—is that caffeine delivers a burst of energy that allows your muscles to delay burning up the stored glycogen, that is, the sugars, that they use for fuel.[7] Supposedly, caffeine increases the amount of fat you metabolize, and your muscles use this fat for fuel before they burn glycogen. This means that the glycogen isn't used up as quickly, which means that you can continue to use the muscle longer—which is to say that you increase your endurance.

If this theory were correct, it would mean that caffeine could benefit only long-term endurance exercise. The reason is simple. Imagine that you are running a race and are given the opportunity of carrying a water bottle during the event. If the race is long and you finally become dehydrated, the water will be useful to you and may improve your performance. In a short race, however, it won't help you. Because the water starts to help only once you are dehydrated, it wouldn't have any effect on sprinting or any other brief activity. Similarly, making your glycogen last longer can only help you once you've reached the point when your glycogen would have otherwise been exhausted. Because this so-called glycogen-sparing hypothesis was widely accepted for decades, it was long assumed that caffeine offered no benefit to short-term athletic performance.

However, recent studies have shown that caffeine's ergogenic effects occur at doses so low that glycogen sparing is not evident. And it now seems that exhaustion occurs when over 50 percent of the glycogen remains available to the muscle, so sparing glycogen may not be a limiting factor in fatigue after all. Finally, the latest studies on caffeine's ergogenic benefits prove that caffeine increases muscle activity in exertion lasting only 60 seconds, a finding that completely explodes the glycogen-sparing theory. Now we know that all, or virtually all, sports and athletic activity—not just cross-country cycling and long-distance running and other endurance activities—can be bolstered by the use of caffeine.

So how *does* caffeine work to increase energy output in athletics? You can get a sense of the complexity of this question when you consider that in addition to the fat oxidation and glycogen-sparing hypothesis discussed above, scientists have suggested that factors as varied as changes in blood glucose, side products of glucose metabolism (such as lactate), the dopamine or adrenaline neurotransmitter systems, intracellular calcium levels, blood flow, and ion balance might be responsible. The latest findings prove that in addition to whatever boost is conferred by its effects on the central nervous system or overall metabolism, caffeine acts directly on muscle tissues by increasing their power to contract.[8] For example, experiments in which caffeine is given to tetraplegics, individuals whose brains are effectively cut off from their peripheral muscles because of spinal chord damage, show that caffeine improves muscle response even when the brain is not sending instructions to the muscles; therefore, caffeine must be acting locally on the muscles themselves.[9] Once again, however, it is not necessary to know how caffeine does what it does to get its benefits. The important thing is to learn what sorts of benefits have been proven and then to determine exactly how it affects you as an individual.

Caffeine Tolerance and Withdrawal in Athletics

With regular caffeine use, most people develop a limited tolerance to caffeine's effects on sleep. That means that regular users find their sleep is less likely to be disturbed by caffeine taken shortly before bedtime. But what

Caffeine Content and Weight Equivalencies

Typical Values

6 ounce cup of instant coffee—100 mg

6 ounce cup filter drip coffee—150 mg

8 ounce cup filter drip coffee—200 mg

Vivarin tablet—200 mg

Body weight equivalencies

1.5 mg per kilogram = 65 mg for 100 pound person

3.0 mg per kilogram = 130 mg for 100 pound person

4.5 mg per kilogram = 200 mg for 100 pound person

1.5 mg per kilogram = 100 mg for 150 pound person

3.0 mg per kilogram = 200 mg for 150 pound person

4.5 mg per kilogram = 300 mg for 150 pound person

1.5 mg per kilogram = 130 mg for 200 pound person

3.0 mg per kilogram = 260 mg for 200 pound person

4.5 mg per kilogram = 400 mg for 200 pound person

about caffeine's energy-producing effects? Do hardened coffee drinkers need extra large jolts of caffeine to get the same lift that a small cup of instant coffee could provide a person who never used caffeine before?

Graham found that tolerance does not develop to caffeine's ergogenic actions. In other words, all other things being equal, 300 mg of caffeine will give the same boost to an athlete who has never tried caffeine and to one who uses caffeine every day, and what's more, it will continue to deliver the same boost indefinitely. This was confirmed in a study reported in the *British Journal of Sports Medicine* in which researchers administered 2 to 2.5 mg per kilogram of caffeine (for a 150 pound person, about what is found in a 6 ounce to an 8 ounce cup of filter drip coffee) to 1500 meter runners

and "found no relationship between caffeine habits and degree of performance response." [10]

Because there is no tolerance to caffeine's ergogenic effects and increasing doses beyond moderate levels serves only to reverse the benefits conferred at moderate doses, caffeine offers no incentive for athletes to engage
in the sinister pattern typical of drugs of abuse, i.e., an inexorable tendency
to take larger and larger amounts, followed by a downhill slide that results
from the growing dangers of the drug and that eventually can destroy a
person's life.

Long-Term Exercise

Endurance in Long-Term Exercise

For many years, research into caffeine's energy-boosting effects was focused
on examining its effects on endurance exercise. As a result, a great deal of
data was accumulated incontrovertibly establishing that caffeine has
ergogenic power in exercise situations in which fatigue occurs in 30 to 60
minutes. [11] For example, if you can run at 85 percent of your maximum
speed for 30 minutes without caffeine, the odds are good that you'll be able
to keep up the same speed for 40 minutes if you take the caffeine before
you start. [12] Endurance advantages of this magnitude can make a critical
difference in competitive sports.

Numerous studies prove the profound benefits of caffeine on endurance. For example, one study of cyclists who were cycling at 80 percent
of their capacity found that after 300 mg of caffeine, endurance increased
from 75 minutes to over 90 minutes, an increase of 17 percent. [13] Another
study of high-intensity intermittent exercise showed that 5 mg per kilogram, the equivalent of about three 6 ounce cups of filter drip coffee for a

Caffeine's Built-In Regulator

Unlike drugs that take you on an accelerating downhill slide of increasing
dosage, decreasing benefits, and increasing side effects, caffeine has a built-in
regulator. You won't need to take more tomorrow to achieve the same athletic
benefits you enjoyed today.

150 pound person, increased endurance from 61 minutes to over 77 minutes, an increase of 21 percent. As a final example, one study, using a total dose of 420 mg, about as much caffeine as is found in three cups of filter drip coffee, showed that runners who could maintain 85 percent of their top speed for 40 minutes increased their endurance to 53 minutes after taking caffeine, an improvement of nearly 33 percent. An interesting regimen of caffeine administration was employed. All participants were given 300 mg of caffeine 1 hour before beginning the test, another 60 mg just prior to the test's beginning, and a final 60 mg after running for 45 minutes.[14]

In endurance athletics the Yerkes-Dodson "less is more" curve of caffeine's activity, explained fully in Chapter 1, has been well documented. This so-called biphasic pattern of activity means that you must be especially careful not to take too much caffeine before training or competition. If you do, you not only will fail to improve your performance over what moderate levels of caffeine could have delivered, you will actually begin to reverse the benefits that the lower doses confer. In other words, if 400 mg is giving you the maximum ergogenic boost, then taking 700 mg will not only *not* help you, it can actually *reduce* your energy output. To determine when you've had enough caffeine, evaluate yourself by taking the self-tests at the end of Chapter 9 and observe the effects of different amounts of caffeine during training.

Speed, Power, and Performance in Long-Term Exercise

It's much harder to collect and analyze data on speed, power, and performance in real or simulated sports situations—in part because of small sample sizes and changing weather conditions—than it is on simple endurance. Therefore, although caffeine's benefits in these respects are widely recognized in the field, fewer studies exist that confirm the actual performance results.

A major study undertaken in 1982 found that caffeine improved the finishing times of well-trained, elite male and female cross-country skiers in a competitive setting.[15] The scientists studied the skiers at both high and low altitudes on a 12 to 14 mile course. At both the halfway point and at the finishing line, 6 mg per kilogram of caffeine (for a 150 pound person, the amount found in four 6 ounce cups of filtered coffee) produced statistically significant faster performance times. The total time for the run at high altitude averaged more than 2½ minutes faster on a race lasting about an hour.

This may not seem like much, but if you're a skier—or a runner, cyclist, or swimmer—who is going for first place, you know that even a few seconds can make the difference between winning and losing a race.

A study conducted in 1995 found that 600 mg of caffeine reduced the time needed to complete a 1500 meter swim by male and female swimmers by 23 seconds.[16] In studies of trained male runners in a 1500 meter run, total time was reduced by over 4 seconds (attaining this advantage even though decaffeinated coffee with caffeine added, not caffeine pills, was used as the source of the drug).[17] Such improvements of a few seconds, which reduce total race time by about 1.5 percent, are a few seconds that could clinch the first-place title. A careful study of power output conducted in 1979 also turned up impressive results: When trained cyclists performed 2 hours of cycle exercise, 250 mg of caffeine increased total power output by 7.3 percent.[18]

Perhaps the best-designed and best-controlled study of power and performance in endurance athletics observed highly trained male cyclists who were assigned the task of completing as quickly as possible a fixed amount of work that was estimated would require approximately 1 hour. A carbohydrate and electrolyte solution proved beneficial. But when the solution also contained caffeine, the power output improvement was much greater—that is, the performance completion time was significantly faster.[19] Doses of 3.2 mg per kilogram and 4.5 mg per kilogram, the equivalent of between 1⅓ and 2 six-ounce cups of filter drip coffee for a 150 pound person, significantly decreased finishing times, the higher dose by more than 6 percent. (It should be noted that a lower dose of caffeine, about 2 mg per kilogram, failed to produce any significant improvement.)

All of these studies confirm what many professional and amateur cyclists, runners, skiers, and swimmers have known for years: that the prudent use of caffeine before and during a race markedly increases endurance and power without adverse side effects.

Short-Term Intense Exercise

Endurance in Short-Term Exercise

Short-term exercise has received much less attention than long-term exercise, in part because old theories held that caffeine couldn't have any short-term benefits and in part because it is more difficult to measure short-term differences with sufficient accuracy.

Recently, scientists have studied caffeine's effects on short-term exercise with progressive work tests, in which subjects undertake high-intensity exercise that results in rapid exhaustion. For example, a 1990 test of the effects of caffeine on subjects who cycled at high speed to exhaustion reported that caffeine significantly increased their endurance over 17 percent from 14.9 to 17.5 minutes.[20] Studies using the imaging technique of nuclear magnetic resonance spectroscopy have shown that maximal power in high-intensity muscular activity was increased 20 percent in subjects using caffeine, and endurance increased over 30 percent, from about 13.5 to nearly 17 minutes. Although the results of other studies have varied and the average benefit is difficult to determine, it is clear that caffeine results in improvements in short-term, intense exercise endurance. In any case, the average benefit isn't really of much interest to you as an individual. Once you understand that caffeine generally produces a significant improvement in short-term performance, you're going to have to do some self-testing if you want to find out exactly what it can do for you.

Speed, Power, and Performance in Short-Term Exercise

When the effects of caffeine on athletic activities of shorter duration are studied, the results have proven more variable than in long-term activity, probably because the improvements in brief, intense activity are invariably smaller and harder to measure. Nevertheless, after evaluating all the existing studies, Graham concludes, "It appears that, in exercise lasting at least 60 seconds, caffeine can be ergogenic." More research needs to be done, and some of the purported benefits of caffeine for intense exercise remain controversial. We can at least say, however, that no studies have ever shown a detrimental effect on short-term performance. In other words, even if we're not quite certain that it will help every aspect of short-term performance, we know that it can't hurt. Once again, the best way to find out what it can do for you is to test it for yourself.

Strength

Caffeine has been used by strength trainers for decades to increase attainments in weight lifting and bodybuilding. In fact, in the United States, weight lifters constitute one of the largest markets for caffeine pills. Unfortunately, few studies exist examining these effects. However, current research strongly suggests that caffeine has direct effects on the strength of muscle performance that are independent of its metabolic effects. That is, it is thought that enhanced muscle contractility is caused by local actions on the muscle itself (probably as a consequence of increased calcium mobilization) and is not related to the other ergogenic effects of caffeine or to its general stimulation of the central nervous system. As Graham explains, caffeine may increase strength by changing the environment of active muscles in a way that can "facilitate force production" by the muscle's cells.[21]

One 1999 study found that caffeine increased the maximal voluntary contraction (MVC), that is, the strength of the force being exerted by a muscle, by 3.5 percent, a significant increase in top capacity.[22] This study also found that the time to fatigue at 50 percent MVC improved by over 25 percent! This means that if you are doing repetitions at 50 percent of your capacity, you should be able to complete 25 percent more curls if you have taken caffeine before you start.[23] Such an increase in MVC would have a dramatic effect in competition. For example, a weight lifter capable of lifting 300 pounds without caffeine should be capable of lifting 310 pounds after taking caffeine, easily a large enough percentage increase to move from second to first place or even to establish a new record. The increase in the fatigue time at 50 percent MVC means that strength trainers can progress much more quickly when using caffeine because they can build their muscles faster by completing more repetitions before running out of steam.

The jury is still out on whether caffeine can increase your maximum strength or power. Some studies suggest that you may not be able to lift a bigger weight when you are on caffeine than when you are not. Others, such as the study cited above, suggest that it confers a modest but significant improvement in maximum exertion. However, because caffeine has a definite beneficial effect on the rate of fatigue and on perceived fatigue, it increases the repetitions that weight lifters can perform before exhaustion. It also increases their tolerance for pain and instills a positive attitude. This means that caffeine is a powerful tool for weight training, a fact that is confirmed by its widespread use for this purpose. It awaits future research to deepen our understanding of the beneficial effects of caffeine for strength athletes and the causes underlying them.

Reaction Time

Careful scientific measurements of individual performances in team sports are almost impossible to make and have rarely been attempted in relation to caffeine's effects. However, it should be apparent that in addition to caffeine's endurance-enhancing and general ergogenic benefits, caffeine's ability to speed reaction time, promote mental clarity, and improve sustained and divided attention offer extraordinary promise in team sports, such as basketball, football, soccer and baseball, and in other fast-moving sports such as tennis, fencing, boxing, and race car driving, in which fast responses and quick thinking are essential. In other words, caffeine will help a runner, a swimmer, and a cyclist to go farther and faster; it should help team players and players of sports like tennis not only in these ways but in other key components of successful competition as well.[24]

Existing data strongly suggest that improvements in reaction time after taking caffeine are significant when subjects are well rested or fatigued.[25] For example, as early as 1975, a major study proved that caffeine reduces the time required "to execute a response," that is, to make a specific movement in a task in which several choices are possible.[26] A similar result was found in a study of simple reaction time, suggesting that "caffeine influences the output side of information processing."[27] These sorts of improvements are discussed extensively in Chapter 4. Here we simply note that fast movements and quick decisions, both of which are facilitated by caffeine, are two critical components of high performance in team sports and other fast-moving competitions. Although average improvements offer provocative guidelines, testing the effects of caffeine on your performance is the only practical way of determining what caffeine can do to speed up your reaction time on the field.

Caffeine's Effects on Athletic Performance

Beneficial Effects

- Long-term exercise: Improved endurance, speed, and power
- Short-term exercise: Improved endurance, speed, and power
- Strength: Increased endurance, possibly increased maximum output
- Faster reaction time
- Increased lung capacity
- Antioxidative muscle protection and healing

There are no known detrimental effects of moderate doses of caffeine on sports performance.

Lung Capacity

Among caffeine's well-established pharmacological effects is the relaxation of the smooth muscles of the bronchi, the passages leading to the lungs.[28] Caffeine has been proven, for example, to help both asthmatic children and adults by opening airways and making it easier to breathe (bronchodilatation). For hundreds of years, caffeine was recommended as a medicine for relieving asthmatic attacks, and even today, one of caffeine's congeners, or chemical cousins, theophylline, is an active ingredient in many medications prescribed for this purpose.

As we exercise, our lungs experience a progressively more limited capacity to take in oxygen (bronchoconstriction), and this limitation is one of the factors that acts to limit the intensity and duration of athletic activity. Caffeine has been found to protect against this exercise-induced bronchoconstriction (EIB).[29] By opening up the airways, caffeine allows more oxygen to reach the bloodstream and enables the athlete to continue playing longer and harder.

Caffeine as an Antioxidant

The human body is a battlefield. Our body's natural defenses are constantly producing antibodies to fight invading bacteria and viruses. When bacter-

Caffeine, Dehydration, and Sports

Dehydration is a concern of every athlete. When the fluid balance of your body starts to fall below normal, your performance will suffer dramatically. For decades, athletes in training and competition have been warned to stay away from caffeine, or at least to limit its intake, because it causes dehydration.

This turns out to be a myth. Especially in sports, study after study has proven that caffeine does not alter the fluid balance, the electrolyte levels, the rate of perspiration, or the core temperature, and it does not increase the likelihood of or contribute to dehydration.[30] This is an old wives' tale, pure and simple. It may have arisen because drinking a couple of cups of hot liquid naturally tends to induce urination.

ial or viral infections multiply faster than they can be neutralized, we become sick. It has come to the attention of the popular press in the past ten years or so that a similar campaign is being waged by the body against free radicals, a potential source of cellular damage that may lead to cancer and may be one of the primary causes of aging.

As researcher J. Caroline Dekkers explains in an article in *Sports Medicine* about using antioxidants to prevent muscle damage, oxygen-free radicals are unstable atoms or groups of atoms with odd or unpaired electrons that are formed when oxygen reacts with certain molecules. These free radicals are highly reactive and try to balance their unpaired electrons by combining with electrons from other substances. Whenever a free radical reacts with a nonradical in this way, another free radical is generated, kicking off a chemical chain reaction, or domino effect, that can be thousands of events long. This chain reaction causes traumatic damage in tissue and leads to changes in cell functions, including making cell membranes more permeable, altering the function of mitochondria (the energy sources of cells), and causing the formation of toxic by-products.[31] Ultimately, this free radical damage can cause cells to function poorly or die.

Our bodies have a complex antioxidant defense system to interfere with free radical activity and prevent this damage from occurring. As a key component in this defense, the body deploys glutathione, the natural biological

Caffeine Even Protects You from Coffee

Free radicals that are found in roasted coffee, instant or brewed, generate free radical production in the body. Caffeine is a potent antioxidant that acts as a "free radical sink," capturing these free radicals and preventing free radical damage to muscles and other tissues.[32]

antioxidant, to soak up and neutralize free radicals and in this way short-circuit damaging chain reactions in cells before they occur. But sometimes the rise in the free radical level exceeds the antioxidant defense capacity of cells. In order to bolster the body's defenses against free radicals, many people take antioxidants, such as vitamin C, vitamin E, beta carotene, and selenium, that act to "wipe up" free radicals in the same way as glutathione does.

Endurance exercise increases oxygen utilization by as much as twenty times its consumption in the resting state. This increased oxygen uptake increases the generation of free radicals, a process thought to promote damage to skeletal muscles and other tissues. That is why it is important for athletes to know that, in the words of a major study of caffeine's antioxidant power, "the antioxidant activity of caffeine is similar to that of the established biological antioxidant glutathione and *significantly higher than ascorbic acid* (Vitamin C)."[33] The same study concludes that if caffeine is present during the time of exercise, it can afford "significant protection" against the damage produced by the free radicals generated by exercise.

The antioxidant power of caffeine may also be part of the reason caffeine can keep you alert and awake. The free radical flux theory of sleep, that free radicals accumulate in the brain while you are awake and that "sleep functions essentially as an antioxidant for the brain," has led some researchers to suggest that the antioxidant power of caffeine may be in part responsible for caffeine's revivifying effects.[34]

In trained athletes, the antioxidant defense system goes into high gear during exercise, and natural antioxidant activity increases markedly. Conversely, inactivity seems to interfere with antioxidant defenses, making cells more vulnerable to free radical damage. Certain tissues, including the heart, have unusually low levels of antioxidant protection and may be even

Block That Radical Damage!

Strenuous physical exertion, especially when you're not used to it, routinely damages the muscles that are being exercised, as is evidenced by a decline in muscle performance, damage to the muscle tissue itself, and muscle aching. In the past, mechanical stress, caused by "high peak forces produced during high-impact activity,"[35] was thought responsible for much of the tissue damage. However, when it was discovered that even low-impact activities produce similar tissue damage, scientists began looking into the possibility that much of the damage was caused by the increased activity of free radicals produced by elevated oxygen consumption during exercise. Recently, it has been proven that lipid peroxidation, or free radical damage to cell membranes, can interfere with cell functions in ways that interfere with muscle recovery time and healing. It also produces toxic metabolites, or poisonous by-products. These toxins travel throughout the body and cause further damage at a distance. The antioxidant power of caffeine works to block this free radical activity and in this way increases muscle performance, protects muscle tissue from damage, and reduces muscle aches.[36]

more susceptible than other tissue types to free radical damage. In addition, the capability of the antioxidant defense varies dramatically from person to person. For all of these reasons, the antioxidant power of caffeine can play an important role in facilitating training and higher performance.

Although controversy still surrounds the full implications of these phenomena, it can be definitely stated that caffeine is a powerful antioxidant that protects against exercise-induced muscle damage. Human studies prove that caffeine, as an antioxidant, supplements the body's natural defenses and can be useful to people performing intense exercise.

Weekend Athletes Get Special Protection from Caffeine

The body seems to know that high levels of activity send free radical levels soaring, and this may be the reason that antioxidant defenses are better tuned and more effective in highly trained athletes who exercise on a regular basis. However, "weekend athletes," people who spend most of their time behind a desk and go in for an occasional bout of energetic athletics, are in a special predicament. Their bodies don't have time to make this adaptation, and therefore they are wide open to the damaging onslaught against their muscles that the increases in free radical activity initiate. That's why caffeine is especially important for people who aren't training regularly. It helps make up for the body's weaker defense system against free radicals and speeds muscle recovery time and healing by delivering a powerful antioxidant at the time it is most needed.

9

How Much to Take and When to Take It
to Boost Athletic Performance

M OST PEOPLE WHO ARE TRYING to enhance their athletic performance take caffeine by mouth, in coffee or caffeine pills.[1] Scientists studying the effects of caffeine on sports activity have used either coffee, caffeine capsules, or caffeine dissolved in water or in decaffeinated coffee. Generally, most controlled studies have evaluated the results of taking a single dose of caffeine before exercising; a few have considered the effects of repeated doses, both before and during the exercise. Which pattern of administration works better or exactly when the dose or doses of caffeine should be consumed for optimal performance remains unknown. However, because caffeine's effects demonstrate individual variation, even if the average optimal pattern of timing and dosing were determined, it would still be vital for each person to evaluate these effects for himself.

In this chapter, we present specific methods for using caffeine to boost your sports attainments and also discuss ethical and practical issues surrounding caffeine use, caffeine's role as a powerful antioxidant, and how caffeine creates a winning attitude in sports. You can take the self-tests at the end of the chapter to determine exactly what caffeine can do for you in training and competition and how to use caffeine strategically for maximum improvements in your athletic attainment.

Timing

Caffeine is rapidly absorbed; the highest blood levels of the drug are generally achieved within 1 hour. Therefore, in most studies, after caffeine is administered, the participants rest for an hour before exercising. However, the half-life of caffeine averages between 3 and 6 hours, which means that caffeine is transformed by the body relatively slowly, and people generally maintain blood concentrations close to the maximum level for about 2 hours.

So when should you take caffeine to attain the maximum ergogenic benefit? We can safely say that caffeine requires at least 15 minutes for its effects to start to become significant, even taken on an empty stomach, and that, on average, it takes 30 minutes to 1 hour for most of its peak effects to kick in. Whether the onset of fat burning, about 3 hours after taking caffeine, contributes to the enhancement of athletic performance is still unknown. In any case, average values are a very poor and misleading guide to the way caffeine will affect each person. As is the case for all the strategic uses of caffeine, if you want to know when you should take caffeine to maximize its ergogenic benefit, you must experiment to find out the time interval before exercise at which caffeine works best for you.

The Variable Half-Life of Caffeine

The degree to which a drug lingers in the body is quantified by what pharmacologists call its half-life, the length of time needed for the body to eliminate one-half of any given amount of a chemical substance. Three factors determine how long caffeine remains active in your system:

- **Genetic predisposition:** Metabolic factors determined by your genes, so the half-life of caffeine varies widely from person to person.

- **Conditioned half-life:** Whether you're smoking, taking oral contraceptives, or drinking grapefruit juice. See Chapter 1 for all the things that can change the rate at which caffeine is metabolized.

- **Dose consumed:** There is a minimum blood level of caffeine necessary for producing its ergogenic effects. If 50 percent of the caffeine you've taken remains active in your system after 4 hours and you have taken 100 mg of caffeine, you will feel the effects of only 50 mg after the 4 hours have passed. However, if you've taken 400 mg of caffeine, you will still be feeling the effects of 200 mg after the 4 hours have

(continued on next page)

passed. The first level, 50 mg, might not be enough to produce any energy benefits. The second level, 200 mg, obviously would. Because of this, the length of time caffeine will work to boost your sports performance depends in part on how much of the drug you have taken.

How long caffeine continues to work as a sport booster depends on the dosage in an additional and surprising way. The half-life of caffeine actually increases with the dosage. This means that the more you take, the longer a higher percentage of what you have taken will remain active in your system. For example, one study found that 150 mg per 150 pounds had a half-life of 4.7 hours, 300 mg per 150 pounds had a half-life of 5.4 hours, and 600 mg per 150 pounds had a half-life of 6.4 hours.[2]

Combining these two effects on the length of activity produces some startling results. Let's assume, for example, that it requires at least 100 mg of caffeine to produce a significant ergogenic effect. One person takes 200 mg of caffeine and another takes 600 mg of caffeine. After about 4.5 hours, the first would no longer be getting any ergogenic benefit; however, over 15 hours later, the second person would still be going strong.

Experiment on yourself with dosing size but also with dosing time, because of the three factors explained above. As a guideline, here are average values for the half-lives of different dosages of caffeine:

Caffeine Dosage for 150 Pound Person	Half-Life in Hours
150 mg	4.7
300 mg	5.4
600 mg	6.4

Dosage

The subject of how much caffeine to take to improve athletic performance can seem confusing. Often scientists have given a fixed or absolute dosage of caffeine to all their study participants, irrespective of the body mass of the participants. When the dosage is not indexed, or adjusted to be proportional to body weight, wide variations in responses can result that are extremely misleading. For example, when given caffeine in proportion to their body weight, men and women generally exhibit almost identical blood levels.[3] However, when investigators use a fixed dosage of caffeine on all their subjects, the lower body weight of women results in caffeine blood levels about 20 percent higher than those of the men who participated in the same study.

Few studies have considered whether it is more effective to take caffeine in a single large dose before exercise or in smaller repeated doses during exercise. Because even a single dose elevates blood levels of caffeine for hours, it is not clear that repeated doses offer any advantage, although repeated dosing could be useful during long-term athletic events that may last several days. For such extended activities, portable caffeine sources, such as caffeine tablets, caffeinated water, and caffeinated mints and chewing gums, provide an excellent way to secure delivery of the exact dose of caffeine you need at exactly the time you need it.

The best current work indicates that in persons of average sensitivity to caffeine, 3 mg per kilogram (for a 150 pound person, about 200 mg or what is found in one and a third 6 ounce cups of coffee) is effective in increasing endurance in prolonged exercise and that the ergogenic benefit continues to increase up to 6 mg per kilogram.[4] It is uncertain, however, what the minimum dosage for attaining a benefit is. Similarly, it is unclear at what point, on average, increasing the dosage of caffeine will not only fail to improve performance further, but will actually begin to reverse the benefits demonstrated at lower dosages. However, these average values are not the most important things for you to know when you are using caffeine to help boost your sports performance. In the end, because individual sensitivities to caffeine vary so greatly, the only way to use caffeine strategically is to complete self-tests such as the ones we include at the end of this chapter, to discover for yourself what works best for you.

"Caffeine Inspiration": Developing a Winning Attitude

There is a constituent of success in sports that is as vital to success as it is hard to quantify: the winning attitude. As we discuss in Chapter 6, caffeine improves self-confidence. It makes people feel more upbeat and more optimistic and puts them in a better frame of mind. In short, caffeine makes people feel like winners. The attitude of success, although it can't be measured, confers an invaluable advantage in athletics, whether you're simply

The Better You Are Already,
the More Caffeine Will Do for You

Trained athletes get better and more predictable benefits from caffeine. The ergogenic effects of caffeine on endurance may be even greater for trained athletes as compared with untrained ones.[5] One study found that "an athlete who placed in the top 10 in an Olympic marathon was able to run for 105 minutes compared with about 75 minutes in the placebo trial," an increase of over 40 percent.[6] As we have observed, it is probable that caffeine has direct actions on muscle tissue, and it is possible that the muscles and other tissues of highly trained athletes are more responsive to caffeine's effects—or perhaps it's simply that trained athletes have the discipline to exercise long enough or hard enough to benefit more from caffeine's stimulating powers.

training to beat your own best time or trying to come in first in a real-world competitive sports event.

One specific way in which caffeine enables us to break through sports performance barriers is by increasing stamina and resistance to pain. Caffeine has been shown not only to increase the power of painkillers such as aspirin, codeine, and ibuprofen and other nonsteroidal anti-inflammatory drugs (NSAIDs), but also to be as strong a pain killer as ibuprofen when used alone. Caffeine reduces the pain of exertion and the perception of pain, making people feel as if they can keep going longer. It's difficult to quantify a benefit like this, which is a combination of pain relief and a better attitude, but there's no doubt that it can help make you a winner.

The Ethical Considerations of Caffeine Use
in Competitive Athletics

If caffeine is a drug that improves athletic performance, shouldn't it be banned, like other drugs, from use in competitive athletics?

There is no question that athletes who use caffeine before engaging in competitive sports are taking a drug for the purpose of improving their performance and gaining an advantage. And there is no doubt that caffeine delivers the improvements they are seeking in training and competition as well.

Caffeine use cannot be justified on the same basis as the use of nutritional supplements to improve performance because caffeine, unlike vitamins, minerals, and some other antioxidants, is not traditionally regarded as a nutrient. Currently, caffeine is permitted in competitive athletic events, although regulatory bodies such as the International Olympic Committee set limits as to how much is acceptable. There is consensus among sports regulatory bodies that the use of drugs to augment performance should be banned from competitive athletics. An exception has been made for caffeine. But the question remains: Is it consistent or right to continue making this exception?

The dilemma is that if you allow caffeine, you are allowing the use of a drug to boost performance, but if you prohibit caffeine, you are excluding athletes from using something that most people rely on to help them through the day. An article in the *American Journal of Sports Medicine* in 2000 raised the drug use objection, arguing that, for consistency, caffeine should be disallowed. Others advance the same point, opening up the question of whether to continue permitting caffeine in competition. However, if you ban caffeine, you are forcing athletes to abstain from a substance on which many, if not most, of them are physically dependent and the cessation of use of which will cause withdrawal symptoms. In effect, banning caffeine from competitive athletics would force most athletes to abstain entirely from their morning coffee or tea in order to avoid experiencing withdrawal symptoms during competition. This seems like an unnecessarily draconian solution, for it would not only deny athletes the benefits of caffeine in training, but would even foreclose them from enjoying its benefits in everyday life, benefits that few of us would voluntarily want to surrender.

The answer might be to recognize, as current Olympic regulations seem to, that caffeine is a unique substance that deserves unique status in competitive sports. There is no denying that it is a drug, but allowing caffeine to remain a part of sports does not obligate us to allow other drugs as well. There are two critical differences between caffeine and the other ergogenic drugs, such as methamphetamine and cocaine, and other drugs used in training, such as steroids.

First, caffeine is essentially a drug of moderation. Tolerance to amphetamines increases to extremely high levels, and people have a strong, almost irresistible craving to consume cocaine in ever greater amounts. In contrast, caffeine use is self-limiting. People find their optimal dosage and tend not to take more than this, no matter how long their caffeine use continues. The reason is twofold. First, beyond the optimal dosage, caffeine's beneficial effects tend to reverse themselves, and unpleasant side effects such as jitteriness, irritability, and insomnia begin to emerge. Therefore, when you take more than the optimal dosage, caffeine does less and less of what you want it to do and more and more of what you don't want it to do. This creates a natural ceiling for caffeine use that is not shared by addictive, stimulant drugs. Second, no tolerance develops to caffeine's ergogenic effects, so there is no tendency to increase its use over time to maintain its athletic benefits.

The other critical difference is that all other stimulant drugs pose serious health hazards. They can seldom become a regular part of anyone's life in the long term without causing major mental and physical problems. In contrast, there are very few adverse health risks from caffeine. Caffeine can be and is a regular part of most people's lives and doesn't cause any disruption or destruction. Surely this is a significant difference that people raising the objection to caffeine must consider.

Passing? Urine Testing for Caffeine

The International Olympic Committee's acceptable maximum level of caffeine is 12 mg per liter of urine. If the IOC's purpose in promulgating this limit is to ban an effective dose of a stimulant, this is a very high level indeed. As little as 3 mg per kilogram—a level that a 150 pound person

Why Caffeine Use Is Doubly Self-Limiting

As you increase your dose of caffeine beyond your optimal level, the beneficial effects that it had been conferring begin to reverse themselves, and unpleasant side effects begin to multiply. The result is that people do not tend to increase their caffeine intake, but instead find a level at which they are satisfied with the benefits and experience no side effects, and maintain that dose indefinitely.

would attain after one and a third cups of filtered coffee or after taking a single Vivarin tablet—has been shown to have ergogenic benefits, but even 9 mg per kilogram, equivalent to over 4 cups of filter drip coffee, results in urinary levels that only approach the levels banned by the IOC. In fact, by drinking coffee or caffeinated soda, it is very difficult to attain a urinary concentration of caffeine that would violate these standards. The result is that, given these standards, competing athletes should effectively be free to consume substantial amounts of caffeine, well beyond those amounts that have been shown to produce significant advantages in athletic performance.

Unfortunately, urine tests are so unreliable that consuming relatively modest amounts of caffeine before an athletic event can create some risk of disqualification.

Countless studies have proven that as Graham states, "urinary caffeine concentrations are notoriously inaccurate reflections of caffeine intake." Urinary levels are extremely variable, too variable to accurately indicate the dose that was ingested. To confuse the issue, some sports offer an opportunity for the participants to urinate during the activity or rest periods, making urine collected after the activity an even less reliable measure. As a result of these factors, the urine test for caffeine may have unfairly resulted in a number of athletes being disqualified from competition. Only blood or saliva analysis can determine the dose taken, so either no tests should be used, or blood or saliva tests should replace urine tests for caffeine.[7]

In fact, because no one can gain an unfair competitive advantage by

Protecting Yourself from the Risk of Disqualification

Urine tests are not very reliable and can result in misleading readings of caffeine levels. Both blood and urine levels peak about 1 hour after taking caffeine. If you take less than 300 mg, you should have nothing to worry about at any time. However, if you are taking more than this, to minimize any chances of being improperly disqualified, we suggest that you strategically time your caffeine consumption by taking it either less than 15 minutes before or more than 2 hours before testing will occur.

One other caveat: See Appendix B for a discussion of medications that can affect the results of urine testing for caffeine.

consuming an excessive amount of caffeine, since larger amounts of caffeine not only fail to augment performance more than moderate amounts but also actually begin to reverse the benefits gained by taking moderate amounts, it seems unnecessary to monitor athletes in order to enforce ceilings of caffeine consumption.

For all the reasons given above, it would seem that the time to recon-

Caffeine and Sports: A Cautionary Tale

Caffeine in moderation is okay before a competition. Right? Tell that to Inger Miller, 1999 world champion in the 200 meter track and field competition, who, following two and a half years of appeals, lost her bronze medal for a 60 meter run in the 1999 world indoor championship because of a positive test for caffeine. As reported in *Runner's World Daily News* (Oct. 17, 2001), the caffeine in her body was detected in routine urine tests conducted by the International Association of Athletic Federations, the world governing body for track and field events. Miller, a twenty-nine-year-old Californian, admits she enjoyed two small cups of coffee before the race. After the race but before the urine test, she drank two cans of Coca-Cola that were provided to her by the meet's organizers. In fact, the meet in Maebashi, Japan, was sponsored by Coca-Cola.

If Miller drank two small cups of coffee and two cans of caffeinated soda, her total caffeine consumption would have been approximately 350 mg. It should have required at least 600 mg to exceed the allowable limits for caffeine. So what happened here? It's impossible to know for certain. Perhaps she downed a couple more cups of coffee than she remembered. Or perhaps she metabolizes caffeine slowly, and some caffeine from after dinner the day before was still circulating in her system. More likely, the urine tests, notoriously unreliable as indicators of actual blood levels of the drug or of the dose ingested, gave the wrong answer. To avoid problems with drug testing, see the guidelines above in "Protecting Yourself from the Risk of Disqualification."

The ruling cost Miller a medal, but won't affect her eligibility to participate in future competition. Still, Miller is angry. She says she still has no idea how much caffeine she had in her system and as long as caffeine levels are an issue, caffeinated drinks should not be provided by an event's sponsors.

sider the use of the urine test—or of any other test—for caffeine in athletic competitions is long past due.[8] Meanwhile, in order to be sure that you avoid any problems, the best advice is to follow the dosage and timing suggestions given in the box entitled "Protecting Yourself from the Risk of Disqualification."

Are There Adverse Effects of Caffeine on Athletic Performance?

High doses of caffeine reduce the benefits gained for exercise performance, and a handful of studies have failed to find any improvement in work output at very high doses. However, we know of no published study that has proven any deleterious effects of moderate amounts of caffeine on exercise or athletic performance.[9]

One point deserves special emphasis. It is almost universally asserted that caffeine is a diuretic and that athletes should use it cautiously or avoid it entirely. However, the truth is that there is no basis in fact for the worry that caffeine will dehydrate athletes. A definitive study by researcher R. D. Wemple in 1997 clearly demonstrated that although caffeine ingestion during rest causes a very mild diuresis, or increase in urinary output, over a 4 hour period, caffeine ingestion coupled with exercise produces no diuretic effect whatsoever and no changes in fluid or electrolyte balance. In other words, caffeine may be a mild diuretic that produces small increases in urinary output over several hours in persons who are not exercising. But caffeine does not increase loss of fluids in people who are exercising. Activity appears to override whatever small diuretic action caffeine would otherwise have had.[10]

Self-Assessments of Caffeine's Effects on Athletic Attainment

In the use of caffeine to boost ergogenic output and athletic achievement, as with all the other benefits of caffeine, careful self-testing is necessary to determine exactly what caffeine will do for you. You must evaluate the effects of different doses, taken at different times, on different categories of athletic activities. Remember that the variations in caffeine metabolism and sensitivity mean that a dose of caffeine that will help one person perform better may do nothing at all for another person. And remember that the Yerkes-Dodson "less is more" phenomenon means that there is a limiting point beyond which increasing your caffeine intake will not only fail to help improve performance further, but will begin to reverse benefits experienced at the lower levels. Using caffeine in athletics requires experimentation, but because of its ergogenic benefits, it is worth investigating as a way of getting more out of your workouts and your athletic training and improving your standing in competitive sports.

No average test scores are given here because the purpose of these tests is to see how much improvement caffeine can give to your athletic performance. Only your improvement relative to your own attainments is significant.

We suggest that you begin with a dosage of about 3 mg of caffeine per kilogram of body weight, which is equivalent to about 200 mg for a 150 pound person. The corresponding dosages for people of different weights is given in the box on p. 136. Then, try increasing your caffeine dosage slowly, by 50 or 100 mg, until you discover the peak of your personal Yerkes-Dodson curve.

At first, try taking your caffeine in a single dose, about 1 hour before you begin the tests. Later, after you've determined your optimum dosage level, try dividing the dosage during the longer tests. Finally, you can try taking some or all of your caffeine 3 hours before exercise to see if increased lipolysis, or fat burning, can improve your performance still further. Remember that normal dosages of caffeine have no adverse side effects on sports performance.

Note: Before embarking on these or any other tests of athletic capacity, it is important that you consult your doctor to determine the safety limits you must observe.

Endurance

For this test, it's best to use a treadmill or a stationary bicycle. In order to take this test, you must first decide what is a moderate and what is a high speed for you in treadmill running or cycling. Once you have made your determination, on different days around the same time, try running or cycling before using caffeine and after using doses of different amounts.

Write down how long you are able to run or cycle at a moderate speed before exhaustion. You can also see how long you can run or cycle at high speed before exhaustion. Evaluate how much improvement, if any, is conferred by different doses of caffeine.

Speed

In these running or cycling tests, you are trying to see how quickly you can complete courses of different lengths. For example, if you are running, you will test to see how fast you can finish a 20 yard course, a 100 yard course, a 1 mile course, and even a 10 mile course. The purpose of the test is to see if you can improve on your best time by using a given dose of caffeine. Take these tests at a time when you are well rested and feeling good.

Strength and Power

For this test, you'll need several weights or an adjustable weight bar with settings of, for example, 2, 5, 10, and 15 pounds. At different weights, how many repetitions can you manage before exhaustion, both before and after taking caffeine? Write down your results after trying these tests on a few different days, and compare your average attainments to see how much boost caffeine gives you and what dose of caffeine works best.

You should try this next test only if you are experienced at weight lifting and are able to work out with a friend. The purpose is to determine the maximum weight you can lift on and off caffeine. Use a barbell or weight resistance machine to gradually increase the weight you are lifting until you reach your maximum level. Then repeat this procedure after taking different doses of caffeine. Write down the maximum weight you've been able to lift and determine if caffeine has given you any additional lifting power.

Reaction Time

You may be able to determine on the field if caffeine is speeding your reaction time when you play tennis or soccer or any other sport that requires quick responses. However, if you'd like to measure the effects of caffeine on your simple reaction time, try taking the test "Reaction Time" on page 91 before taking caffeine and after taking different doses.

10

Weight Loss

I F YOU'VE BEEN SEARCHING for a safe, effective fat-burning diet aid that
can help you to control how much you eat so you will lose weight and
keep it off, ordinary caffeine may be the answer to your prayers. In fact,
caffeine helps control your weight in four entirely separate ways:

- Suppresses appetite
- Increases metabolism
- Increases fat burning
- Enhances the benefits of exercise

In this chapter, we explain how you can put caffeine's power to work for
you to enable you to shed fat and stay slim. Clinical experience suggests
that caffeine is an effective therapy "for bodyweight loss in obese
patients."[1] Best of all, caffeine can help you cut down on what you're eating without feeling hungry. These effects are additive. The amount you lose
by eating less must be added to what you lose by increasing your metabolism, increasing fat burning, and increasing exercise levels to estimate the
total effect caffeine will have on your weight.

The "Satisfaction Diet": How Caffeine Suppresses Appetite

Caffeine, like most other stimulants, is an anorectic, that is, a pharmacological agent that suppresses appetite. It delays the onset of hunger, and
taking it before meals reduces the amount of food you need to feel full.
Most people have coffee after eating. Although this is a pleasant custom, it's

really doing things backward if you want to get the full weight-loss benefits from caffeine. To capitalize on the ability of caffeine to help you eat less, you should take an effective dose of caffeine at least 15 minutes *before* you begin your meal. Caffeine pills can be very handy. It may be difficult to secure a strong cup of coffee 15 minutes before lunch or dinner, but you can always find a glass of water and take a caffeine pill. If you do this, by the time you begin eating, you will find that your appetite has been reduced.

What is the evidence that caffeine can help curb your appetite? Throughout its history, the natural sources of caffeine have all been used for their ability to stave off hunger. The Galla warriors, semilegendary highland raiders of Ethiopia, carried balls of fat mixed with crushed coffee beans to help keep them from growing hungry during their military expeditions. In the 1556 annals of a man who was in Cortés's company during his conquests in Central America, we read of a strong cacao preparation common in that region: "This drink is the healthiest thing, and the greatest sustenance of anything you could drink in the world, because he who drinks a cup of this liquid, no matter how far he walks, can go a whole day without eating anything else."[2] And when a mini ice age in Europe in the seventeenth century ruined crops and cut off the food supply, peasants relied on the caffeine in coffee and tea to help them endure the long wait between meals. You could say that natural sources of caffeine have been proven in the field as appetite suppressants under a variety of harsh conditions in which controlling hunger was vital.

Modern scientific research has confirmed the experience of history by proving that caffeine is an anorectic. Although there are very few studies of the appetite-suppressing effect of orally consumed caffeine on people, animal tests leave little doubt about its anorectic power. For example, after an experiment in which a caffeine and water solution equivalent to about three cups of coffee for a 150 pound man was orally administered to rats, researcher Paul J. Kulkosky, Ph.D., a professor of psychology at the University of Southern Colorado, concluded that "a prominent finding in the present study is that orally consumed caffeine strongly suppresses feeding behavior."[3]

Lurid testimony of caffeine's power to stop hunger is found in clinical accounts of patients suffering from anorexia nervosa, a serious psychophysical eating disorder, usually afflicting young women, that is marked by a pathological fear of gaining weight that leads to a persistent unwillingness to eat, often to a point close to starvation. It may result in death if medical treatment is not successful. Research has revealed that sufferers from this condition frequently rely on caffeine to curtail their appetites so they can achieve their goal of eating almost nothing. In an article published in the *American Journal of Psychiatry,* John A. Sours, M.D., reports that "many patients with anorexia nervosa drink large quantities of beverages containing caffeine—e.g., coffee and diet cola—which have few calories and suppress the appetite while increasing energy."[4] Sours describes the clinical aspects of "caffeinism," the word psychiatrists use to designate the chronic or long-term ingestion of large amounts of caffeine, in two patients with anorexia nervosa. He notes that one of the women he studied drank as many as 12 cups of coffee and 1 gallon of diet cola a day.

Caffeine's use in enormous amounts by anorectics provides a graphic demonstration of caffeine's appetite-killing power. However, the fact that anorectics find that caffeine can reduce or even virtually stop their intake of food is good evidence that, used in moderation, caffeine can help people to lose weight in a healthy way. Another extreme example is found in a story sent to us by Dr. Kulkosky:

> I teach a course entitled "Drugs and Behavior." I had a student a few years ago who wanted to do an independent study on caffeine's behavioral effects in rats, so we bought a pound or so of the pure white crystal and began injecting rats. It has a truly powerful anorectic effect; you can dramatically curtail feeding in hungry rats with a large dose (50 mg/kg). I presented the finding at a meeting and noted that it would be the human equivalent of 35 cups of strong coffee, and it is unlikely a human would ingest such a quantity at a single sitting. After the talk, a member of the audience came up and said he knew many people who drank such quantities daily, himself included![5]

While it's true that few people would want to consume thirty-five cups of coffee daily, this amount apparently causes a loss of appetite averaging over 35 percent in most rats and reaching over 90 percent in some sensitive rats. And if caffeine in large doses can dramatically reduce hunger, it seems reasonable that, in small doses, it should significantly reduce the amount you eat. Remember that if you can reduce your appetite and your food intake by even 10 percent, you've turned yourself into a thin person in the long run.

How does caffeine suppress appetite and enable us to lose weight? The answers seem to lie in its effects on our intricate system of neurotransmitters, the chemical substances such as serotonin, dopamine, or acetylcholine that, among other things, tell us when to be hungry, how much energy to produce, and how much fat to burn. G. A. Bray, M.D., a prominent obesity researcher at the Pennington Biomedical Research Center in Baton Rouge, traces caffeine's appetite-reducing power to its ability to activate the sympathetic nervous system (SNS), a part of the autonomic nervous system that reacts to food intake by making us feel full, raising our metabolic rate, and burning body fat. Bray's hypothesis, published in the *International Journal of Obesity,* is that low SNS activity can lead to obesity. Bray says that by boosting SNS activity, caffeine inhibits food intake, increases energy expenditure, and decreases fat stores.[6] "The reciprocal relationship between food intake and sympathetic activity is robust," comments Bray. "We conclude that the inhibition of feeding by activating the SNS is an important satiety [fullness] system which helps regulate body fat stores."

Regulating serotonin and other neurotransmitter systems may be one of the keys to caffeine's appetite-suppressing power. After eating, especially after eating carbohydrates and dairy products, the brain releases serotonin and other neurotransmitters that determine whether we feel hungry or full and that also have a relaxing effect. Lower serotonin levels can cause people to crave food at the same time as they feel depressed. Many antidepressant and antianxiety medications achieve their therapeutic effects by increasing serotonin levels or by making the brain more sensitive to serotonin. Eating foods rich in carbohydrates produces similar effects. So when you are edgy or depressed and consume carbohydrate-rich foods, you are medicating yourself.[7] By helping you avoid this calorie-rich "medicine," caffeine can spare you the additional fat you would have accumulated from pasta, candy, and bread.

Other mechanisms by which caffeine may help to limit your appetite have also been postulated. According to Miriam E. Nelson, Ph.D., and Sarah Wernick, Ph.D., in their best-selling book *Strong Women Stay Slim.* "When food leaves the stomach and enters the small intestines, the intes-

Fighting the "Being Down, Chowing Down" Syndrome

Almost all of us have had the experience of feeling depressed or lethargic and turning to food for comfort and a lift. This syndrome might be called "eating your way to happiness," and it is a downward spiral that results in Americans' gaining millions of pounds every year. You could pay a therapist to try to dissipate your gloom and get you going again. Or you could try caffeine. Caffeine may give you the mental and emotional lift you need to break out of depression. It also supplies a burst of physical energy. Together, these effects encourage you to increase your level of daily activity and exercise. Because exercise increases endorphin output, it helps to dissipate your depression. Instead of a downward spiral of eating more and feeling worse, you can begin moving in an upward spiral of doing more and feeling better.

tinal lining releases several hormones. We know from experiments in animals that these hormones are powerful appetite suppressants. One of them, called cholecystokinin (CCK), also seems to contribute to the calming effects we experience after eating. CCK is especially responsive to fat in the diet."[8] Coffee has been shown to stimulate the release of cholecystokinin. This means that caffeine could help our bodies to generate a hormone that actually makes us feel full and keeps us from wanting to eat.

Finally, some researchers have proven that people who have taken caffeine show "reduced time to perceived gastric fullness" and that caffeine significantly delays "gastric emptying."[9] In other words, when you eat, caffeine makes you feel full faster and keeps your hunger satisfied longer. These effects were tested using an herbal preparation containing an extract of maté leaves and guarana seeds, both high in caffeine, and damiana leaves. The researchers concluded that the preparation "induced significant weight loss over 45 days in overweight patients treated in a primary health care context." Furthermore, maintenance treatment enabled the patients to keep their weight off. The researchers add that further clinical studies of the active principles, especially the caffeine, in the herbal preparation are now indicated. Unfortunately, as we explain in the Introduction to this book, such studies are unlikely to be funded by the major pharmaceutical companies.

The important thing to remember is that caffeine has been proven to reduce your appetite, to make you feel full, and to keep you from wanting to eat. For a dieter, that's really all the good news you need.

Experiment with your own eating habits. For a week, write down what you have for lunch every day, making careful note of the size of your portions. Don't try to limit your food intake. Simply eat until you feel full. When you have completed your log, determine how many calories you are consuming, and find the average. Then, for a week, take a 100 mg or 200 mg caffeine pill, depending on your body weight and individual sensitivity to the drug, 15 minutes before you sit down at the table. Keep the same record as you did the previous week. Again, don't try to force yourself to eat less. Eat until you feel satisfied. At the end of the week, calculate your average calories per lunch, and compare your two logs. Were your portions smaller? Did you have fewer side dishes? Were you able to skip desserts? And, most important, was the average calorie count reduced during the week you were taking caffeine?

Don't forget that everyone has a different caffeine sensitivity level. Only by trial and error can you determine how much caffeine you should use to achieve a weight-loss benefit from the drug. If you take caffeine before your meal, you may want to drink decaf coffee after your meal to get a weight-loss benefit while keeping your total intake of caffeine the same.

You don't have to take caffeine before every meal. It's not all or nothing. Depending on your needs and dietary habits, you might want to use caffeine only on special occasions. For example, if you are on a diet and are planning to attend a lavish buffet lunch, and you know that you usually succumb to the temptation to take large portions and go back for second or even third helpings, you might want to take caffeine before this affair. Or you might be unable to use caffeine as an appetite suppressant before dinner, because dinnertime occurs after your personal caffeine cutoff point, and it would therefore interfere with getting a good night's sleep. One approach is to remember that, if taken before breakfast, caffeine may work to suppress your appetite for the entire day.

The beauty of using caffeine to suppress your appetite is that you can eat less and still feel that you enjoyed a complete meal. You don't have to go hungry. Many stimulants, including amphetamines and cocaine, can accomplish the same thing, but the other stimulants are illegal and dangerous to your health. In the 1960s doctors began widely prescribing

Dexedrine and other prescription medications containing dextroampheta-mine for their patients who wanted to lose weight. At first, this seemed like a good idea. There was no question that 5 mg of Dexedrine taken three times a day reduced appetite and increased energy expenditures. Unfortu-nately, the nation was to learn the hard way about the hazards of prescrib-ing dextroamphetamine to dieters. Tens of thousands of people, mostly younger and middle-aged women, became addicted to the drug. Unlike caffeine, dextroamphetamine produces a craving to increase the dosage to higher and higher levels. So like all other amphetamine users, Dexedrine users developed a tolerance to its effects that required them to increase the dosage regularly. Although guidelines stated that Dexedrine should be pre-scribed only for a few weeks for weight loss, the patients being treated with it demanded of their doctors that their supplies continue and that the dosages even be increased. Poorly informed or simply unscrupulous doc-tors readily acceded to their requests. Some doctors even pushed the drug, because it kept patients coming back on a regular basis to refill prescrip-tions. Eventually, the FDA and the medical community, recognizing a growing drug abuse problem, put a halt to the use of Dexedrine for weight loss.

Dangerous Duo: Caffeine and Ephedrine

Ephedrine is a stimulant drug that works primarily by increasing the actions of epinephrine, that is, adrenaline. It is extracted from the ephedra plant, a leafless desert bush related to pine trees that is native to arid regions through-out the world. Ma-huang, an ephedrine preparation made from the Chinese species of ephedra, has been used as a traditional medicine in China since before the introduction of tea in that country. Synthetic ephedrine and a closely related compound, pseudoephedrine, are ingredients in dozens of prescription and over-the-counter allergy and cold medications today. Ephedrine and ma-huang are common components of over-the-counter weight-loss products, and they are often sold in formulas that combine them with caffeine.

Although the FDA has issued warnings about the use of products con-taining ephedrine as an active ingredient, its sale as an over-the-counter drug is still permitted.

Ephedrine and the ephedrine-caffeine combination are effective for weight loss. However, questions have arisen about the safety of both. A report in the *Mayo Clinic Proceedings* in January 2002 concluded that ma-huang use is related to stroke, heart attack, and sudden death and that these dangers exist even in healthy people who use small dosages. Dramatic stories, such as that of the death of a healthy twenty-year-old professional athlete, have led many health experts to advise people to avoid the drug.

When caffeine is sold as part of a diet pill, is it almost always in combination with ephedrine. The idea is that the combination of these two drugs is more effective in producing weight loss than either would be separately. This is probably true. But in evaluating drugs, we must consider safety as well as efficacy, and the caffeine-ephedrine combination probably poses greater risks than ephedrine alone and certainly poses more risks than caffeine alone.

Ephedrine products do deliver weight-loss benefits, but their safety is questionable. Caffeine also delivers weight-loss benefits, but its safety profile is outstanding. If you're looking for a weight-loss agent, we recommend sticking to pure caffeine.

Increasing Your Metabolic Rate

Many books have been written to unravel the question of what makes people gain weight and how they can lose it. The basic truth, however, is simple: The amount of weight you gain is proportional to the difference between the number of calories you take in and the number of calories you burn. For every 3500 calories you take in and fail to burn, you will gain 1 pound. Conversely, every time you burn off 3500 calories without increasing the amount of food you take in, you will lose 1 pound. If you are consistently taking in 100 calories a day more than you are burning, you will gain 10 pounds a year.

You burn calories by doing exercise and doing work. But you also burn calories simply by being alive, breathing, circulating your blood, and keeping warm. The speed at which you burn calories in this way is a function of your basal metabolism. The faster your basal metabolism is, the more quickly you burn calories. We all know people with a fast metabolism, they're the ones who seem to stay thin their whole lives no matter how much they eat.

Calories are burned in three basic ways. First, there is your basal metabolism, accounting for about 50 to 75 percent, which means the energy you consume just by being alive, without using any calories to move about. Second, there is digestion, accounting for about 10 percent, which is the energy you consume when you are processing your food. Third, there is physical activity, accounting for about 15 to 40 percent, which includes all activities, from walking to your refrigerator to swimming a 1500 meter race. If you could increase your basal metabolism by 10 to 20 percent, you would be burning between 5 and 15 percent more calories overall.[10]

Your basal metabolic rate is initially determined by genetic factors. However, your actual metabolic rate at any given time can be influenced by many things. For example, if you are deprived of food for a prolonged period, your metabolic rate will slow down. Conversely, if you are briefly exposed to a cold climate, your metabolic rate will increase to help keep you warm.

Caffeine increases your metabolic rate, which causes you to burn more calories and therefore to tend to lose weight. Even if it increases your metabolism by only 5 percent, this is enough to make the difference between being fat and being thin. According to researcher Robert Conlee, Ph.D., caffeine increases the metabolic rate through its effects on the neurotransmitter systems: "Caffeine increases the metabolic rate of muscle, either directly or indirectly, through release of catecholamines." In fact, caffeine, as many studies have proven, will speed up your metabolism for 24 hours after ingestion.[11]

Small increases in metabolic rate cause the body to release energy as body heat instead of converting it into body fat. Even when the differences in energy expenditure are so slight that they are difficult to measure, explains Cornell nutritional biochemist T. Colin Campbell, they can make a big difference in your weight over time. As little as 50 to 100 calories a day in a 2500 calorie diet, "if unburned . . . can add up to 10 additional pounds a year."[12]

A similar conclusion was reached in a peer-reviewed article about caffeine published in the *Navy Health Book* in 1997, in which a navy researcher states, "Caffeine, at doses equivalent to one cup of coffee, raises the metabolic rate slightly for a couple of hours. If a person wanting to lose weight could refrain from making up this energy deficit with food, these small changes in the metabolic rate (75–100 calories/day) could lead to a substantial weight loss."[13]

Research suggests that on the average, 200 mg of caffeine will speed up your metabolism by about 15 percent for about 2 or 3 hours. If you took this dosage of caffeine three times a day, the total increase would result in burning about 75 to 100 calories more than you would have otherwise burned. It may not seem like much, but, as we have seen, a difference of 100 calories a day results in a net difference in weight of 10 pounds a year. That means that if you never consumed any caffeine, then suddenly began drinking one strong cup of coffee three times a day, without increasing the amount of food you were eating, you would lose about 1 pound a month,

---

How Many Extra Calories Can You Burn by Boosting Your Metabolic Rate with Caffeine?

To find out, you must first determine your basal metabolic rate (BMR), that is, the number of calories you need just to stay alive. Use the Harris-Benedict equation to estimate this value:

1. Multiply your weight in pounds by 4.4.
2. Multiply your height in inches by 4.7.
3. Add 1 and 2.
4. Multiply your age in years by 4.7.
5. Subtract 4 from 3.
6. Add 655. If you're a man, add 10 percent. The result is a reasonably good estimate of your BMR.
7. Take 10 percent of this amount. This will tell you about how many extra calories you can burn by increasing your metabolic rate 10 percent with caffeine.

Because women have about 10 percent more body fat than men and fat is metabolically less active than muscle, when all other factors are equal, men generally have a higher BMR.

If your BMR is 1500 calories, and your caffeine use increases your metabolism by 10 percent, you will be burning an additional 150 calories a day, enough to lose 15 pounds a year![14]

or 10 pounds a year. After a few years, a difference like that would really begin to add up.

Most of us already consume more than one cup of coffee a day, and the metabolic benefits of that amount of coffee have been compensated for by our diet. Without consciously deciding to do so, we allow ourselves to eat a little more than we would otherwise have because we can do so without putting on any additional weight. Therefore, to capitalize on the metabolism-increasing and fat-burning benefits of caffeine, we must increase the total amount of caffeine we are taking daily. This can be done by taking a caffeine pill before lunch while continuing to consume your regular cup of coffee or tea after lunch. This additional caffeine before the meal may be enough to help you lose weight by increasing your metabolic rate. If you are increasing the amount of caffeine you are taking by doing this, you may want to drink decaf during your afternoon coffee breaks to limit your total intake. Otherwise, your total caffeine intake may be higher than you'd be comfortable with.

One final note on metabolism. When you're fatigued, your metabolic rate slows. In addition to restoring your energy and brightening your mood, caffeine boosts your metabolism up to the levels of a well-rested person.[15]

Increasing Fat Burning and the Benefits of Exercise

In addition to reducing your appetite and increasing your metabolism, caffeine can help you lose weight by increasing lipolysis, or fat burning, especially when you are exercising. This means that caffeine literally helps to speed up the rate at which fat is eliminated from your body. In one study, trained male and female cyclists were instructed to perform 2 hours of cycle exercise to produce the greatest amount of work possible. Those who had ingested two doses of 250 mg of caffeine (one taken before and one during the exercise) burned 31 percent more fat than those who did not take caffeine before and during cycling! They also expended about 7.5 percent more energy.[16]

It's also well established that caffeine increases the burning of brown adipose tissue—ordinary fat, like the stuff we carry around in our "love handles"—even when we are at rest.[17] Levels of free fatty acid (FFA) in the blood increase after caffeine is taken, which proves that more fat is being burned up by the body. This fat-burning effect begins to show up about 3 hours after taking caffeine, but probably occurs only when using larger doses of the drug.[18]

Whether we are at rest or working out, caffeine increases fat burning by increasing the release of catecholamine neurotransmitters, including dopamine and epinephrine, which activate the enzymes, or biological catalysts, "responsible for lipolysis in muscle and adipose tissue."[19] In other words, caffeine tells your body to burn fat.

When taken before exercise, caffeine also has the specific ability to burn off the fat stored in the viscera, the soft internal organs of the body, including the intestines and those contained within the abdominal and thoracic cavities. Although you can't see such fat deposits from the outside, high levels of fatty buildup in these organs are bad for your health. By taking caffeine before exercise, we potentiate the fat-burning effects of exercise in these areas of the body. Scientists suggest that such effects on "visceral adipocytes," or fat cells in internal organs, can boost insulin sensitivity as well.[20]

Caffeine is metabolized, or transformed, by the body largely into paraxanthine, a related chemical. Scientists have shown that the activity of paraxanthine is directly responsible for the increase in lipolysis that occurs after caffeine ingestion. As caffeine is metabolized and paraxanthine is formed, there is a simultaneous increase in free fatty acid levels, indicating that paraxanthine is an active lipolytic agent, that is, something that facilitates the burning of fat. Once again, caffeine's effects on the adenosine neurotransmitter system seem to be the key to how it accomplishes this. Caffeine and its metabolites, including paraxanthine, increase fat burning primarily by blocking adenosine receptors on the surface of fat cells.[21]

Although caffeine in large enough doses does increase adrenaline, studies indicate that this is not the primary way that caffeine increases the amount of fat we burn and that increases in fat burning occur even when adrenaline levels are kept constant. Within normal dosage levels, caffeine directly stimulates specific tissues, including fat cells.[22] So caffeine does not rely on a centralized mechanism of boosting adrenaline production to cause increased fat burning. Caffeine acts directly on fat cells to cause them to shrink.

Everyone knows that if you want to lose weight, it is important, even

Caffeine and Cellulite: Can Caffeine Actually Melt Away Fat on Your Thighs?

It has long been known that caffeine and closely related compounds, such as aminophylline, literally cause cells to burn fat. As long ago as 1985, scientists Frank L. Greenway of UCLA and George A. Bray, M.D., of the Pennington Biomedical Research Center at Louisiana State University, patented an anti-cellulite cream based on aminophylline.

Very little was known about the composition of anticellulite creams by the dermatological community until a 2000 article in the *European Journal of Dermatology* examined thirty-two anticellulite products containing forty-four different emollients and thirty-nine different botanicals. Caffeine, present in fourteen of these anticellulite products, was the most common additive.[23] The study found that all the creams were microbiologically pure and concluded, "In spite of the large number of substances used in cellulite creams, their safety seems acceptable for most users."

David Heber, M.D., Ph.D., a professor of medicine and chief of clinical nutrition at UCLA, explains that if you put fat cells in a culture dish with caffeine, "you can literally watch them release their stores of fat." The question remains, however, whether these creams really deliver a substantial practical benefit in actual use. One study found that after six weeks of application, in which women used the cream on only one thigh, they lost only about a half-inch from thighs treated with the creams as compared with untreated thighs. There is anecdotal evidence that these creams can have at least a temporary effect that is significant. Some models apply them before photo shoots to help shrink their thighs. And Neutrogena Anti-Cellulite Treatment, sold in a spray bottle, which contains retinol and seaweed as well as caffeine, is advertised to reduce cellulite visibly by 50 percent after twelve weeks, as proven by clinical tests "under dermatological control."

necessary, to get more exercise. One of the remarkable benefits of caffeine, discussed extensively in Chapters 8 and 9, is that caffeine increases your ability to walk, run, and participate in sporting activities by boosting your endurance and speed and even by instilling an attitude of success. What this means is that by using caffeine, you will be able to exercise longer and

Tea Box

The caffeine contained in all kinds of tea works to increase the burning of fatty tissue, but tea probably contains other chemicals that work with caffeine to burn even more fat than caffeine could burn alone.

The antiobesity effects of oolong tea are "due partly to the enhancing effect of caffeine . . . on noradrenaline-induced lipolysis in adipose tissue. . . ." However, researchers also found that inhibitory action on pancreatic enzymes, caused by some other substance in oolong tea, also contributed to the increase in fat burning. The results suggest that "oolong tea may be an effective crude drug for the treatment of obesity and fatty liver caused by a high-fat diet."[24] Another study confirms that "green tea stimulates brown adipose tissue thermogenesis to an extent which is much greater than can be attributed to its caffeine content per se." That is, the researcher attributes a large part of this effect to a "synergistic interaction between catechin-polyphenols and caffeine," stimulating fat burning to a extent that "could be of value in assisting the management of obesity."[25]

harder and, what is more, that you will look forward to doing so. There are no double-blind studies of exactly how many more pounds you will lose as a result. But it is certain that even if caffeine had no other weight-loss benefit apart from increasing the amount and quality of your exercise, it would be an immensely valuable tool in the fight to become and stay slim.

What difference will increasing your level of exercise make to how much weight you lose? For many people, the difference between being slender and fat is as small as 50 to 100 calories a day, and 100 calories a day make a net difference in your weight of 10 pounds a year. If you increase your level of exercise or even your overall activity level even slightly and boost your caloric expenditures in this way, you should experience a significant weight loss over time.

One good idea is to take 100 mg to 200 mg of caffeine, depending on your weight and your individual sensitivity to the drug, 15 minutes or more before doing an early morning workout on a treadmill or stationary bicycle or even some calisthenics or weight lifting. Taking this dose of caffeine will help you to work out longer and harder, thus helping you to lose

The Four Ways Caffeine Works to Help You Lose Weight

- Decreases your appetite and makes you feel full faster and keeps you feeling full longer
- Increases lipolysis, or fat burning
- Increases your basal metabolic rate, thus burning calories instead of storing them
- Increases your ability to exercise and the amount of energy you expend and the amount of fat you burn when you do exercise

more weight. If you feel no problems taking 200 mg, you may want to try increasing your dose to 300 mg or even more. Because you are taking it early in the morning, it probably won't keep you awake at night.

Self-Assessments

Many fitness experts and physicians say that walking is the best exercise you can get. It's low impact, low stress, and low risk. It's something nearly everyone can do, and it's an effective way of losing weight and keeping it off. A simple walking test can enable you to measure your aerobic fitness. It can also help you to estimate the effects of caffeine on your exercise and keep track of how your physical condition is progressing as you implement your program of using caffeine.

If you are able to walk 1 mile, try seeing how you measure up on the table, walking the mile as fast as you can do so comfortably or running if you are able to do so. Then try it again on other days, after taking 100 mg, 200 mg, and 300 mg of caffeine. Compare your results without caffeine and after taking different doses to find out how much caffeine can help boost your athletic prowess. You can walk, run, or jog, but the goal is to complete the mile as quickly as possible.

One Mile Walking, Running, or Jogging Time (minutes)

Age	Excellent	Very Good	Good	Fair	Poor
20–39	<12	<14	<16	<18	18>
40–49	<13	<15	<17	<19	19>
50–59	<14	<17	<19	<21	21>
60–69	<15	<18	<20	<22	22>
70+	<16	<19	<21	<23	23>

Note: < = "less than"; > = "more than."
Source: Adapted from M. Nelson and S. Wernick, *Strong Women Stay Slim*, New York: Bantam Books, 1998, p. 162.

11

An Elixir of Life? Caffeine and Staying Younger

Si le café est un poison, c'est un poison lent.
(If coffee is a poison, it is a slow poison.)

Remarked late in life by Fontanelle (b. 1657),
a coffee lover, who lived to be 100

MOST PEOPLE THINK that the fountain of youth and the elixir of life are just myths, fabulous dreams concocted out of the hopeless desire of people throughout history to recapture the mental sharpness and physical vitality they enjoyed in their youth. Yet the remarkable fact is that caffeine not only improves the performance of people in general, but it also specifically acts to increase the intellectual and physical capacities of older people and to restore them close to the levels of the young. In addition, caffeine is a powerful antioxidant and works to keep the body youthful by protecting it from free radicals, one of the major sources of age-related deterioration. Caffeine also has powerful brain-protective and -restorative functions, enabling it to reduce dramatically the incidence of degenerative conditions such as Parkinson's disease and possibly Alzheimer's as well. Finally, research has shown that caffeine causes the brain to grow new cells in the areas responsible for long-term memory, a special blessing for people who have a long life to remember.

Perhaps because many of the detrimental changes that occur with increasing age resemble the effects of fatigue, caffeine has the specific power to reverse these changes. The age-reversing effects of caffeine include restorative effects on:

- Memory
- Reasoning
- Reaction time
- Physical stamina
- Motivation, focus, and self-confidence

Some researchers say that caffeine does more for older people because they do not work as close to their full capacity as younger people, so they have more room for improvement. In their best-selling book *Biomarkers: The 10 Keys to Prolonging Vitality*, William Evans, Ph.D., and Irwin H. Rosenberg, M.D., argue that most of the decrements in athletic performance associated with advancing age are simply a result of older people not trying as hard as young people do.[1] For example, a twenty year old has strong motivation to train and compete to win in a track meet. A fifty year old has far less reason to push himself to attain a record time when running the same distance. Evans and Rosenberg found that when fifty year olds trained hard and tried hard, their running times and endurance approximated those of average people thirty-five years younger. They concluded that by increasing motivation, focus, and self-confidence, an older person can improve levels of performance greatly, frequently to the same levels he achieved decades before, especially if he did not train hard in his youth. Trying harder usually means believing in yourself. As we have seen in Chapter 6, one of caffeine's most prized powers is the ability to restore our spirits and give us a sense of optimism and confidence. As the complexities and challenges of life mount up over time, perhaps it is natural that this benefit should come to mean even more to us as we age.

Whatever the reason, caffeine has stronger beneficial effects on middle-aged and older people than it does on younger people. For example, when people in their twenties and people in their sixties are given caffeine, all of them will tend to improve in parameters of physical and mental performance. However, the older group will improve significantly more, closing the gap in performance between the groups.

An illustration of this difference is found in the results of a 1988 study by two English scientists who examined how certain of the effects of caffeine on cognitive and psychomotor performance change with age.[2] A series of tests were administered to twelve subjects: Six were ages eighteen to thirty-seven and the other six were ages sixty-five to seventy-five. Both age groups demonstrated clear improvements in performance with caffeine use, but researchers concluded that the older group overall showed a greater benefit from caffeine use than the younger one. Although the younger group improved more on tasks depending on motor speed, the older group experienced more improvement in attention span and choice reaction time—the abilities to concentrate and make quick decisions—both of which are important when working at our jobs and in life in general. This greater improvement among older people has been confirmed by other studies, such as a 1997 British study that showed that higher levels of caffeine consumption are associated with improved cognitive functioning in older people and that older people are more susceptible to the cognitive performance–improving effects of caffeine than are younger people.[3]

An additional curiosity is that although the performance benefits of caffeine to reaction time, memory, and reasoning are greater for older people

"Sarcopenia": Why We "Poop Out" As We Get Older

In discussing the travails of aging, Evans and Rosenberg describe a generalized condition, characterized by spending most of your day sitting and walking tentatively and by the loss of muscle tone and vitality. People exhibiting this condition suffer from what is a generally undiagnosed disease that Evans and Rosenberg call "sarcopenia." It refers to "an overall weakening of the body caused by a change of body composition in favor of fat at the expense of muscle."[4] According to these writers, sarcopenia is responsible for a preponderance of the decline in performance experienced by older people. Their theory is that if we can just jump-start our motivation, change our attitude, and begin participating in exercise and in life, we can effectively reverse most of the losses that people generally think inevitably accompany aging.

Caffeine could have been invented simply to treat this condition. By helping us to build muscle by exercising longer and harder, burning fat, and increasing motivation and focus, caffeine gives older people an effective weapon for combating sarcopenia. If nothing else, caffeine can help people in middle age and beyond to be more active, which, according to these writers, postpones aging in and of itself. Caffeine can put the "oomph" back into your life. Once you have recovered that, say Evans and Rosenberg, you will be well on your way to enjoying the capacities you had in your youth.

than for younger ones, its relaxation effects follow just the opposite pattern. A recent study found that although 200 mg of caffeine conferred more objective benefits on older people—that is, it improved attention and reaction time in older people more than it did in younger ones—some of the subjective effects of caffeine on older people were less noticeable. The researcher reports that "young subjects reported feeling more alert, calmer, more interested, and steadier on caffeine," while less dramatic changes were reported by the elderly.[5] Parallel results have been found for sedative drugs, with the young but not the old reporting "acute subjective effects" of drowsiness and dizziness, but the significance of this dichotomy remains unclear. Whatever the reason, older people are either less aware of the effects of psychoactive drugs or less inclined to report their awareness of these effects.

One special caveat for older users of caffeine is that people over age fifty average as much as 2 hours less sleep a night than younger people, so additional loss of sleep time, such as can be caused by using caffeine too late in the day, can represent a proportionally greater decrement.[6] Further, caffeine's half-life tends to become extended in older people, which means that its effects last longer in them.[7] Unfortunately, many older people who have difficulty falling asleep are unaware that their medicines contain caffeine. For example, Anacin and Excedrin, over-the-counter painkillers, and Darvon Compound-65, a prescription painkiller, contain doses of caffeine that might keep many people awake. The Iowa 65+ Rural Health Study of 3,000 people over age sixty-five found that 5 percent were using medicines that contained caffeine, and that the ones who were doing so were twice as likely as the others to report problems falling asleep. The same study failed to discover any such correlation between sleep problems and coffee drinking. The conclusion is obvious. People are universally aware that coffee contains caffeine and therefore avoid drinking it in the evening, but because they don't think about the caffeine in their medicines, they make

Perking Up Your Sex Life?

We don't know if caffeine is an aphrodisiac or whether it just gives you more energy to perform, but researchers have found that people over age 65 are more likely to remain sexually active if they are coffee drinkers.

The Three Ages of Man

How old are you? There can be more than just one way to answer this question. We've all known people over age sixty-five who think and perform like people half their age. In fact there are three types of age:

- Chronological age: How many years you have lived
- Biological age: How much age has affected the different systems of your body and how many age-related decrements you have
- Virtual age: How well you function at a given time in relation to the parameters that decline with age

Caffeine probably helps slow the progression of or even decrease your biological age because it is a powerful antioxidant and may offer strong protection to brain cells from the effects of aging and degenerative disease. Caffeine decreases your virtual age by improving reaction time and memory to the levels of younger people and by boosting your energy levels and physical endurance. Nothing can help you decrease your chronological age short of a time machine.

no effort to take caffeine-containing medications early enough in the day to avoid sleep problems.[8]

"I'll Never Forget What's-His-Name": Combating Memory Loss

Memory loss is one of the most dreaded banes of aging. Some of caffeine's strongest restorative effects are evident in its ability to improve the memory of older people.

A 2001 study published in *Psychological Science,* the journal of the American Psychological Society, highlighted some of caffeine's memory-enhancing powers for people over age sixty-five. It is well known that the memory of older people is better in the morning and that it suffers a distinct decline over the course of the day. Researcher Lee Ryan, director of the Cognition and Neuroimaging Laboratory of the University of Arizona, wanted to see if caffeine could help reverse this decline. She divided forty subjects, all over age sixty-five, into two groups. Both groups were given memory tests at 8 A.M. and at 4 P.M. Before each test, the first group was given a 12 ounce cup of coffee containing about 220 to 270 mg of caffeine. The other group drank decaf, containing 10 mg or less of caffeine. The group that drank decaf "suffered a significant decline in memory perform-ance from morning to afternoon." However, the group that drank regular coffee showed no decline on the memory tests. "Caffeine, in a dose that most adults readily consume daily," says Ryan, "ameliorates memory impairment arising from time-of-day effects in older adults. The fact that these effects are easily reduced is . . . vindication for those of us who live with a coffeepot always at the ready."

A major 1992 study using data gathered by the epidemiological Health and Lifestyle Survey of over 9,000 adults living in the United Kingdom found that caffeine in coffee or tea also improved the overall memory of older people and that this improvement was significantly greater than the improvement experienced by the young. In this study, the population of daily coffee or tea drinkers was broken into three approximately equal groups, ages sixteen to thirty-four, thirty-five to fifty-four, and fifty-five and older. Improvements on memory tests were nearly fifteen times greater in the oldest group as compared with the youngest.[9]

The researchers also discovered a dose-dependent increase in memory performance that seems to outlast caffeine's immediate effects in the body: The daily consumption of any amount of caffeinated coffee or tea improved memory, but those who regularly drank more had correspond-ingly higher scores on memory tests, regardless of whether they had con-sumed caffeine just prior to taking the test.

The benefits discussed above are for short-term memory. However, new research strongly suggests that regular caffeine use may grow functional new branches in brain cells in the areas of the brain responsible for long-term memory and may even protect the brain against certain forms of dete-rioration and degenerative disease.

A recent startling discovery by Menachem Segal, professor of neuro-sciences at the Weizmann Institute in Rehovot, Israel, and one of the world's leading experts in neuromodulators in the brain, suggests that caf-feine causes changes to brain cells that are likely to have profoundly benefi-cial effects on long-term memory.[10] In earlier research, Segal had discovered that increasing the amount of calcium absorbed by brain cells is one way of improving long-term memory. Because caffeine augments the ability of these cells to metabolize calcium, Segal conjectured that adding caffeine directly to the hippocampus, an area of the brain that is "the site of continual neuronal birth in adulthood,"[11] and is critical to learning and determining what incoming information will be stored in long-term memory, would increase these calcium levels inside the cells and probably improve long-term memory function as a result. The outcome of his experiments confirmed that caffeine does increase calcium metabolism in the brain, which means that regular caffeine use, because it exposes brain cells to caffeine, should also produce an improvement in long-term memory performance.

Segal also observed an even more astonishing phenomenon: Caffeine caused existing dendritic spines, the branching extensions at the ends of nerve cells that allow them to make synaptic connections with each other, to grow longer and even caused new spines and branches to develop as well. Neuroscientists have long believed that better "wiring" does in fact improve both long-term memory and learning, and it seems that these new connections may help explain how caffeine works to boost long-term memory performance. If this finding is borne out in future studies, caffeine would be confirmed as the only known substance that can augment brain functions by altering the physical structure of the brain.

Combating Parkinson's Disease and Alzheimer's Disease

Parkinson's disease, named for English surgeon James Parkinson, who first described it in 1817, is a degenerative brain disorder initially characterized by trembling lips and hands and muscular rigidity and later by body tremors, a shuffling gait, and, often, nearly complete incapacity. It usually appears after age forty. Over half a million Americans suffer from the disease, which strikes men and women with equal frequency, and 50,000 new cases are diagnosed every year, incurring a total annual cost of over $5.6 billion. In addition to causing physical disabilities, Parkinson's disease can affect emotions and impair mental capacity, although assessment of such effects is difficult because depression often accompanies the disease. Parkinson's disease occurs when the brain cells that produce dopamine die.

A Caffeine Success Story

The story of Edith, an eighty-one-year-old woman living in an affluent retirement community in Scottsdale, Arizona, may not be as probative as a scientific study, but it vividly illustrates the potential benefits of caffeine for older people.

Edith is a well-educated, witty, articulate woman who always enjoyed the best things in life. She had a loving husband and a good job, and was financially comfortable. After she retired, she depended more and more on her husband's companionship, and, when he died two years ago, she slipped into a lassitude that bordered on depression. She seemed to lose interest in life.

Always a moderate coffee drinker, when she heard about the potential advantages of caffeine pills, she decided to give up her favorite drink for a while and try the pills instead. She began her experimentation with 100 mg of caffeine at breakfast. When she failed to notice any effects, she increased the dose to 200 mg.

"Suddenly, things began to happen for me," Edith told us. "I can concentrate much better, and I keep my apartment much cleaner. But the big news is that I bought a computer and began writing and editing the community newsletter. My children were astonished and wanted to know what got into me."

On busy days, she takes a second 200 mg caffeine pill around noon. Now her favored morning routine is a caffeine pill and a chaser of herbal tea.

The lack of dopamine causes brain cells to fire erratically, producing the muscular symptoms that mark the condition. Although its symptoms are treatable with various drugs, including deprenyl (selegiline), L-dopa, and amantadine, there is no cure.

A high intake of caffeine over a long period of time is strongly correlated with a dramatically lower incidence and slower progression of Parkinson's disease. A study reported in the *Journal of the American Medical Association* in 2000, led by G. Webster Ross, M.D., a staff neurologist at the Department of Veterans Affairs in Honolulu, analyzed thirty years of data from the Honolulu Heart Program, which has followed more than 8,000 Japanese-American men since 1965. The researchers uncovered a dose-dependent decrease of Parkinson's disease that correlated with caffeine use. That is, the more caffeine the men in the study consumed, the less likely they were to contract the illness. Age-adjusted incidence of Parkinson's disease dropped over 80 percent in men who drank more than 28 ounces of coffee, or about five 6 ounce cups a day. A similar decline was observed from caffeine intake from sources other than coffee. Ross concluded that "caffeine has a medicinal effect. It could be treating motor symptoms." [12]

Commenting on these findings in an interview in *HealthScout,* Abraham Lieberman, professor of neurology at the University of Miami and medical director of the National Parkinson's Foundation, attributes the possible role of caffeine in preventing Parkinson's disease to its ability to block adenosine receptors and increase the levels of dopamine, which are low in people suffering from the disease. [13] Although Lieberman maintains that further long-term studies of the progression of the disease are needed to establish caffeine's treatment potential for Parkinson's disease, caffeine obviously provides remarkable protection for brain cells against the ravages of the condition. In fact, assuming that the results of the Honolulu Heart Program can be generalized to the entire population, if everyone consumed 500 to 600 mg of caffeine daily, there would be 40,000 fewer cases of Parkinson's disease in the United States every year.

Because of caffeine's now proven powers to preserve, protect, and even grow new brain cells, some researchers speculate that caffeine may offer significant protection against the development of Alzheimer's disease and other degenerative brain diseases. Alzheimer's is a degenerative brain disease that usually strikes in late middle or old age. It begins with memory loss for recent events and progresses over a period of five to fifteen years to a pervasive intellectual decline, marked by dementia and incapacity. Its effects on the cellular level include the degeneration of brain neurons, especially in the cerebral cortex. Only about 1 percent of people between ages sixty-five and seventy-four have Alzheimer's disease or a related condition, but these diseases afflict more than 25 percent of people over age eighty-five. As our population ages, Alzheimer's disease is expected to become a greater and greater problem.

Alzheimer's disease is associated with a loss of memory due in part to a loss of cells in the cortex and the hippocampus. Caffeine grows new cells in the hippocampus and causes existing dendritic cells to grow longer and develop new branches. Therefore, some researchers think that caffeine may have a protective or even therapeutic effect on the progression of the condition.

Most scientists think that Alzheimer's disease is the result of chronic inflammation in the brain,[14] and therefore it is also widely conjectured that nonsteroidal anti-inflammatory drugs (NSAIDs) might reduce its incidence by warding off the brain-damaging effects of inflammation. A major study conducted in Rotterdam, reported in 2001, of nearly 7,000 men and women over age fifty-five who did not have signs of Alzheimer's disease at the start were followed for about seven years. Those who took NSAIDs were significantly less likely to develop Alzheimer's disease, and furthermore, the longer someone had been taking NSAIDs, the less likely that person was to develop Alzheimer's.[15] Caffeine, while not an NSAID, is an anti-inflammatory, and therefore it is reasonable to suppose that it might also have similar protective powers. Only future research can determine if this is true.

And finally and perhaps most important, as Alzheimer's disease progresses, healthy tissue is displaced by plaque. As a result, the brain gradually loses its ability to produce acetylcholine, a neurotransmitter that, as we have seen, is critical to memory and cognition. Because caffeine increases the activity of acetylcholine, it may well function to help forestall or even reverse this accumulation of plaque and combat the attendant memory loss as well.

The Antioxidant Power of Caffeine

Antioxidants, including vitamin C, vitamin E, beta carotene, and selenium, are commonly taken as nutritional supplements. Few people know that caffeine is a stronger antioxidant than vitamin C and is actually equal in strength to the body's natural biological antioxidant, glutathione.

What benefit are people expecting when they add antioxidants to their diets? Nothing less spectacular than slowing the aging process. Free radicals are unstable atoms or groups of atoms that kick off a chain reaction of oxidation. The cumulative cellular damage caused by this oxidation is thought to be one of the underlying causes of aging. Antioxidants soak up harmful free radicals and neutralize them before they can initiate a chain reaction damaging to the body's cells. In this way, they are thought to fight the

Wake Up and Smell the Coffee: A Treasure Trove of Antioxidants

Professor Takayuki Shibamoto maintains that the aroma of brewing coffee delivers phytochemicals, including antioxidants, to your system. If smelling your morning coffee makes you feel good, perhaps it's more than simply sensual enjoyment or anticipation of the delights of caffeine. But the coffee must be sniffed immediately after brewing, because the phytochemicals degrade quickly.

physical deterioration that we associate with getting older. By protecting the body's cells from the damaging effects of oxidation, caffeine works on the cellular level to keep us younger longer.

Coffee contains as many as 1,000 chemical compounds. About 300 of these are phytochemicals (from the Greek word *"phyto,"* meaning "plant")—nonnutritive, bioactive plant substances thought to have a beneficial effect on human health. Several of coffee's phytochemicals, in addition to caffeine, are powerful antioxidants.

Phytochemicals also abound in other foods and drinks. They include flavonoids, found in red wine, apples, and tea, which reduce the risk of heart disease; isoflavones (also known as phytoestrogens), found in soybeans, which reduce the risk of breast and ovarian cancer and osteoporosis and may help relieve hot flashes in premenopausal women; and carotenoids, found in yellow, orange, and dark green vegetables, which reduce the risk of macular degeneration, a leading cause of blindness. According to Takayuki Shibamoto, Ph.D., an eminent professor of environmental toxicology at the University of California at Davis, a cup of coffee has the antioxidant power of three oranges, and the antioxidants in coffee can remain effective in your body for up to 30 days.[16]

Self-Assessments of Virtual Age

As we have noted, "virtual age" is defined as how well you function at a given time in relation to performance parameters that decline with age.

Caffeine: A Nutritional Supplement?

Some researchers argue that caffeine should be classified as a nutritional supplement, because it is a substance that can be introduced into the diet to fight cancer, Parkinson's and other diseases, and the effects of aging, and prevents free radical damage to muscles during exercise.

Caffeine can help to improve your performance parameters and, therefore, can act to decrease your virtual age.

Reaction Time

Reaction time increases very predictably with age, that is, it takes longer and longer to respond to a stimulus. For this reason, tests of reaction time can be used to measure a person's virtual age. To estimate your virtual age after taking different doses of caffeine, take the test on page 91.

You can try this test before using caffeine and after using 100 mg, 200 mg, and if you can tolerate it comfortably, 300 mg of caffeine. See if caffeine can enable you to catch the ruler more quickly, nearer to the 11 inch mark—if it really makes you "quicker on the draw." (On average, scores decrease progressively from the 11 inch mark at age twenty to the 6 inch mark at age sixty, although what you are most interested in when taking this test is not how you stack up against average performance but how much you can improve your score after taking caffeine.)

Static Balance Youth Test

The following test of static balance is supposed to be the best test you can take at home for measuring your biological age. It is very simple, consisting of seeing how long you can stand on one leg with your eyes closed without needing to prop yourself up with your other leg. When you take this test, stand on your left leg if you are right-handed and on your right leg if you are left-handed. On average, a 100 percent decline in performance is experienced between the time a person is twenty years old and eighty years old. People around twenty years old can usually hold themselves upright on one leg with their eyes closed for thirty seconds or longer. People around eighty can do so for only a few seconds.

Take this test either in bare feet or in a low-heeled shoe, on a hard surface, with both feet together. Close your eyes and lift your foot 6 inches from the floor, bending your knee at 45 degrees. Try to hold as still as possible. Have someone stand by with a watch (and to catch you if you fall!) to determine how long you can maintain this position without opening your eyes or falling over. Take the test three times, and take the average. Try this procedure before taking caffeine and after taking doses of different amounts to see if your virtual age declines with caffeine. You can also make the same comparison over a period of several months of regular caffeine use to see if you are actually creating long-term improvements. Use the chart to evaluate your score.

Time in Seconds Before Losing Your Balance	Virtual Age
28 seconds	20 years
25	30
15	40
10	45
8	50
6	60
5 seconds or less	65+

12

Caffeine and Good Health

As we have seen, caffeine delivers immediate improvements to your mental abilities, your mood, and your athletic performance. And that is not the whole story of its benefits. In this chapter, we'll explore the many ways caffeine can contribute to health and fight disease. And because any drug can have adverse effects on some people in certain circumstances, we'll also review the few caveats that attend caffeine use.

The scientific report card on the health effects of caffeine is outstandingly favorable: It has very few and very minimal detrimental effects, if any, and an astounding number of good ones. But, historically, full confidence in caffeine's safety and benefits was a long time coming.

About four hundred years ago, when coffee, tea, and chocolate arrived in Europe from distant, exotic lands, people across the Continent became excited about the pharmacological effects of the new beverages, effects that we now know are produced by caffeine. In fact, when these infusions were first encountered, they were thought of only as drugs and not as items of food or drink, and they were available for purchase exclusively at pharmacies. The bitter, murky potion produced by boiling coffee beans even tasted like medicine, so no one would have dreamed of consuming it for enjoyment. The first coffeehouse in London, opened by Pasqua Rosée in 1652, was advertised with the following broadside that, after recommending that a half-pint of water in which the ground beans had been boiled should be downed on an empty stomach, promised:

> It much quickens the spirits, and makes the heart lightsome; it is good against sore eyes. . . . It suppresseth fumes exceedingly, and

therefore is good against the head-ache, and will . . . prevent and help consumptions and cough of the lungs.

It is excellent to prevent and cure the dropsy, gout, and scurvy. It is known by experience to be better than any other drying drink for people in years, or children that have any running humours upon them as the king's evil, &tc. . . . It will prevent drowsiness, and make one fit for business, if one have occasion to watch, and therefore you are not to drink of it after supper, unless you intend to be watchful, for it will hinder sleep for three or four hours.

It is observed that in Turkey, where this is generally drunk, that they are not troubled with the stone, gout, dropsy, or scurvy.[1]

Some of the benefits commonly associated with caffeine today are included in Rosée's list, such as keeping you awake and alert when you need to get work done. More astonishing is the fact that many of the conditions supposed by the author to have been treatable with caffeine, including headaches, pulmonary conditions, and gallstones, have turned out in modern studies to be ameliorated by caffeine use.

Cornelius Buntekuh, court physician to Friedrich William after the Thirty Years' War, a colorful figure who opened the first coffeehouse in Hamburg in 1679, is a good example of a physician who promoted caffeine use in the early years. Buntekuh published a book advising people to drink enormous quantities of tea—even hundreds of cups—daily in order to enjoy the full benefits of its rejuvenating and life-extending powers. However, other physicians thought the new beverages were harmful to health. Simon Pauli, a German who was the personal physician to the king of Denmark, was the first and fiercest of Buntekuh's adversaries. He published a medical tract with dire admonitions about the detrimental effects of coffee, tea, and chocolate and believed that they were all equally injurious to physical and mental health, producing, among other ills, "effeminacy and impotence." However, the public seemed to like the new drinks so well that despite the medical disagreements, acceptance and use of all three became nearly universal.

Caffeine has remained a central interest of research scientists, and as we begin the twenty-first century, we have the results of decades of randomized, double-blind studies, performed under controlled conditions, to reveal caffeine's true effects on human health. As it turns out, some of the more expansive claims by early physicians for caffeine's health benefits were proven true, and many other unsuspected benefits have been discovered as well. Also, as it turns out, several concerns about caffeine have been laid to rest, including the theories that caffeine causes or affects the progression of heart disease, kidney and bladder cancers, pancreatic cancer, fibrocystic breast disease, increased blood sugar, and high cholesterol levels.[2] Other concerns have been put into perspective. For example, the fact that caffeine slightly increases calcium loss has been shown to be significant only in older women who have a specific gene mutation, and, even in them, the loss can be entirely offset by consuming a tablespoon of milk daily, about what you get when you have cream with your coffee.

Controlling Pain

Caffeine is a potent painkiller. The relief it delivers to nociception, that is, pain perception, results from at least two distinct mechanisms. Caffeine delivers pain relief by exerting peripheral action, that is, relief at the site of an injury. In doing so, it acts directly on muscle tissue, relieving pain by repairing tissue damage and reducing inflammation. Caffeine also has profound CNS effects that block the central processing of pain signals in the brain and increase the effectiveness of the body's natural painkilling mechanisms. In addition to reducing pain on its own, caffeine in even low doses has been shown to magnify the painkilling power of aspirin and ibuprofen and even of narcotic analgesics.[3] That is the reason that caffeine is an active ingredient in over-the-counter painkillers like Anacin and in prescription painkillers like Darvon Compound-65. Leading caffeine researchers Jan Snel and Monique M. Lorist state that the studies of caffeine alone and in combination with other painkillers show that "different pain states can, to different degrees, be mediated by different mechanisms that may be caffeine-sensitive."[4] This means that different mechanisms enable caffeine to relieve pain of different kinds and differing intensities. Snel and Lorist add that caffeine's power to alleviate intense pain suggests that the neural mechanisms that cause this pain are "directly sensitive to caffeine."

One creative study, using a 200 mg caffeine pill, found that caffeine by itself was a potent pain reliever for muscle pain. Conducted by Daniel E. Myers, D.D.S., associate professor in the department of oral medicine and pathology at the University of Pittsburgh School of Dental Medicine, this experiment measured the effects of caffeine on ischemic muscle contraction pain, that is, the intense pain (such as that experienced during a heart attack) caused by blocking the flow of blood to an area of the body. Each participant in the study was given either a 200 mg caffeine pill or a placebo. One hour later, subjects raised their arms to drain the blood, and blood pressure cuffs were attached to prevent blood flow to the arm. The participants then did wrist curls while holding a small weight, activity that would give rise to ischemic muscle pain. The subjects were then asked to rate pain levels after 15, 30, and 45 seconds of wrist curl exercises. At 15 seconds, the mean pain rating of those who had taken caffeine was half that of those who had taken a placebo. A similar profile but less pronounced pattern of effects was found at 30 seconds and 45 seconds. Myers attributes the painkilling power of caffeine in his study and in over-the-counter and prescription medications to its action in blocking adenosine receptors in muscles, concluding that caffeine alone delivers considerable analgesic efficiency and that the "implication is that there is a rationale for the use of caffeine in the treatment of muscle pain when blood flow is reduced."[5]

As this experiment demonstrates, caffeine alone is a strong analgesic. But there have been relatively few studies of the effects of caffeine alone on pain in human beings. Most scientists have concentrated on examining caffeine's use as an adjuvant, or added ingredient, in preparations of drugs like acetaminophen, acetaminophen and aspirin combinations, and ibuprofen. A thorough review of these studies, published in *Pharmacological Review* in 1993, concluded that caffeine potentiated the pain relief of other analgesics, especially of ibuprofen, to a significant degree in postpartum pain, postsurgical pain following a dental extraction, and headache pain.[6] Another metastudy reviewing thirty pain studies in which caffeine was used in combination with nonsteroidal anti-inflammatory drugs (NSAIDs) to treat postpartum, dental, and headache pain found that the addition of 65 mg to 200 mg of caffeine (the amount in about a half-cup to about one and a third cups of filter drip coffee) resulted in a clear increase in the power of the NSAIDs to relieve pain.[7]

Caffeine has an especially powerful effect in relieving tension headaches. A landmark 2001 study, conducted by Dr. Seymour Diamond and Dr. Frederick G. Freitag of Chicago's Diamond Headache clinic, tested hundreds of people who suffer from severe tension headaches at least three times a month.[8] The researchers split participants into four groups, which were given either 400 mg of ibuprofen (e.g., Advil) alone, 400 mg of ibuprofen combined with 200 mg caffeine, 200 mg of caffeine alone, or a placebo. Caffeine alone delivered as much pain relief as the ibuprofen, completely eliminating the headaches in nearly two-thirds of the participants. (In other studies, as little as 130 mg of caffeine was effective at relieving headache pain.)[9] Caffeine also worked faster, ending the headaches a half-hour more quickly than the ibuprofen. However, the best results were achieved with the combination of caffeine and ibuprofen, which stopped the headaches in nearly three-fourths of the participants. The combination of caffeine and ibuprofen also worked much longer, providing an extra 4 hours of pain relief as compared with ibuprofen alone. So, if your doctor is aware of these facts, perhaps he might be telling you, "Take 200 mg of caffeine—and call me in the morning."

As has been known to physicians for nearly 500 years, caffeine also has a special power to relieve migraine headaches. Coffee was one of the earliest pharmacological remedies used against migraines, and caffeine has been a therapeutic ingredient in some modern migraine medicines for decades. In the 1970s the theory arose that caffeine alleviates migraines by con-

How Caffeine Kills Pain

Scientists speculate that caffeine's analgesic power arises from three different mechanisms:

- The blockade of peripheral pronociceptive actions of adenosine, which means that caffeine interferes with a neurotransmitter that is responsible for carrying pain signals from a specific area of the body to the brain (for example, caffeine could prevent adenosine's ability to activate a nerve ending and block its ability to signal pain)[10]

- Activation of central noradrenergic [adrenaline] pathways that constitute an endogenous pain suppressing system, which means that caffeine stimulates the body's own painkilling mechanism

- Central nervous system (CNS) stimulation, which means that caffeine's overall stimulating effects somehow change the way pain signals are processed in a way that reduces pain[11]

stricting cranial blood vessels. In the late 1990s, it was discovered that even though caffeine does constrict these blood vessels, its ability to relieve migraines is unrelated to this action and depends instead on its effects on the neurotransmitter serotonin. It turns out that migraines are not caused by vascular engorgement but rather by a disorder of the serotonin system. This discovery helped explain why bad moods so often precede or accompany migraines. Caffeine has the power to help restore the balance of the serotonin system, and this is the key to its ability to relieve migraines. One lesson we can learn from this is that it is not always important to know why caffeine does what it does in order to get the benefits of using it. After all, people were using caffeine to treat migraines hundreds of years before anyone had ever heard of the serotonin system. You don't have to know why it works, but you do have to know how to use it.

One additional statement that we found interesting was made by Jan Snel and Monique Lorist: "The positive effect of caffeine on lowering sensitivity to pain," combined with the ways in which caffeine intensifies our sense perceptions, "may mean that caffeine . . . may form a major contribution to the enjoyment of life." [12]

Hypertension and the Cardiovascular System

Contrary to a popular myth, caffeine does not affect the incidence or development of hypertension or congestive heart failure or cause or exacerbate any cardiovascular condition. Although people persistently worry over the

Stopping Migraines in Their Tracks

Caffeine does more than mask the pain of migraines. It actually changes the course of the migraine headache. Left untreated, migraines typically progress into intense headache pain and nausea. Many people find that by taking a 200 mg caffeine pill (or more if they can tolerate higher doses) at the first sign of migraine, followed by a 100 mg supplement after a few hours, and another 100 mg after another few hours if necessary, they stop the migraine in its tracks and prevent it from developing into a full-blown episode. The only way to find out if caffeine can do this for you is to try it for yourself.

way caffeine will raise their blood pressure, the medical facts indicate that they should simply stop being concerned and relax, perhaps by enjoying a cup of coffee. If they do so regularly, studies show that their blood pressure should actually go down.

People have been studying the cardiovascular effects of caffeine for over a hundred years, and studies have proliferated since the 1970s. It is now well established that giving caffeine to people without a history of caffeine use produces a transient elevation of blood pressure and a slowing of the heart rate, but that these effects disappear when caffeine is used for a few days.[13] Virtually all long-term studies reveal no long-term harm to the heart of any kind from caffeine. In fact, if certain major studies are to be believed, caffeine actually has some protective effects against cardiovascular damage. Constituents of coffee made in an infusion pot or in a percolator, which are eliminated when filter drip coffee is consumed, can increase cardiovascular risk by raising cholesterol. Caffeine helps protect users against this risk. (However, despite this protective effect, long-term consumption of unfiltered coffee is correlated with higher cholesterol levels and their associated cardiovascular problems.)

An article published in the *Journal of the American Medical Association* reported a 1996 study of more than 85,000 women examining data col-

Cardiovascular Report Card: Mixing Caffeine and High Blood Pressure

It is time for people concerned about caffeine's cardiovascular effects to breathe a sigh of relief and accept the conclusions of large-scale, well-designed studies. For example, the noted MR FIT study of more than 12,000 men and women with high blood pressure and high cholesterol levels, the first large-scale prospective study of caffeine and all causes of death, concluded that there was "no relationship between coronary heart disease events or total mortality and coffee consumption" in this high-risk group.[14] The same result—that is, an absence of any relation between caffeine consumption and all or any causes of death—was found by a 1990 study of 45,000 men, published in the *New England Journal of Medicine*,[15] and also by the Framingham Heart Study,[16] the Evans County study (1960–1969),[17] and the Gothenburg, Sweden, study.[18]

lected over a ten-year period. The researchers found that women consuming six or more cups of coffee a day were not at increased risk of cardiovascular disease.[19] A 1990 study of more than 45,000 men also found no link between coffee, caffeine, and cardiovascular disease, even for those drinking four or more cups of coffee a day.[20] These results confirm the findings of the famous Framingham Heart Study of 6,000 adults, conducted over twenty years, which concluded that levels of coffee consumption had "no influence on the rate of coronary heart disease" and found no evidence to support the hypothesis that levels of caffeine consumption are related to death rates from strokes in hypertensive patients.[21] Similar findings were published in the *New England Journal of Medicine*[22] and the *American Journal of Epidemiology,*[23] based on analyses of the data from the massive Honolulu Heart Program, which followed over 8,000 men for thirty years. Finally, we may note that in 1997, the National Institutes of Health (NIH) evaluated the caffeine research to date and found that "no direct relationship between caffeine intake and elevated blood pressure has been found in most epidemiological surveys."[24]

Does caffeine have any effect on blood pressure? As we mention above, caffeine seems to cause a transient increase in blood pressure for the first few days you use it. After that, this effect disappears in most people. In a 1990 study of the effects of using high and low doses of caffeine, researchers concluded that in normal subjects, after five days of use, complete

Drink Coffee Daily—and Lower Your Blood Pressure

Coffee use has been shown to have a direct correlation with lowered blood pressure. A provocative 1998 study of over 3,000 Japanese men between forty-eight and fifty-six years of age found "a significant inverse relation" between regular coffee consumption and blood pressure. The benefit was proportional to the number of cups of coffee consumed, with a decrease in diastolic and systolic pressure of about 1 point each for every two cups of coffee consumed per day. Investigators concluded, "Habitual coffee drinkers had lower blood pressure than non-drinkers at any levels of alcohol use, cigarette smoking, obesity, and glucose intolerance. Our findings consolidate the previous observation that habitual coffee consumption was associated with lower blood pressure."[25]

tolerance develops to the effects of caffeine on blood pressure and heart rate.[26] This means that the slight increase in blood pressure that is seen when you start to use caffeine does not continue. If you use it for a few days, it should not raise your blood pressure at all thereafter.

"Sure," you may say, "caffeine doesn't actually cause heart problems or high blood pressure. But what about people who already have high blood pressure? Shouldn't they avoid caffeine?" *If you have hypertension, or are being treated for any other medical condition, you should follow your doctor's advice about caffeine use and the use of all other drugs and medications.* However, research strongly suggests that hypertensive patients have no more to fear from caffeine than people without hypertension. In 1984, D. Robertson, a medical researcher, undertook a study of hypertensives and found that increases in blood pressure and slowed heart rate in this group lasted only one day. Robertson concluded that the acute response to caffeine was actually less in hypertensives than in people with normal blood pressure and that "tolerance developed rapidly and completely."[27] Other researchers have concluded that there was no association between caffeine consumption and all or any causes of death among hypertensives. If you are hypertensive but don't use caffeine and suddenly begin using it, your blood pressure should go up a little, but only for a couple of days. After that, it will no longer be elevated by caffeine. If you are hypertensive and use caffeine regularly, you should experience no long-term increase in blood pressure as a result.[28] This means that people with high blood pressure may be safer drinking coffee every day than they would be doing so once or twice a week.

In fact, not only does caffeine not raise blood pressure, but small amounts of it daily may help reduce the risk of developing high blood pressure in high-risk groups. A 1989 Norwegian study of 30,000 middle-aged men and women demonstrated that drinking more than one cup of coffee a day is positively correlated with a reduction in both systolic and diastolic blood pressure. In other words, people in a high-risk group for hypertension who drink more than one cup of coffee a day tend to have lower blood pressure than people who do not.

But What If You're over Sixty-Five?

In "Coffee and Cardiovascular Diseases: A Personal View After 30 Years of Research," Siegfried Heyden, Department of Community and Family Medicine, Duke University Medical Center, provides a comprehensive review of his experience with "community surveys, epidemiological studies, animal experiments, and, most important, with a prospective study in a large hypertensive population."[29] He sums up the evidence about the effects of caffeine on the blood pressure of people over age sixty-five: "Older caffeine users showed no increase in blood pressure or heart rate" and even continuous heavy coffee consumption does not increase the risk of developing hypertension.[30]

Preventing Strokes and Stroke Damage

A stroke is the sudden loss of consciousness, sensation, and ability to move that is caused by the obstruction (or sometimes the rupture) of an artery that normally brings blood to the brain. It can cause significant brain damage or death as brain cells, cut off from the blood supply, starve and die from lack of oxygen. Surprisingly, regular caffeine use reduces the brain damage caused by strokes. One leading researcher put it succinctly: "In man chronic consumption of caffeine is inversely related to the risk of fatal and non-fatal stroke."[31] Caffeine protects the brain against ischemic damage, that is, the damage caused when a blood clot blocks blood flow. In addition, studies have found that clot-dissolving time is reduced by drinking coffee but remains unaffected by drinking decaffeinated coffee, and many researchers think that caffeine is the agent responsible for this difference. This means that if you are a regular caffeine user and you have a stroke, the resulting harm is likely to be significantly reduced.

What about using caffeine after you've had a stroke? Irish coffee, because of its caffeine and alcohol content, when administered immediately after a stroke, seems to offer almost complete protection against the damage to brain cells that would otherwise have occurred. According to a presentation at the 124th Annual Meeting of the American Neurological Association in Seattle by James Grotta, M.D., professor of neurology and director of the stroke program at the University of Texas Medical School, the latest findings about caffeine suggest that it has neuroprotective functions.[32] In experimental rats, a combination of 10 percent ethanol and as much as 10 mg per kilogram of caffeine, the equivalent of about six cups of coffee for a 150 pound person, is a powerful way of reducing the damage to brain cells caused by strokes. When Grotta and his colleagues induced strokes in laboratory rats, they found that the administration of this drink reduces infarct, the area of tissue destroyed by the obstruction of local blood supply that occurs in a stroke, by nearly 90 percent. Neither caffeine nor alcohol has this effect separately. Grotta speculates that the combination may "tweak the neurotransmitter systems optimally," although the precise mechanism of neuroprotection remains unknown. Phillip Gorelick, M.D., M.P.H., professor and director of the Cerebrovascular Disease section in the Department of Neurology at Rush Medical Center, Chicago, said antioxidant effects might be responsible for these benefits and added that "caffeine must upregulate certain receptors" and in this way limit ischemic damage. There are enough similarities between the brains of rats and the brains of people for these results to merit further study. Grotta comments, "We found that if we gave a combination of alcohol and caffeine, equivalent to, say, one drink of alcohol and two or three cups of coffee, that there's almost complete protection from a stroke. . . . The striking thing to me isn't just that it's effective but how great the effect is. It is really very dramatic." However, he adds, "Obviously no pharmaceutical company is going to fund a study of alcohol and caffeine since they won't be able to make money from those substances." Unfortunately, the state of current knowledge makes this therapy too speculative to recommend at present.

Protecting Your Brain Cells from Harm

Neuroprotectors are a relatively new class of drugs that insulate or safeguard brain cells while they are being threatened by the nutrient and oxygen deficits caused by blood clots during a stroke. Providing this protection reduces brain damage and gives doctors time to make the best treatment choice, because it frees them from the immediate necessity of restoring blood flow to the brain. Research proves that caffeine is a powerful neuroprotector, and it may be able to give doctors the time to save the lives of more stroke victims.

Fighting Cancer

Major studies have proven that using caffeine does not increase your chances of getting cancer of any kind. In fact, caffeine offers protection against some kinds of cancer and may even offer protection against carcinogens like cigarette smoke and against tumor growth in general.

In a 1988 retrospective analysis of 10,000 people from the Hypertension Detection and Follow-up Study, "no association was found between caffeine consumption and mortality from cancer or any other cause."[33] A prospective study following over 40,000 men and women between thirty-five and fifty-four years of age for ten years also found "no association between caffeine consumption and overall risk of cancer."[34] Many studies have confirmed this lack of association for cancers at specific organ sites, such as the bladder and pancreas.

The really astonishing fact is that caffeine may well lessen the risk of developing some cancers. In his "Evaluation of Coffee and Caffeine for Mutagenic, Carcinogenic, and Anticarcinogenic Activity," published in 2000, Richard H. Adamson, Ph.D., summarizes four epidemiological studies concluding that the level of caffeine intake is correlated with a protective effect on the development of breast cancer. Two of the studies he cites found that three or four cups of coffee daily significantly reduced the incidence of breast cancer.[35]

Coffee consumption has also been tied to lower rates of colon cancer. A 1998 meta-analysis of seventeen published studies by Professor Edward Giovannucci, a Harvard University epidemiologist, showed that drinking several cups of coffee daily reduces the incidence of colorectal cancer by 30 percent as compared with not drinking any coffee. The studies included samples of the populations of ten countries: the United States, China, Japan, Italy, Spain, Belgium, France, Norway, Sweden, and Denmark. Giovannuci concluded that "anti-mutagenic" components in coffee, including caffeine, probably inhibit the mutagenic, or cancer-causing, effect of various microorganisms and in this way protect the body against colon cancer.[36]

Studies with rats suggest that caffeine may protect against cancerous tumors generally and indicate that caffeine specifically "decreased the incidence of tumors that developed . . . in mice treated with cigarette smoke condensate, ultraviolet light," or other mutagenic agents in the skin and lungs.[37]

No one knows for sure how caffeine fights the onset of cancer, but one theory is that CYP1A2, the liver enzyme that metabolizes caffeine, activates "a large number of procarcinogens . . . and can ultimately trigger carcinogenesis."[38] This means that by effectively keeping some of the CYP1A2 enzyme out of circulation, caffeine blocks some of the cancerous activity that would otherwise have been initiated by the enzyme. (For more about this enzyme, see Appendix B.)

An additional consideration is that epidemiological studies show lower cancer rates in people whose diets are rich in fruits and vegetables, leading some researchers to conclude that the high levels of antioxidants found in those foods fight cancer. As we have observed, caffeine is a powerful antioxidant and may also exert this protective effect.

When Undergoing Surgery

When you stop using caffeine abruptly, you risk a headache. You might even become depressed or, if you were a heavy user before stopping, develop a runny nose or muscle aches. Discomforts like these, although not usually serious enough to constitute clinical problems in themselves, can become problematical when stopping caffeine before surgery.

Because patients are routinely advised not to consume any food or beverages, including their usual cup of coffee, on the morning before an operation, surgical patients often wake up from their anesthesia with a caffeine withdrawal headache. The solution is simple: Unless there are medical contraindications, give them some caffeine as soon as they open their eyes. If they can't drink coffee yet, the caffeine can be administered intravenously. This "caffeine rescue" technique is being increasingly practiced by nurses in hospitals across the country. In fact, if patients who consume caffeine daily are undergoing minor surgical procedures, several studies have recommended that they should be permitted to ingest caffeine before surgery to reduce the risk of developing a headache after the operation.[39]

If you are told to cut out caffeine and you don't anticipate being able to resume caffeine use immediately, you should follow the procedures for quitting outlined in Chapter 2. By eliminating caffeine over a period of several days, you also eliminate the discomforts that would otherwise attend suddenly stopping your intake of it.

Glaucoma

Glaucoma is the name for a group of eye diseases characterized by abnormally high intraocular fluid pressure. If untreated, it can result in partial or complete loss of vision. Some scientists have speculated that caffeine, by constricting blood vessels, may increase intraocular pressure and affect the incidence or course of the disease. One study indicated that in people genetically predisposed to developing glaucoma, coffee can increase their risk. Although most studies show no effect of caffeine on intraocular pressure, one found that glaucoma patients who drink two cups of coffee a day show an increase in pressure, especially if they drink it quickly, while normal patients who consume the same amount of coffee show no such increase.[40] If you are suffering from inadequately controlled glaucoma, consult your ophthalmologist before continuing or increasing caffeine use.

Preventing Gallstones

Gallstone disease afflicts more than 20 million Americans and results in 800,000 hospitalizations a year at a direct cost of over $2 billion. Current research suggests that caffeine provides significant protection against the development of symptomatic gallbladder disease.

According to a major study, men who drank two to three cups of coffee a day had a 40 percent lower risk of developing the disease, and the risk declined slightly more for those who drank four or more cups a day. The study evaluated the frequency of new symptomatic gallstone disease, diagnosed by ultrasound or X-ray, and cholecystectomy, that is, gallbladder removal. The analysis was part of the Health Professionals Follow-up Study, a prospective study of the dietary habits and health histories of over 50,000 men, ages forty to seventy-five, conducted between 1986 and 1996. Although investigators speculated that several constituents of coffee may contribute to the protective effect, caffeine is regarded as the primary source of this protection, because no reduction in risk was associated with drinking decaffeinated coffee. Caffeine has demonstrated the ability to increase bile flow, decrease gallbladder fluid absorption, and inhibit biliary cholesterol crystallization, factors that help explain how caffeine works to limit the risk of developing gallstones.[41]

Creating Beautiful Skin

Atopic dermatitis, a form of eczema, is a chronic skin disease characterized by itchy, inflamed skin. It most often afflicts infants and young children, but it can continue into adulthood and can cause significant physical suffering, even extending to complete disability. Among the treatments suggested for atopic dermatitis is "caffeine administered topically, 10% to 30% in a petrolatum or water-in-oil base." In other words, rubbing on Vaseline with some caffeine dissolved in it may well reduce the symptoms of this serious condition.[42]

Healthy skin may also benefit from the application of caffeine, if some of the new products flooding the cosmetics counters are any indication. All kinds of wrinkle and skin-firming creams are being introduced with caffeine as an active ingredient. (Anticellulite creams are discussed in Chapter 10.)

Osteoporosis

Osteoporosis is a devastating disease in which the bones become dangerously fragile and more likely to fracture. It is caused by the gradual loss of the mineral calcium, which helps make bones hard. Osteoporosis occurs most often in women following menopause. Many physicians believe that the disease can be prevented through regular exercise and a diet high in calcium and vitamin D. Some studies have seemed to show that caffeine causes the body to excrete calcium more readily, which could mean that caffeine increases the hazard of developing osteoporosis. However, Robert Heaney of Creighton University, a leading caffeine researcher, reporting on his review of the scientific literature pertaining to caffeine's effect on bone and calcium, dismissed the idea that caffeine has anything to with calcium loss. He says that lower calcium levels in caffeine users result from the fact that, overall, many people who use caffeine fail to eat a calcium-rich diet, so if you maintain an adequate intake of calcium, caffeine shouldn't affect your bones at all. He concludes that even if high caffeine intake has an effect on calcium absorption, this effect is "very small," and it can be eliminated by as little as 1 or 2 tablespoons of milk daily. His overall conclusion is clear: "There is no evidence that caffeine has any harmful effect on bone status or the calcium economy in individuals ingesting currently recommended levels of calcium."[43]

But what about the studies that seemed to show calcium loss from high caffeine intake? Typically, such as in the 2001 long-term study of osteoporosis lead by Dr. Prema B. Rapuri from Creighton University, the women who participated did not take either calcium or vitamin D supplements, two factors strongly associated with increased bone loss in their peers. Even absent proper nutritional support, high caffeine use did not cause significant bone loss except in a subgroup of women who carry two copies of a mutated vitamin D receptor gene. Only about 12 percent of the population have this "tt genotype," and even for them, the intake of small amounts of milk would probably completely compensate for the calcium losses observed.[44]

Asthma, Pulmonary Problems, and Smoking Cigarettes

Asthma is a respiratory disorder in which the airway becomes obstructed, causing difficulty in breathing and wheezing, coughing, and thick mucus production. It is the most common breathing affliction, and as many as 10 percent of children suffer from asthma to the extent that they require medical treatment. Caffeine, at first administered in strong coffee, has been used to relieve the symptoms of asthma for hundreds of years. Although caffeine's primary respiratory effect is to increase the rate of breathing, today we know that caffeine is also a bronchodilator, that is, an agent that relaxes bronchial tissue, and that it also reduces respiratory muscle fatigue. Because of these powers, caffeine improves airway functioning for several hours after consumption.[45] Caffeine's cousin, theophylline, has almost twice the brochodilating potency of caffeine and is widely used in asthma medications. Studies have shown that asthmatics who drink between two and three cups of coffee daily have 25 percent fewer attacks. Because of caffeine's ability to open the breathing passages, it is also commonly used in treating newborns for neonatal apnea, or arrested breathing, which often occurs in premature infants.[46]

In 1989, medical researcher D. R. Lima investigated the theory that because of its bronchodilating effects, caffeine might help protect smokers against the development of chronic bronchitis and pulmonary edema.[47] He tested the lung capacity of both smokers and nonsmokers after they smoked a cigarette with or without an accompanying cup of coffee. Coffee was found to provide protection against the adverse pulmonary effects of smoking. In the words of leading caffeine researcher Jack James, "The investigators concluded that regular intake of coffee might be beneficial to smokers in delaying the development of chronic obstructive lung disease."[48] Although more research is needed to define these benefits precisely, current findings about caffeine's effects on pulmonary function suggest that caffeine may have important therapeutic potential in forestalling or treating the pulmonary complications of smoking.

Alcohol and Alcoholism

One of the earliest historical claims made on behalf of coffee and tea was that they acted to negate or reverse the intoxicating effects and mental

If You're Quitting Cigarettes, Watch Out for Caffeine

We now know that cigarettes approximately double the rate of caffeine metabolism, that is, they cut in half the time it takes to clear caffeine from the body. This means that its effects will wane in them more quickly than in nonsmokers. In order to maintain caffeine's effects, smokers must consume caffeine more frequently than nonsmokers, which may be one reason smokers drink more coffee than nonsmokers do.

When smokers are cutting down or eliminating tobacco, they should be aware that the caffeine they consume will continue to exert its effects much longer. In other words, if you stop smoking, caffeine use throughout the day could be more likely to keep you awake at night.[49]

impairment produced by opium and alcohol. In fact, although blood alcohol levels are not lowered by caffeine (this can only be accomplished over time by the liver), caffeine can in a sense make people "less drunk" by reducing the bad effects alcohol has on performance. Most studies have shown that caffeine reduces the impairments in both cognitive and psychomotor tasks produced by alcohol. This confirms the common experience that taking a strong cup of coffee after drinking makes you more clear-headed, better coordinated, and better able to conduct yourself at more nearly normal levels.[50]

Heavy drinkers might get an even more important benefit from regular caffeine use. In an account published in the *Annals of Internal Medicine* in 1991, researchers Roseane Santos and Darcy Lima reported on a study of coffee's effects on twenty chronic alcoholics, aged thirty-five to fifty-three years. To qualify, participants had to have each consumed at least half a quart of alcohol a day for at least one year. They were given either five cups of strong instant coffee or five cups of decaf coffee daily for thirty days. The results were impressive. On tests of concentration and short-term memory, the performance of the coffee group improved dramatically, while the performance of the decaf group remained the same. Perhaps even more fascinating, the average daily intake of alcohol in the group drinking coffee decreased by two-thirds, from 600 ml to 200 ml daily. The researchers concluded that coffee might be useful in controlling alcoholism.[51]

Caffeine and Diabetes

People suffering from type 1 diabetes live precarious lives. They must continually inject themselves with insulin to meet all of their metabolic needs for the hormone, and therefore they constantly risk taking a little too much insulin and forcing their blood sugar to plummet catastrophically. When this happens, the diabetic person can pass out or even go into a coma. People with diabetes who can sense the onset of low blood sugar can avert this problem by having something to eat before it drops further. Caffeine has been shown in several studies to "increase an individual's sensitivity to hypoglycemia," which means it makes people aware that their blood sugar is falling earlier than they would otherwise have known about it. Some diabetics, with hypoglycemia unawareness, have special problems sensing when their sugar is low and are at high risk of becoming unconscious. One researcher concluded that "caffeine may be a useful adjuvant therapy for patients with hypoglycemia unawareness," adding, "For once here is a therapy which is inexpensive, safe, and remarkably popular with its consumers." [52]

Fertility

Even before caffeine had been isolated, coffee was suspected of reducing fertility in both men and women and with reducing the sexual appetites of men. Recent studies have not only dispelled these fears, but even suggest that, properly used, caffeine might even reduce the time it takes to become pregnant.

If a woman is trying to conceive, most studies show no correlation between caffeine use and the risk of either delayed conception or persistent infertility. For example, a study of more than 2,000 postdelivery women found that the average time to conception, four to five months, remained unchanged whether women consumed as little as one cup of coffee a week or more than two cups every day. [53]

So a woman can't expect caffeine use to make much change in her chances of conceiving a child. But what about caffeine's effect on the man in her life? As we have seen, caffeine permeates every cell of the body with ease, and the concentrations of caffeine in seminal fluid are virtually identical to those that occur in the blood. Some scientists have wondered what effects, if any, caffeine might have on the activity levels of the sperm. Incredibly, sperm seem to get a charge from caffeine that increases their likelihood of fertilizing an egg. The effects on so-called sperm motility are well documented. When semen is exposed to high concentrations of caffeine immediately prior to artificial insemination, the increased motility is sufficient to double a woman's chances of getting pregnant.

The profile of some of caffeine's effects on sperm observed both in vitro and in vivo closely resembles that predicted by the Yerkes-Dodson principle, which states that the "relationship between arousal and performance efficiency takes the form of an inverted-U." This means that the effects of caffeine on sperm cells increase with the dose until a certain level is reached, whereupon additional doses of the drug have less and less effect, and still higher doses progressively reverse its initial benefits. If you are going for these effects, therefore, less definitely means more. Researchers Dlugosz and Bracken sum up their findings with the comment, "In a study of 446 men attending an infertility clinic, men who drank 1–2 cups of coffee per day had *increased* sperm motility and density compared with subjects who drank no coffee. However, men who drank more than 2 cups per day had *decreased* sperm motility and density."[54]

So, whereas small to moderate doses of caffeine may even help a man to father a child, the dynamics of caffeine's effects on sperm seem to resemble those ascribed to alcohol on sexual performance in the traditional aphorism, "A little stimulates; a lot depresses."

Summary of Health Effects of Caffeine

- Controls pain, especially migraine headaches
- Has some protective effects on hypertension and the cardiovascular system; no bad effects
- Protects against stroke damage
- Probably offers protection against many types of cancer; does not increase risk of any cancer
- May affect glaucoma in large doses consumed all at once
- Prevents gallstones
- Is useful in controlling some skin conditions
- Does not generally increase risk of developing osteoporosis
- Helps breathing problems caused by asthma and smoking cigarettes
- May help alcoholics to overcome their affliction
- Helps prevent catastrophic episodes of low blood sugar in some diabetics
- May increase male fertility; little or no effect on female fertility
- Does not cause major birth defects, but may create hazards in pregnancy of more subtle long-term problems, and sufficient amounts may increase likelihood of miscarriage

Pregnancy: A "No-Caffeine" Zone?

For most people, caffeine is about as safe as a drug can be. But it may not be such a good idea for pregnant women to use much caffeine, if any. The good news is that caffeine use during pregnancy does not cause any major morphological damage; that is, it doesn't produce children with observable physical deformities or obvious birth defects. However, despite this important and reassuring fact, there are several reasons we suggest that women avoid caffeine during gestation.

When pregnant women consume caffeine regularly, their children are born with caffeine withdrawal symptoms. We've all heard about "crack babies," delivered from cocaine-dependent mothers. The principle here is the same. Although no damage to the infant has been shown to result from this dependence, do you really want your child to start life in withdrawal, plagued with headaches, muscle aches, and increased tension? A 1988 study found that the children of heavy-caffeine-using mothers had unusual levels of irritability, jitteriness, and vomiting.[55] Some studies show that more than 75 percent of infants tested had caffeine in their blood at birth.[56] (Surveys also show that 75 percent of women cut down the level of their caffeine use early in pregnancy.)

Some recent studies have found no increased risk of miscarriage even from large amounts of caffeine. However, other recent studies show caffeine in doses of more than 300 mg a day may increase the likelihood of miscarriage or premature birth.[57] Cautious researchers, assuming that a cup of coffee contains 100 mg of caffeine, often tell expectant mothers that they can have up to three cups of coffee a day. However, as we have seen, a cup of coffee commonly contains 150 to 200 mg of caffeine and may even contain as much as 400 mg. Because the amount of caffeine in a cup is so difficult to determine, even one cup a day may put a woman's pregnancy into the danger zone.

Gross physical deformities aren't the only forms of birth defects. Less obvious problems, such as long-term, subtle neurological deficits, can be serious as well. For example, because of caffeine exposure in the womb, children may grow up with a reduced ability to concentrate or a tendency to get angry more quickly. Without long-term controlled studies, it would be nearly impossible to associate such problems with caffeine use during pregnancy. No such problems have been established with caffeine, but, so far, no studies of the question have been made. Studies are being done to see if caffeine slows habituation to stimuli in the womb—that is, when mothers use caffeine, do their fetuses become accustomed to sounds and vibrations more slowly?—which is a sign that brain function is being interfered with. And the evidence from the animal studies is cautionary. Rat studies show that the neurological effects of caffeine given to the mother persist to the second generation. Although one cannot assume that there are similar effects in people, effects like this in mammals at least raise a warning signal. Perhaps this signal should not be ignored until some good studies show that caffeine exposure in the womb is harmless to long-term development. One researcher has come close to acknowledging this risk. "I raise the issue of the neurodevelopment of the offspring," states Brenda Eskenazi, professor of maternal and child health and director of Children's Environmental Health Resources at the University of California, Berkeley, School of Public Health. "If I were pregnant, I would be consuming less than 1 to 2 cups a day. Why take the risk?"[58]

Indeed, why take any chance at all? Why not simply skip the caffeine entirely until your baby is born and then return to enjoy its life-enhancing and energy-boosting powers when you need them the most, that is, when you face the demands of caring for your new child.

Appendix A

Tables of the Caffeine Content of Common Sources of Caffeine

Caffeine Content of Coffee and Tea

Most people think that an espresso has more caffeine than an ordinary cup of coffee. This is a myth. While espresso has much more caffeine per ounce, it is usually served in cups of between 1.5 and 2 ounces. Because regular filter drip coffee usually is served in cups that are 6 ounces or larger, the amount of caffeine in an espresso is actually smaller than the amount in a cup of regular filter drip coffee.

The reason for the question mark in the table for decaffeinated coffee is that sometimes so-called decaffeinated coffees aren't really as caffeine free as they pretend to be. Instant decaffeinated coffees like Sanka are reliable and contain only a few milligrams of caffeine at most.

Remember that the caffeine content of robusta beans is twice that of arabica beans.

	Preparation Method	Caffeine Content (mg)
Coffee (6 oz. cup, arabica coffee)	Filter drip	130–180 (average 150)
	Percolated	75–150
	Espresso (1.5–2 oz.)	100
	Instant	50–130
	Decaffeinated	2–6 (?)

	Type of Leaf	Caffeine Content (mg)
Tea (6 oz. cup, 3 minute brew)	Green tea	10–15
	Orange tea	25
	Black tea	50

	Brand	Caffeine Content (mg)
Bottled iced tea	Snapple iced tea (all varieties)	31
(16 oz. bottle)	Lipton iced tea (all varieties)	18–40
	Nestea iced tea (all varieties)	16–26
	Arizona iced tea (all varieties)	15–30

Sources: Adapted from Weinberg and Bealer, *The World of Caffeine*, p. 327; National Soft Drink Association web site: www.NSDA.com

Caffeine Content of Chocolate Candy, Drinks, and Miscellaneous Foods

Chocolate contains two substances that can give you a boost: caffeine and theobromine, caffeine's chemical cousin. Theobromine's effects are very similar to caffeine's, but theobromine is much weaker than caffeine. However, it is found in much larger amounts than caffeine in chocolate. Although no one is certain, most scientists believe that the total stimulant effect of caffeine and theobromine in chocolate is about twice that of the caffeine alone. Therefore, in evaluating the lift you will get from chocolate, approximately double the amount of caffeine given in this table. As you can see, except for dark chocolate, the amount of caffeine in most candy is relatively small.

Brand Name	Serving Size	Milligrams per Serving
Hershey's Milk chocolate bar	1.55 oz. (43 g)	10
Hershey's Milk chocolate bar with almonds	1.45 oz. (41 g)	6
Hershey's Special Dark Chocolate Bar	1.45 oz. (41 g)	31
Perugina Milk Chocolate Bar with Cappuccino Filling (⅓ bar)	1.2 oz. (33 g)	24
M&M's	1.75 oz. (49 g)	15
Rolo Caramels in milk chocolate	1.93 oz. (54 g)	4
Reese's Peanut Butter Cups	1.60 oz. (45 g)	4
Mr. Goodbar chocolate bar	1.75 oz. (49 g)	5
Hershey's Kisses	1.55 oz. (43 g)—8 kisses	11
Coffee Nips (hard candy)	Two pieces	6
Kit Kat wafer bar	1.50 oz. (42 g)	6

Chocolate Product	Caffeine Content (mg)
Hot chocolate (mix, 6 oz.)	10
Chocolate milk (6 oz.)	4
Milk chocolate (28 g)	6
Dark chocolate (28 g)	20
Baking chocolate (28 g)	35

Miscellaneous Foods	
Cocoa Puffs breakfast cereal (4 oz.)	2
Penguin Mints (1 mint)	7
Dannon Coffee Yogurt (8 oz.)	45
Dannon Light Cappucino Yogurt (8 oz.)	<1
Yoplait Café Au Lait Yogurt (6 oz.)	5
Stonyfield Farm Cappuccino Yogurt (8 oz.)	0
Häagen Dazs Coffee Ice Cream (1 cup)	58
Häagen Dazs Coffee Frozen Yogurt, fat-free (1 cup)	40
Starbucks Coffee Ice Cream, assorted flavors (1 cup)	40–60
Ben & Jerry's No Fat Coffee Fudge Frozen Yogurt (1 cup)	85

Sources: Hershey's web site: www.hersheys.com; Center for Science in the Public Interest web site: www.cspinet.org; and B. A. Weinberg and B. K. Bealer, *The World of Caffeine,* New York: Routledge, 2001, p. 327.

Caffeine Content of Soft Drinks

Most soft drinks contain about 40 mg of caffeine in a 12 ounce serving. Note in the table, however, that Coca-Cola Classic contains only 34 mg, while Diet Coke contains 46 mg. If you are drinking a few servings or are unusually sensitive to caffeine, this difference may matter. Also note that Sunkist orange soda contains 42 mg of caffeine in a 12 ounce serving, while Minute Maid orange soda has no caffeine. This underscores the importance of checking the labels.

Drink (12 oz.)	Caffeine Content (mg)
Jolt Cola	70
Mountain Dew	55
Diet Mountain Dew	55

(continued on next page)

Drink (12 oz.)	Caffeine Content (mg)
Surge	52
Tab	47
Diet Coke	45
Shasta Cola	45
Shasta Cherry Cola	45
Shasta Diet Cola	45
RC Cola	43
Diet RC	43
Dr Pepper	42
Diet Dr Pepper	42
Sunkist Orange Soda	42
Pepsi-Cola	38
Diet Pepsi	36
Aspen	36
Diet Rite	36
Coca-Cola Classic	34
Canada Dry Cola	30
A&W Cream Soda	29
Diet A&W Cream Soda	22
Barq's Root Beer	22
Canada Dry Diet Cola	1
Diet Barq's Root Beer	0
Minute Maid Orange Soda	0
Sprite	0
Diet Sprite	0
7-Up	0

Source: Adapted from FDA statistics, 1984, published in *FDA Consumer.*

Caffeinated Waters

Brand	Serving Size	Caffeine Content (mg)
Java Water	½ liter (16.9 ounces)	125
Krank 20	½ liter (16.9 ounces)	100
Aqua Blast	½ liter (16.9 ounces)	90
Water Joe	½ liter (16.9 ounces)	60–70
Aqua Java	½ liter (16.9 ounces)	50–60

Source: Center for Science in the Public Interest web site, www.cspinet.org

Caffeine Content of Medications

Type of Medication	Caffeine Content (mg per pill or capsule)
Analgesics	
Vanquish	33
Anacin	32
Excedrin	65
Midol	32
Cold Remedies	
Coryban-D	30
Dristan	0
Triaminicin	30
Appetite Suppressants	
Dexatrim	200
Prolamine	140
Diuretics	
Aqua Ban	100
Prescription Medications	
Cafergot	100
Darvon Compound-65	32
Fiorinal	40
Migralam	100
Alertness Aids	
Vivarin	200
NoDoz	200

Source: Adapted from Weinberg and Bealer, *The World of Caffeine*, p. 320.

Caffeine Content of Coffeehouse Coffees

Brand	Net Serving Size	Total mg	Mg per 6 oz.
Dunkin' Donuts, regular	12.6 oz.	275	147.6
Cooper's, medium	9.9 oz.	146	99.6
West Side Deli, medium	13.5 oz.	295	103.8
Dalton's Coffee, regular	8.9 oz.	148	99.7

Decaffeinated

Starbucks decaffeinated			25
Dunkin' Donuts decaffeinated			10
Au Bon Pain decaffeinated			7
Starbucks decaffeinated espresso			6
McDonald's decaffeinated			5
7-Eleven decaffeinated			4
Tetley decaffeinated tea			4
Cooper's decaffeinated			4
Dalton's decaffeinated			2
Sanka			1.5

Source: Adapted from Weinberg and Bealer, *The World of Caffeine*, p. 229.

Appendix B

Drug and Food Interactions

Enzymes are complex proteins that act as catalysts to help other organic molecules undergo chemical reactions. Over the past thirty years, scientists have made many discoveries about the role that enzymes play in the metabolism of drugs. Their findings have revealed surprising ways that drugs interact with other drugs and with foods to make their effects stronger and longer lasting or weaker and of shorter duration. Don't expect your doctor to tell you about the drug and food interactions we discuss in this appendix; few pharmacists and even fewer physicians were ever taught much about them in school.

The human polycyclic aromatic hydrocarbon-inducible cytochrome P450(CYP1) family of enzymes, otherwise called "CYP450" enzymes, was first linked to drug metabolism in the 1970s, and since then, the many ways in which CYP450 enzymes affect drug interactions have become one of the exciting topics in the world of pharmacology. When a medication is metabolized by a CYP450 enzyme, the amount of CYP450 available can determine the speed with which the medication is cleared from the body. Some medications compete with each other for CYP450 enzymes, while others increase or decrease the production of these enzymes. In each case, the rate of clearance of the medications in question is correspondingly increased or decreased.

In fact, CYP450 enzymes have many functions in addition to metabolizing drugs. They also metabolize environmental toxins, dietary components, and various endogenous substances (e.g., steroids, prostaglandins) that are produced within the body, and the activity of these substances is also a factor in determining the speed at which various drugs are cleared from the body. Usually, CYP450 enzymes inactivate a drug or compound, but sometimes they make it more active.

Most of the caffeine you ingest is metabolized by a CYP450 liver enzyme called "CYP1A2." This means that the body uses CYP1A2 to "demethylate" caffeine molecules, transforming them into other substances, chiefly paraxanthine, which are ultimately excreted in the urine. CYP1A2 is one of the most abundant CYP liver enzymes and is responsible for the metabolism of several clinically important medications.

There are three ways in which a drug can influence the amount of CYP450 that is available to metabolize other drugs: It can use some of the enzymes, it can inhibit the production of the enzymes, or it can stimulate the production of the enzymes.

When caffeine and another drug are each metabolized by CYP1A2, they compete for the enzyme. As a result, each is said to partially block the enzymatic metabolism of the other, and the speed with which they are excreted from the body decreases. When another drug interferes with the production of CYP1A2, the speed with which caffeine is excreted is reduced. Finally, when a drug increases the production of CYP1A2, the speed at which caffeine is metabolized will be increased.

It was recently discovered that CYP1A2 is the major enzyme used by the body to metabolize not only caffeine but many drugs that are commonly used as medications.[2] Other drugs metabolized by this enzyme include theophylline, warfarin, and several antidepressants and antipsychotics. When caffeine is introduced, there is less of the enzyme available to metabolize these drugs. What this means is that each acts as a metabolic inhibitor—and sometimes as a very potent metabolic inhibitor—of the

One Reason Caffeine's Half-Life Varies So Greatly

Caffeine is metabolized by the liver enzyme CYP1A2. However, CYP1A2 exhibits "pronounced interindividual variation in activity."[1] The speed with which caffeine is cleared from the body is proportional to the amount of available CYP1A2, and highly variable activity levels of the enzyme mean a highly variable half-life for caffeine users. That's one reason that two cups of coffee in the late afternoon might not keep you awake at night, while one cup in the late morning can disturb another person's sleep.

other, slowing the speed with which the body can break down, or eliminate, the drugs. The result is that blood level of these drugs, or of caffeine, or of both, increases. For example, a woman who was a heavy coffee drinker who was also taking clozapine (an antischizophrenic medication) was found to have about two and a half times higher blood levels of the drug when she took caffeine. Because schizophrenic patients commonly consume remarkably high doses of caffeine, such interactions could conceivably constitute a relatively common problem for patients taking that medication.

Alternatively, other drugs can inhibit the production of CYP1A2 and in this way dramatically slow the metabolism of caffeine and inhibit the clearance of caffeine from the body. Several antibiotics and antidepressants are potent inhibitors of several CYP450 enzymes, including CYP1A2. For example, the selective serotonin reuptake inhibitors Prozac (fluoxetine), Paxil (paroxetine), and Luvox (fluvoxamine), commonly used to treat depression, social anxiety, and obsessive eating disorders, are inhibitors of the CYP1A2,[3] and therefore interfere with the body's ability to catalyze the biotransformation of caffeine. Luvox is a particularly potent inhibitor of the enzyme, and people taking it can "exhibit unexpected toxicity or intolerance to caffeine as plasma levels of caffeine rise."[4] Research has shown that when Luvox is being used in treatment, the half-life of a caffeine dose between 100 mg and 200 mg increases 500 percent, that is, from 5 hours to over 30 hours.[5] If large amounts of caffeine are consumed over a period of several days, such an enormous extension of caffeine's activity could lead to blood levels associated with undesirable side effects, including sustained sleep disturbances, anxiety, and even, in extreme cases in which unusually large amounts of caffeine had been consumed, caffeine intoxication.

The consequences of these drug interactions are highly variable. Caffeine may cause therapeutic failure in patients receiving lithium (a mood stabilizer), may cause toxic reactions in patients receiving clozapine (another antipsychotic), may augment the efficacy of aspirin and acetaminophen (Tylenol), and may have no significant consequences, despite metabolic interactions, on the effects of mexiletine (an antiarrhythmic). For this reason, some scientists have suggested that the FDA should require that drugs interacting with caffeine be labeled with an advisory about these interactions.[6]

Finally, certain substances other than drugs can activate the production of CYP1A2 and thus increase its activity. The polycyclic hydrocarbons found in cigarette smoke, charbroiled foods, and so-called cruciferous vegetables, such as broccoli and cauliflower, are capable of inducing this enzyme, that is, of increasing its production.[7] If you smoke cigarettes, the amount of CYP1A2 available in your body to metabolize caffeine increases, and the speed with which you metabolize caffeine increases correspondingly.

In sum, the medications you are taking, the foods you are eating, even the cigarettes you are smoking can change the way caffeine is metabolized by your body. And caffeine can also change the way certain other drugs are metabolized. The charts that follow summarize some of the primary interactions between caffeine and medications and other common substances.

Medications Whose Rate of Metabolism Is Slowed by Caffeine and That Slow the Metabolism of Caffeine

These are drugs whose metabolism is partially or entirely dependent on CYP1A2, which means that they will be metabolized more slowly—and remain active in the body longer—when caffeine is being used. It also

Luvox and "Time-Release" Caffeine?

Although these interactions can create problems, if they are understood and used strategically, they might offer some opportunities to caffeine users to improve caffeine's effects. Caffeine does not affect the metabolism of the antidepressant Luvox. However, Luvox dramatically slows the metabolism of caffeine. As a result, if Luvox users take a low dose of caffeine, say 100 mg, once or twice a day, the extended half-life would effectively give them a "time-release" caffeine. Because caffeine has powerful antidepressant effects, this extended activity could help alleviate their condition. Half of the caffeine from a caffeine pill taken at noon would still be active at 7 A.M. the next morning, which would mean that the person could wake up cheerful and in good spirits, without the symptoms of depression—even before he's taken any more caffeine. As we've observed, the uses of caffeine as a treatment for clinical depression must be investigated further, but existing data strongly suggest that even a small amount of caffeine can lift a depressed person out of the doldrums for an entire day.

means that they will slow the rate at which caffeine is metabolized, extending the time during which it will continue to exert its effects.

Drugs Whose Metabolism Is Dependent on CYP1A2

Class of Drug	Generic Name
Antiandrogens	Flutamide
Antidepressants	Amitriptyline
	Clomipramine
	Fluvoxamine
	Mianserin
	Imipramine
Antipsychotics	Clozapine
	Haloperidol
	Olanzapine
	Thioridazine
Cardiovascular drugs and anticoagulants	Lidocaine
	Mexiletine
	Propafenone
	Propranolol
	Triamterene
	Verapamil
	Warfarin
Cholinesterase inhibitors	Tacrine
Local anesthetic	Ropivacaine
Nonsteroidal anti-inflammatory drugs	Acetaminophen
	Phenacetin
	Methotrexate
Quinolones	Pefloxacin

Source: Adapted from J. A. Carrillo and J. Benitez, "Clinically significant pharmacokinetic interactions between caffeine and medications," *Clinical Pharmacokinetics, 39,* 127–153, 2000.

Medications That Affect the Rate of Metabolism of Caffeine

Here are some examples of medications and the amounts by which they facilitate or inhibit the ability of the body to metabolize caffeine by affecting the production of CYP1A2. Some of these medications are not affected by caffeine, but they all affect the rate at which caffeine is metabolized. A recent journal article by Dr. Juan Carrillo warned that "pharmacokinetic interactions at the CYP1A2 enzyme level may cause toxic effects during concomitant administration of caffeine and certain drugs used for cardio-vascular, CNS, gastrointestinal, infectious, respiratory and skin dis-orders."[9] He advises physicians that unless a lack of interaction has been established, "dietary caffeine intake should be considered when planning, or assessing response to, drug therapy." Women should note that oral con-traceptives decrease caffeine clearance by 40 percent, which means that caf-feine's effects will be considerably prolonged in women taking them. Athletes should also be aware that medications that slow caffeine clearance can affect urine caffeine concentrations and might cause a competitor to exceed the current regulatory limit even with an intake of as little as 400 mg of caffeine.[10]

Examples of Drugs Slowing or
Speeding the Metabolism of Caffeine

Type of Drug	Name of Drug	Change in Speed of Caffeine Clearance[a]
Antimycotic	Fluconazole	-25%
	Ketoconazole	-11%
	Terbinafine	-21%
Cardiovascular drugs	Diltiazem	-22%
	Mexiletine	-50%
	Verapamil	-20%
	Propafenone	Slows clearance
	Propranolol	Slows clearance
	Triamterene	Slows clearance
	Warfarin	Slows clearance
	Lansoprazole	+10%
	Omeprazole	+40%
CNS drugs	Clozapine	Slows clearance
	Fluvoxamine	-80%
	Olanzapine	Slows clearance

	Antiserotonergic	Slows clearance
	Ondansetron	Slows clearance
Oral contraceptives	All brands	-40%
Psoralens	Methoxsalen	-70%
	5-methoxypsoralen	-31%
Quinolones	Ciprofloxacin	-33%
	Enoxacin	-80%
	Grepafloxacin	-50%
	Norfloxacin	-35%
	Pefloxacin	-47%
Other	Cimetidine	-31%
	Idrocilamide	Slows clearance
	Methotrexate	Slows clearance
	Phenylpropanolamine	Slows clearance
	Theophylline	Slows clearance

[a] + = speeds clearance of caffeine. - = slows clearance of caffeine.
Source: Adapted from J. A. Carrillo and J. Benitez, "Clinically significant pharmacokinetic interactions between caffeine and medications," *Clinical Pharmacokinetics*, 39, 127–153, 2000.

Miscellaneous Factors Affecting the Speed of Caffeine Metabolism

The factors listed in the table have been found to affect CYP1A2 activity and therefore to increase or decrease the amount of time it takes for caffeine to be cleared from the body. When a factor increases the speed of caffeine metabolism, that means that it enables the body to eliminate caffeine from your bloodstream more quickly and that it will cause caffeine to affect you for a shorter time. When a factor decreases the speed of caffeine metabolism, it causes caffeine to remain at active levels in your bloodstream for longer and causes caffeine to affect you for a longer time. For example, narigenin, the chemical that makes grapefruit juice bitter, by inhibiting the production of CYP1A2, slows the clearance of caffeine from the body and prolongs its half-life by over 30 percent.[8]

Factors Affecting the Speed of Caffeine Metabolism

Increases Speed of Caffeine Metabolism (makes caffeine's effects abate more quickly)	**Decreases Speed of Caffeine Metabolism (makes caffeine's effects last longer)**
Cruciferous vegetables (broccoli, cauliflower, cabbages, radishes, etc.)	Grapefruit juice
Coffee	Alcohol
Grilled meat	Pregnancy
Tobacco smoke	Liver disease
Lean people	Obese people
Younger people	Older people

Source: Adapted from J. A. Carrillo and J. Benitez, "Clinically significant pharmacokinetic interactions between caffeine and medications," *Clinical Pharmacokinetics,* 39, 127–153, 2000.

Appendix C

Children and Caffeine

The information in this book is intended for adults in good health. However, there can be no doubt that many children and young adults, who get most of their caffeine from carbonated soft drinks and iced tea, consume large amounts of caffeine and are consuming more caffeine every year. Studies have even shown a trend of increased caffeine ingestion by infants in recent decades. Whereas parents in the 1930s and 1940s tried to keep caffeine out of the mouths of young children, more and more of them, especially in poorer neighborhoods, are now giving their children caffeine in the form of Coca-Cola and chocolate bars.

Should we be worried about caffeine use by children? Caffeine can have a beneficial effect on children who use it. In fact, in both younger children and in adolescents, scientists have documented the same favorable effects on vigilance and sustained attention as in adults.[1] Also, like adults, children usually self-select in their use of caffeine. The ones who experience unpleasant side effects avoid caffeine, while those who get benefits continue using it.[2] Overall, children under eighteen years old average 1 mg per kilogram a day, which is the equivalent of a 4 ounce cup of filter drip coffee for a 150 pound person.

However, caffeine is a psychoactive substance that supports a physical dependence, and we don't ordinarily assume that children have the judgment to regulate their own consumption of such substances. Some studies show that caffeine, in addition to increasing attention to detail and manual dexterity, may also increase anxiety in high doses. Therefore, even though there is no reason to panic or to ban caffeine use by children, parents should nevertheless monitor how much caffeine their children consume.

Remember that although small children and adolescents usually use less caffeine than adults, their body weight is also less, and therefore their exposure in terms of blood concentrations of the drug may be higher. In the age group six to eleven months, a National Academy of Sciences survey found that the average intake of the minority who consumed caffeine was 77 mg a day, a great deal of caffeine for a tiny child's body weight.

Parents should especially be aware of caffeinated soft drinks like Coca-Cola, Dr Pepper, and Mountain Dew and iced tea, and stay alert to the possibility of sleep disturbances or even increased levels of anxiety if large amounts are being used. An additional concern is raised by some who assert that, because most soft drinks have a high sugar content, and children may increase their consumption of these beverages because they like caffeine's effects, the addition of caffeine to soft drinks may increase the risk of childhood obesity and tooth decay.

Liking the smell of coffee may be an adult preference. As one researcher reported, "A striking change was found from dislike to like for coffee odour from 8 to 16 years of age. This change in coffee liking was the greatest as compared with the change in liking of nine other odourants."[3] Some studies suggest that the psychopharmacological effects of caffeine may be responsible at least in part for this change.[4] So there actually may be a certain age, sometime after puberty, at which caffeine helps to turn us on to coffee, one of its most pleasurable vehicles.

Notes

Introduction: The World of Caffeine

1. P. Quinlan et al., "Effects of hot tea, coffee, and water ingestion on physiological responses and mood: The role of caffeine, water, and beverage type," *Psychopharmacology*, *134*, 164–173, 1997.
2. Editorial, *British Medical Journal*, *1* 1031, 1976.
3. Committee on Military Nutrition Research: Food and Nutrition Board, *Caffeine for the Sustainment of Mental Task Performance: Formulations for Military Operations*, Washington, D.C.: National Academy Press, 2001.
4. Weinberg, B. A., and B. K. Bealer, *The World of Caffeine*, New York: Routledge, 2001, p. 126.

1: Getting Started with Caffeine

1. "It is often difficult, however, to measure with consistency the effects of caffeine on performance because these effects have been found to be both task and situation specific and biphasic." Meyers, J. P., et al., "Caffeine in the modulation of brain function," in *Caffeine and Behavior*, B. S. and U. Gupta, eds., Boca Raton, FL: CRC Press, 1999, p. 22.
2. Smith, A., and A. C. Miles, "Acute effects of meals, noise and nightwork," *British Journal of Psychology*, 77, 377–387, 1987.
3. Committee on Military Nutrition Research: Food and Nutrition Board, *Caffeine for the Sustainment of Mental Task Performance: Formulations for Military Operations*, Washington, D.C.: National Academy Press, 2001.
4. Lorist, M. M., "Influence of caffeine on selective attention in well-rested and fatigued subjects," *Psychophysiology*, *31*, 525–534, 1994.
5. Quoted in Lorist, 1994. Citing Dews, P. B., 1984, "Behavioral effects of caffeine," *Caffeine Perspectives from Recent Research*, New York, Springer-Verlag, p. 90.
6. Blanchard, J., and S. J. A. Sawers, "The absolute bioavailability of caffeine in man," *European Journal of Clinical Pharmacology*, *24*, 93–98, 1983.
7. Experiencing a rapid heartbeat does not mean that your heart is being damaged. It no more suggests cardiovascular problems than a sneeze augurs pneumonia. See T. B. Graboys et al., "Coffee, arrhythmias, and common sense," *New England Journal of Medicine*, 308, 1983.
8. Lamberg, L., "Brew it or chew it? Military seeks ways to caffeinate," *Journal of the American Medical Association*, *281*, 885–886, 1999.

9. Kaplan, G. B., et al., "Dose-dependent pharmacokinetics and psychomotor effects of caffeine in humans," *Journal of Clinical Pharmacology, 37*(8), 693–703, 1997.

10. Wiles, J. D., et al., "Effect of caffeinated coffee on running speed, respiratory factors, blood lactate and perceived exertion during 1500m treadmill running," *British Journal of Sports Medicine, 26,* 116–120, 1992.

11. Bridge, N., "Coffee-drinking as a frequent cause of disease," *Transactions of the Association of American Physicians, 8,* 281–288, 1893.

12. Rogers, Peter J., et al. "Caffeine use: Is there a net benefit for mood and psychomotor performance?" *Neuropsychobiology, 3,* 195–199, 1995; Terry E. Graham, "Caffeine and exercise: Metabolism, endurance and performance," *Sports Medicine* 31(11), 785–807, 2001.

13. Rogers et al., 1995.

2: Caffeine and Your Body Clock

1. Quoted in Lorist, M. M., "Influence of caffeine on selective attention in well-rested and fatigued subjects," *Psychophysiology, 31,* 525–534, 1994.

2. Dement, W. C., and C. Vaugham, *The Promise of Sleep,* New York: Random House, 1999, p. 65.

3. Dement and Vaughan, 1999, p. 84.

4. Lambert, L., "Brew it or chew it?" Military seeks ways to caffeinate," *Journal of the American Medical Association, 281,* 885–886, 1999.

5. Lamberg, 1999.

6. Bonnet, M. H., and D. L. Arand, "Metabolic rate and the restorative function of sleep," *Physiological Behavior, 59,* 777, 1996.

7. Penetar, D., et al., "Caffeine reversal of sleep deprivation effects on alertness and mood," *Psychopharmacology, 112,* 359–365, 1993.

8. Penetar et al., 1993.

9. Craig, A., et al., "The effects of lunch on sensory-perceptual functioning in man," *International Archives of Occupational and Environmental Health, 49,* 105–114, 1981.

10. Christie, M. J., and E. M. McBreaty, "Psychophysiological investigations of post-lunch state in male and female subjects," *Ergonomics, 22,* 307–323, 1979.

11. Smith, A., and C. Miles, "Acute effects of meals, noise and nightwork," *British Journal of Psychology, 77,* 377–387, 1986.

12. Smith, A., et al., "Effects of breakfast and caffeine on performance and mood in the late morning and after lunch," *Neuropsychobiology, 26,* 198–204, 1992.

13. Smith et al., 1992.

14. Smith et al., 1992.

15. Smith A., et al., "Effects of evening meals and caffeine on cognitive performance, mood and cardiovascular functioning," *Appetite, 22,* 57–65, 1994.

16. Regina, E. G., et al., "Effects of caffeine on alertness in simulated automobile driving," *Journal of Applied Psychology, 59,* 483–489, 1974.

17. Baker, W. J., and G. C. Theologus, "Effects of caffeine on visual monitoring," *Journal of Applied Psychology, 56,* 422–427, 1972.

18. Dement and Vaughan, 1999, pp. 51–53.

19. Dement and Vaughan, 1999, pp. 4, 225.

20. Horne, J. A., and L. A. Reyner, "Counteracting driver sleepiness: Effects of napping, caffeine, and placebo," *Psychophysiology, 33,* 306–309, 1966.

21. Dement and Vaughan, 1999, p. 394.

22. Borland, R. G., et al., "Performance overnight in shiftworkers operating a dog-night schedule," *Aviation, Space and Environmental Medicine, 57,* 241–249, 1986.

23. Sugerman, J. L., and J. K. Walsh, "Physiological sleep tendency and ability to maintain alertness at night," *Sleep, 12,* 106–112, 1989.

24. Walsh, J. K., et al., "Effect of caffeine on physiological sleep tendency and ability to sustain wakefulness at night," *Psychopharmacology, 101,* 271–273, 1990.

25. Griffiths, R., et al., "Low-dose caffeine discrimination in humans," *Journal of Pharmacology and Experimental Therapeutics, 252,* 970–978, 1990.

26. Lamberg, 1999.

27. Dement and Vaughan, 1999, p. 225.

28. Goldstein, A., and S. Kaizer, "Psychotropic effects of caffeine in man, III. A questionnaire survey of coffee drinking and its effects in a group of housewives," *Clinical Pharmacology and Therapeutics, 10,* 477–488, 1969.

29. Karacan, I., "Dose-related sleep disturbances induced by coffee and caffeine," *Clinical Pharmacology and Therapeutics, 20,* 682–689, 1976.

30. Goldstein and Kaizer, 1969.

31. Regestein, Q. R., "Pathologic sleepiness induced by caffeine," *American Journal of Medicine, 87,* 587–588, 1989.

3: The Jet Lag Program

1. Dement, W. C., and C. Vaughan, *The Promise of Sleep,* New York: Random House, 1999, p. 84.

2. Mothernature.com web site (http://library.mothernature.com/bookstore/19/index.cfm?chp=137), citing Sharon Faelton, ed., *The Doctors Book of Home Remedies for Women,* Emmaus, PA: Rodale Press, 1997 (http://library.mothernature.com/bookstore/19/index.cfm?chp=137).

3. British Airways web site, "Jet Lag," http://www.britishairways.com/health/docs/jet_lag/.

4. Recht, L. D., et al., "Baseball teams beaten by jet lag," *Science, 377,* 583, 1995.

5. Shiota, M., M. Sudou, and M. Ohshima, *Aviation, Space and Environmental Medicine, 67,* 1155–1160, 1996.

4: Sharpening Your Mind

1. Jarvis, M., "Does caffeine enhance absolute levels of cognitive performance?" *Psychopharmacology, 110,* 45–52, 1993.

2. Smith, A., and C. Miles, "Acute effects of meals, noise and nightwork," *British Journal of Psychology, 77,* 377–387, 1987.

3. Smith, B., et al., "Caffeine and arousal: A biobehavioral theory of physiological, behavioral, and emotional effects," in B. S. and Uma Gupta, eds., *Caffeine and Behavior,* Boca Raton, FL: CRC Press, 1999, pp. 87–135.

4. Gupta, Uma, and B. S. Gupta, "Caffeine, impulsivity and performance," in Gupta and Gupta, *Caffeine and Behavior,* pp. 191–205.

5. Hasenfratz, M., and K. Battig, "Acute dose-effect relationships of caffeine and mental performance, EEG, cardiovascular and subjective parameters," *Psychopharmacology, 114,* 281, 1994.

6. Smith, B., et al., "The lateralized processing of affect in emotional labile extroverts and introverts: Central and autonomic effects," *Biological Psychology, 39,* 143, 1995; F. Roman, et al., "Sex differences and bilateral electrodermal activity," *Paul. J. Biol. Sci., 24,* 150, 1989.

7. De-Brabander, B., "Effect of short lateralized signals on arousal vs. activation on tasks requiring visuospatial or elementary semantic visual processing," *Perceptual and Motor Skills, 67,* 783, 1988.

8. Smith, B., "The effects of caffeine and gender on physiology and performance: Further tests of a biobehavioral model," *Physiology and Behavior, 54,* 415–422, 1993.

9. Gupta, B. S., and U. Gupta, "Caffeine, impulsivity, and performance," in *Caffeine and Behavior,* B. S. and U. Gupta, eds., Boca Raton, FL: CRC Press, 1999, pp. 191–205.

10. Daly, J. W., et al., "The role of adenosine receptors in the central action of caffeine," in Gupta and Gupta, 1999, p. 3.

11. Smith, A., "Effects of caffeine on attention at low levels of arousal," in *Nicotine, Caffeine and Social Drinking,* J. Snel and M. M. Lorist, eds., Amsterdam: Harwood Academic Publishers, 1998.

12. Warburton, D. M., "Effects of caffeine on cognition and mood without caffeine abstinence," *Psychopharmacology, 119,* 66–70, 1995.

13. Eysenck, H. J., *Intelligence: A New Look,* New Brunswick, NJ: Transaction Publishers, 1998, pp. 57–58.

14. Rodgers, P., et al., "Caffeine use: Is there a net benefit for mood and psychomotor performance?" *Neuropsychobiology, 31,* 195–199, 1995.

15. Jarvis, M., "Does caffeine intake enhance absolute levels of cognitive performance?" *Psychopharmacology, 110,* 45–52, 1993.

16. Lumley, M., et al., "Ethanol and caffeine effects on daytime sleepiness/alertness," *Sleep, 10,* 306–12, 1987; Zwyghuizen-Doorenbos A., et al., "Effects of caffeine on alertness," *Psychopharmacology, 100,* 36–39, 1990.

17. Eysenck, pp. 57–58. See also Battig, K., and R. Buzzi, "Effect of coffee on the speed of subject paced information processing," *Neuropsychobiology, 16,* 12, 1986.

18. Van der Stelt, O., "Caffeine and attention," in Gupta and Gupta, 1999, pp. 231–240.

19. Rogers et al., 1995.

20. Frewer, L., and M. Lader, "The effects of caffeine on two computerized tests of attention and vigilance," *Human Psychopharmacology, 6,* 119–128, 1991.

21. Smith, B., et al., "Caffeine and arousal: A biobehavioral theory of physiological, behavioral, and emotional effects," in Gupta and Gupta, 1999, pp. 87–135.

22. Lorist, M. M., and J. Snel, "Caffeine effects on perceptual and motor processes," *Electroencephalography and Clinical Neurophysiology, 102,* 401, 1997.

23. Debrah, K., et al., "Effect of caffeine on recognition of and physiological responses to hypoglycaemia in insulin-dependent diabetics," *Lancet, 347,* 19, 1996.

24. Groopman, J., "Medical dispatch: Eyes wide open," *New Yorker,* Dec. 2, 2001, p. 53.

25. Holck, H.O.G., "Effect of caffeine on chess problem solving," *Journal of Comparative Psychology,* 301–311, 1933.

26. Warburton, 1995.

27. Smith, A. P., et al., "Investigation of the effects of coffee on alertness and performance during the day and night," *Neuropsychobiology, 27,* 217–223, 1993; Smith, A. P., et al., "Effects of breakfast and caffeine on cognitive performance, mood, and cardiovascular functioning," *Appetite, 22,* 39–55, 1994.

28. Gupta and Gupta, 1999, pp. 191–205.

29. Riedel, W. J., and J. Jolles, "Cognition enhancers in age related cognitive decline," *Drugs and Aging, 8,* 245, 1996.

30. Riedel and Jolles, 1996.

31. Cattell, R. B., "The effects of alcohol and caffeine on intelligent and associate perform-ance," *British Journal of Medical Psychology, 10,* 20–33, 1930.
32. Gillilan, A. R., and D. Nelson, "The effects of coffee on certain mental and physiological functions," *Journal of General Psychology, 21,* 339–348, 1939.
33. Anderson, K., and W. Revelle, "The interactive effects of caffeine, impulsivity, and demands on visual search task," *Personality and Individual Differences, 4,* 127–134, 1983.
34. Rodgers et al., 1995.
35. Jarvis, 1993.
36. Jacobson, B. H., and S. R. Thurman-Lacey, "Effect of caffeine on motor performance by caffeine-naïve and -familiar subjects," *Perceptual and Motor Skills, 74,* 151–157, 1992.
37. Streufert, S., et al., "Excessive coffee consumption in simulated complex work settings: Detriment or facilitation of performance?" *Journal of Applied Psychology, 82,* 774, 1997.
38. Streufert, S., et al., "Effects of caffeine deprivation on complex human functioning," *Psy-chopharmacology, 118,* 377, 1995.
39. Cole, K. J., et al., "Effect of caffeine ingestion on perception of effort and subsequent work production," *International Journal of Sports Nutrition, 6,* 14, 1996.
40. Sargeant, J., and P. Solbach, "Stress and headache in the workplace: The role of caffeine," *Medical Psychotherapeutics, 1,* 83, 1996.
41. Some have felt that caffeine actually released the human potential to create the modern world. "Would we have had the Industrial Revolution, absent caffeine . . . ? Could a British population that awoke to a breakfast of beer soup and continued drinking alcohol throughout the day have functioned as a disciplined industrial work force—up and at their machines, energized at mid-shift rather than languishing in alcohol-fueled lethargy? Would democratic revolution have come at the times and places it did, absent the fuel of caffeine? What does the twin rise in Seattle of coffee and Microsoft tell us about the neu-rochemistry of computer programming?" "Caffeine: Stimulant to Better Living or a Dan-gerous and Sinful Vice?" article on the web site of the Wharton School of the University of Pennsylvania, Dec. 2001, www.knowledge.wharton.edu/121901_556.html.
42. Jarvis, 1993.
43. Jarvis, 1993, notes that "because of measurement error, the relation between coffee and tea intake and cognitive performance is probably even stronger than it appears in these data."
44. This test is adapted from Walford, R. L., *120 Year Diet,* New York: Pocket Books, 1986, pp. 44–45.

5: Enhancing Your Creativity

1. Weinberg, B., and B. Bealer, *The World of Caffeine,* New York: Routledge, 2001, p. 216.
2. de Balzac, H., *Traité des excitants modernes,* P. Alechinsksy and M. Butor, eds., Arles, 1994.
3. Poincaré, H., *Science and methods,* London: St. Augustine Press, 2001, p. 121.
4. Found at www.paulerdos.com, referencing *The Man Who Loved Only Numbers: The Story of Paul Erdos,* New York: Hyperion, 1998.
5. Myers, J., et al., "Caffeine in the modulation of brain function," in *Caffeine and Behavior,* B. S. Gupta and U. Gupta, eds., Boca Raton, FL: CRC Press, 1999, p. 22.
6. Snel, J., and M. M. Lorist, "Caffeine and information processing: Its role in sensory per-ception," in *Pleasure and Quality of Life: Proceedings of the ARISE Meeting,* D. M. War-burton and N. Sherwood, eds., New York: Wiley, 1996, pp. 97–114.

7. Tharion, W. J., et al., "Effects of caffeine and diphenhydramine on auditory evoked cortical potentials," *Perception and Motor Skills, 70,* 707–715, 1993.

8. Diamond, A. L., and R. E. Cole, "Visual threshold as a function of test area and caffeine administration," *Psychonomic Science, 20,* 109–111, 1974.

9. Diamond, A. L., and E. M. Smith, "The effects of caffeine on terminal dark adaptation," in *Sensation and Measurement,* H. R. Moskowitz et al., eds., Dordrecht: D. Reidel, 1979, pp. 339–349.

10. Bohme, M., and H. R. Bohme, "The influence of hormonal contraceptives and caffeine on the Farnsworth-Munsell-100-Hue-Test," *Zentralblatt Gynakologie, 107,* 1305–1316, 1985.

11. Bohme and Bohme, 1985; Kravkov, S. V., "The influence of caffeine on color sensitivity," *Acta Ophthalomologica, 17,* 89–92, 1939.

12. Fine, B. J., and M. McCord, "Oral contraceptive use, caffeine consumption, field-dependence, and the discrimination of colors," *Perceptual and Motor Skills, 73,* 931–941, 1991.

13. Kole, A., J. Snel, and M. M. Lorist, "Effects of background odour on visual ERP (Evoked Response Potential)," unpublished study.

14. Gupta, U., and B. S. Gupta, "Caffeine, impulsivity, and performance," in Gupta and Gupta, 1999, pp. 191–205.

15. Schiffman, S. S., et al., "Methylxanthines enhance taste: Evidence for modulation of taste by adenosine receptor," *Pharmacology, Biochemistry, and Behavior, 24,* 429–432, 1985; Schiffman, S. S., et al., "Caffeine intensifies the taste of certain sweeteners: Role of adenosine receptor," *Pharmacology, Biochemistry, and Behavior, 24,* 429–432, 1986.

16. Mela, D. J., et al., "Relationship between ingestion and gustatory perception of caffeine," *Pharmacology, Biochemistry and Behavior, 43,* 513–521, 1992.

6: Getting in a Good Mood

1. Griffiths, R. R., et al., 1989, "Reinforcing effects of caffeine in coffee and capsules," *Journal of the Experimental Analysis of Behavior, 52,* 127–140; Stern, K. N., et al., 1989, "Reinforcing and subjective effects of caffeine in normal volunteers" *Psychopharmacology, 98,* 81–88, 1989.

2. Loke, W. H., et al. "Caffeine and diazepam," *Psychopharmacology, 87,* 344–350, 1985.

3. Roache, J. D., and R. R. Griffiths, "Interactions of diazepam and caffeine." *Pharmacology Biochemistry, and Behavior, 26,* 801–812, 1987.

4. Warburton, D. M., and D. H. Thompson, "An evaluation of the effects of caffeine in terms of anxiety, depression and headache in the general population," *Pharmacopsychoecologia, 7,* 55, 1994.

5. Smith, A., private correspondence, Jan. 5, 2002.

6. Warburton, D. M., "Effects of caffeine on cognition and mood without caffeine abstinence," *Psychopharmacology, 119,* 66–70, 1995.

7. Smith, B., "Caffeine, performance, mood and states of reduced alertness," *Pharmacopsychoecologia, 7,* 75, 1984; Rogers, P., et al., "Caffeine use: Is there a net benefit for mood and psychomotor performance?" *Neuropsychobiology, 31,* 195, 1995.

8. Ratliff-Crain, J., et al., "Cardiovascular reactivity, mood, and task performance in deprived and nondeprived coffee drinkers," *Health Psychology, 8,* 427, 1989.

9. Penetar, D., et al., "Caffeine reversal of sleep deprivation effects on alertness and mood," *Psychopharmacology, 112,* 359–365, 1993.

10. Griffiths, R. R., et al., 1989; Stern et al., 1989; Penetar et al., 1993, referencing "long-lasting improvements in mood" (p. 365).
11. Goldstein, A., et al., "Psychotropic effects of caffeine in man: I. Quantitative and qualitative differences associated with habituation to coffee," *Clinical Pharmacology and Therapeutics, 10,* 489, 1969.
12. Ratliff-Crain, J., "Cardiovascular reactivity, mood, and task performance in deprived and non-deprived coffee drinkers," *Health Psychology, 8,* 427, 1989.
13. Quinlan, P., et al., "Effects of hot tea, coffee and water ingestion on physiological responses and mood: The role of caffeine, water and beverage type." *Psychopharmacology, 134,* 164, 1997.
14. Bonnet, M. H., et al., "The use of caffeine vs. prophylactic naps in sustained performance," *Sleep, 18,* 97, 1995.
15. Perrine, D., *The Chemistry of Mind-Altering Drugs,* Washington, D.C.: American Chemical Society, 1996, p. 23.
16. Rush, C. R., et al., "Intravenous caffeine in stimulant drug abusers: Subjective reports and physiological effects," *Journal of Pharmacology and Experimental Therapeutics, 273,* 351, 1995.
17. Azcona, O., et al., "Evaluation of the central effects of alcohol and caffeine interaction," *British Journal of Clinical Pharmacology, 40,* 393, 1995.
18. White, J. M., "Behavioral effects of caffeine coadministered with nicotine, benzodiazepines, and alcohol," in B. S. and Uma Gupta, eds., *Caffeine and Behavior,* Boca Raton, FL: CRC Press, 1997, pp. 75–83.
19. Smith, A. P., et al., "The effects of caffeine, impulsivity, and time of day on performance, mood, and cardiovascular function," *Journal of Psychopharmacology, 5,* 120, 1991; Frewer, L. J., and M. H. Lader, "The effects of caffeine on two computerized tests of attention and vigilance," *Human Psychopharmacology, 6,* 119, 1991.
20. Gauvin, D. V., and F. A. Holloway, "The subjective effects of caffeine: Bridging the gap between human and animal research," in Gupta and Gupta, 1999, p. 277.
21. Kawachi, I., et al., "A prospective study of coffee drinking and suicide in women," *Archives of Internal Medicine, 156,* 521, 1996.
22. Weinberg, B., and B. K. Bealer, *The World of Caffeine,* New York: Routledge, 2001, p. 299.
23. Mainous, R. O., "Research utilization: Pharmacological management of neonatal pain," *Neonatal Network, 14,* 71, 1995; Kawachi et al., 1996.
24. Worthington, J., et al., "Consumption of alcohol, nicotine, and caffeine among depressed outpatients: Relationship with response to treatment," *Psychosomatics, 37,* 518, 1996.
25. Kawachi, 1996.
26. Cherek, R. D., et al., "Regular or decaffeinated coffee and subsequent human aggressive behavior," *Psychiatry Research, 11,* 251–258, 1984.
27. Smith, B., et al., "Caffeine and arousal: A biobehavioral theory of physiological, behavioral, and emotional effects," in Gupta and Gupta, 1997, p. 97.
28. DeFreitas, B., and G. Schwartz, "Effects of caffeine in chronic psychiatric patients," *American Journal of Psychiatry, 136,* 1337, 1979.
29. Roache, J. D., and R. R. Griffiths, "Interactions of diazepam and caffeine: Behavioral and subjective dose effects in humans," *Psychopharmacology, Biochemistry, and Behavior, 26,* 801–812, 1987.
30. Davidson, R., and B. Smith, "Arousal and habituation: Differential effects of caffeine, sensation seeking, and task difficulty," *Personality and Individual Differences, 10,* 111, 1989.

31. Kawachi et al., 1996.
32. Goldstein, 1969.
33. Cole, K. J., et al., "Effect of caffeine ingestion on perception of effort and subsequent work production," *International Journal of Sports Nutrition, 6,* 14, 1996.
34. Adapted from Bond, A., and M. Lader, "The use of analogue scales in rating subjective feelings," *British Journal of Medical Psychology, 47,* 211–218, 1974.

7: Relaxation and Meditation

1. Quinlan, P., et al., "Effects of hot tea, coffee and water ingestion on physiological responses and mood: The role of caffeine, water and beverage type," *Psychopharmacology, 134,* 164, 1997.
2. Goldstein, A., "Psychotropic effects of caffeine in man. III A questionnaire survey of coffee drinking and its effects in a group of housewives," *Clinical Pharmacology and Therapeutics, 10,* 477–488, 1969.
3. Kaplan, G. B., et al., "Dose-dependent pharmacokinetics and psychomotor effects of caffeine in humans," *Journal of Clinical Pharmacology, 37*(8), 693–703, 1997.
4. Graham, T. E., "Caffeine and exercise: Metabolism, endurance and performance," *Sports Medicine, 31,* 785–807, 2001; Smith, A. P., "Effects of caffeine on attention: Low levels of arousal," in *Nicotine, Caffeine, and Social Drinking,* J. Snel and M. Lorist, eds., Amsterdam: Harwood Academic Publishers, 1998.
5. Goldstein, 1969.
6. Roach, J. D., and R. R. Griffiths, "Interactions of diazepam and caffeine: Behavioral and subjective dose effects in humans," *Pharmacology, Biochemistry, and Behavior, 26,* 801–812, 1987.
7. Chait, L. D., and R. R. Griffiths, "Effects of caffeine on cigarette smoking and subjective response," *Clinical Pharmacology and Therapeutics, 34,* 612–622, 1983.
8. Loke, W. N., et al., "Caffeine and diazepam," *Psychopharmacology, 87,* 344–350, 1985.
9. Penetar, D., et al., "Caffeine reversal of sleep deprivation effects on alertness and mood," *Psychopharmacology, 112,* 359–365, 1993.
10. Graham, 2001.
11. James, J. E., *Caffeine and Health,* London: Harcourt Brace Jovanovich, 1991, p. 294.
12. Smith, B., et al., "Caffeine and arousal: A biobehavioral theory of physiological, behavioral, and emotional effects," in *Caffeine and Behavior,* B. S. Gupta and J. Gupta, eds., Boca Raton, FL: CRC Press, 1997, p. 105.
13. There is some evidence that caffeine may contribute to post-traumatic stress disorder (PTSD), a syndrome that first appears in the literature in 1755 in the story of a peasant family trapped in their house by an avalanche in the Italian Alps. However, the jury is still out on this finding. Parry-Jones, B., and W. Parry-Jones, "Post-traumatic stress disorder: Supportive evidence for an eighteenth century natural disaster," *Psychological Medicine, 24,* 15, 1994.
14. NewScientist.com, Feb. 2002.
15. Bruce Krulwich, private correspondence.
16. Daisetz, T. S. *Zen and Japanese Culture,* Princeton: Princeton University Press, 1959, p. 293.

8: Improving Your Athletic Performance

1. Weinberg, B. A., and B. K. Bealer, *The World of Caffeine,* New York: Routledge, 2001, p. 44.
2. Even children seem to know about caffeine's ergogenic power. "A large survey of Canadian teenagers reported that 27% of respondents had used caffeine in the last year for the specific purpose of enhancing athletic performance." Graham, T. E., "Caffeine and exercise: Metabolism, endurance, and performance," *Sports Medicine, 31,* 787, 2001.
3. There were serious scientific studies reporting the ergogenic benefits of caffeine over 100 years ago. Graham, 2001, p. 786.
4. Graham, 2001.
5. Graham, T. E., et al., "The metabolic and exercise endurance effects of coffee and caffeine ingestion," *Journal of Applied Physiology, 85,* 883–889, 1998.
6. Although increases in free fatty acids and adrenaline levels were noted only in the caffeine-only trials and were not observed in the coffee drinking trials, this difference cannot explain the differences in outcome either, because it is unlikely that either change contributes to caffeine's ergogenic effects.
7. Essig, D., et al., "Effects of caffeine ingestion on utilization of muscle glycogen and lipids during leg ergometer cycling," *International Journal of Sports Medicine, 1,* 86–90, 1980. The supposed mechanism, called the Randle effect, is that caffeine increases blood levels of free fatty acids (FFA). The muscles use this FFA for fuel, allowing them to delay burning up their primary fuel supply of stored glycogen.
8. Graham, 2001.
9. Graham, T. E., et al., "Caffeine ingestion and metabolic responses of tetraplegic humans during electrical cycling," *Journal of Applied Physiology, 85,* 979–985, 1998.
10. Wiles, J. D., et al., "Effect of caffeinated coffee on running speed, respiratory factors, blood lactate and perceived exertion during 1500m treadmill running," *British Journal of Sports Medicine, 26,* 116–120, 1992.
11. Dozens of studies confirm this phenomenon. A few recent examples are given here: Trice, I., and E. M. Haymes, "Effects of caffeine ingestion on exercise induced changes during high intensity, intermittent exercise," *International Journal of Sports Nutrition, 5,* 37–44, 1995; Greer, F., et al., "Comparison of caffeine and theophylline ingestion: Exercise, metabolism, and endurance," *Journal of Applied Physiology, 89,* 1837–1844, 2000; Van Soeren, M. H., and T. E. Graham, "Effect of caffeine on metabolism, exercise endurance, and catecholamines responses after withdrawal," *Journal of Applied Physiology, 85,* 1501, 1998.
12. The same study found no effect from caffeine in coffee. Graham, 1998.
13. Costil, D. L., et al., "Effects of caffeine ingestion on metabolism and exercise performance," *Medicine and Science in Sports and Exercise, 10,* 155–158, 1978.
14. Sasaki, H., et al., "Effect of sucrose and caffeine ingestion on performance of prolonged strenuous running," *International Journal of Sports Medicine, 8,* 261–265, 1987.
15. Berglund, B., and P. Hemmingsson, "Effects of caffeine ingestion on exercise performance at low and high altitudes in cross-country skiing," *International Journal of Sports Medicine, 3,* 234–236, 1982.
16. MacIntosh, B. R., and B. M. Wright, "Caffeine ingestion and performance of a 1500 meter swim," *Canadian Journal of Applied Physiology, 20,* 168–177, 1995.
17. Wiles et al., 1992.

18. Ivy, J. L., et al., "Influence of caffeine and carbohydrate feedings on endurance perform- ance," *Medicine and Science in Sports and Exercise, 11,* 6–11, 1979.
19. Kovacs, E. M. R., et al., "Effect of caffeine drinks on substrate metabolism, caffeine excre- tion, and performance," *Journal of Applied Physiology, 85,* 709–715, 1998.
20. Flinn, S., et al., "Caffeine ingestion prior to incremental cycling to exhaustion in recre- ational cyclists," *International Journal of Sports Medicine, 11,* 188–193, 1990.
21. Graham, 2001, p. 786.
22. Kalmar, J. M., and E. Caffarelli, "Effects of caffeine on neuromuscular fatigue," *Journal of Applied Physiology, 87,* 801–808, 1999.
23. Kalmar and Caffarelli, 1999.
24. One study did demonstrate significant improvements in tennis playing, showing an increase in winning percentages with 5 mg per kilogram of caffeine. Ferrauti, A., et al., "Metabolic and ergogenic effects of carbohydrate and caffeine beverages in tennis," *Jour- nal of Sports Medicine and Physical Fitness, 37,* 258–266, 1997.
25. Lorist, M. M., et al., "Influence of caffeine on selective attention in well-rested and fatigued subjects," *Psychophysiology, 31,* 525–534, 1994.
26. Smith, D. L., et al., "Combined effect of tobacco and caffeine on the components of choice-reaction time, heart rate, and hand steadiness," *Perceptual and Motor Skills, 45,* 635–639, 1977.
27. Jacobson, B. H., and B. M. Edgley, "Effects of caffeine in simple reaction time and move- ment time," *Aviation, Space, and Environmental Medicine, 58,* 1153–1156, 1987.
28. Kivity, S., et al., "The effect of caffeine on exercise-induced bronchoconstriction," *Chest, 97,* 1083–1085, 1990.
29. Kivity et al., 1990.
30. Many studies confirm these findings—for example: Falk, B., et al., "Effects of caffeine ingestion on body fluid balance and thermoregulation during exercise," *Canadian Journal of Physiological Pharmacology, 68,* 889–892, 1990; Engels, W. J., and E. M. Haymes, "Effects of caffeine ingestion on metabolic responses to prolonged walking in sedentary males," *International Journal of Sports and Nutrition, 2,* 386–386, 1992.
31. Dekkers, J. C., et al., "The role of antioxidant vitamins and enzymes in the prevention of exercise-induced muscle damage," *Sports Medicine, 21,* 213–238, 1996.
32. Devasagayam, T.P.A., et al., "Caffeine as an antioxidant: Inhibition of lipid peroxidation induced reactive oxygen species," *Biochimica et Biophysica Acta, 1282,* 63–70, 1996.
33. Devasagayam et al., 1996.
34. Reimund, E., "Free radical flux theory of sleep," *Medical Hypotheses, 43,* 231–233, 1994.
35. Dekkers et al., 1996.
36. Dekkers et al., 1996.

9: How Much to Take and When to Take It to Boost Athletic Performance

1. In addition to oral ingestion, caffeine can be administered by suppository, intramuscular injection, or infusion into a vein. Whether the avenue of delivery affects caffeine's ergogenic effects is unknown.
2. Penetar, D., et al., "Caffeine reversal of sleep deprivation effects on alertness and mood," *Psychopharmacology, 112,* 359–365, 1993.
3. Graham, T. E., and C. McLean, "Gender differences in the metabolic responses to caffeine," in *Gender Differences in Metabolism: Practical and Nutritional Implications,* M. Tarnopolsky, ed., Boca Raton, FL: CRC Press, 1999, 201–227.

4. Graham, T. E., "Caffeine as an ergogenic aid," *Sports Medicine, 31,* 785–807, 2001.
5. LeBlanc, J., et al., "Enhanced metabolic response to caffeine in exercise-trained human subjects," *Journal of Applied Physiology, 59,* 832–837, 1985.
6. Graham, T. E., and L. L. Spriet, "Metabolic, catecholamine, and exercise performance response to various doses of caffeine," *Journal of Applied Physiology, 78,* 867–874, 1995.
7. Graham, T. E., "Caffeine and exercise: Metabolism, endurance, and performance," *Sports Medicine, 31,* 785–807, 2001.
8. Graham, 2001.
9. Graham, 2001.
10. Wemple, R. D., et al., "Caffeine vs. caffeine-free sports drinks: Effects on urine production at rest and during prolonged exercise," *International Journal of Sports Medicine, 18,* 40–46, 1997.

10: Weight Loss

1. Carrillo, J. A., and J. Benitez, "Clinically significant pharmacokinetic interactions between caffeine and medications," *Clinical Pharmacokinetics, 39,* 127–153, 2000.
2. Coe, S. D., and M. D. Coe, *The True History of Chocolate,* London: Thames and Hudson, 1996, p. 51.
3. Kulkosky, P. J., et al., "Effect of CCK-8 on intake of caffeine, ethanol, and water," *Bulletin of the Psychonomic Society, 29,* 441–444, 1981.
4. Sours, J. A., "Case reports of anorexia nervosa and caffeinism," *American Journal of Psychiatry, 140,* 235–236, 1983.
5. P. Kulkosky to the authors, Feb. 2002.
6. Bray, G. A., "Reciprocal relation of food intake and sympathetic activity: Experimental observations and clinical implications," *International Journal of Obesity, 24,* s8–s17, 2000.
7. Nelson, M. E., and S. Wernick, *Strong Women Stay Slim,* New York: Bantam Books, 1998.
8. Nelson and Wernick, 1998, p. 31.
9. Andersen, T., and J. Fogh, "Weight loss and delayed gastric emptying following a South American herbal preparation in overweight patients," *Journal of Human Nutrition and Dietetics, 14,* 243–250, 2001.
10. Nelson and Wernick. 1998, p. 22.
11. Astrup, A., et al., "Caffeine: A double-blind, placebo-controlled study of its thermogenic, metabolic, and cardiovascular effects in healthy volunteers," *American Journal of Clinical Nutrition, 51,* 759–767, 1990; Horton, T. J., and C. A. Geissler, "Post-prandial thermogenesis with ephedrine, caffeine, and aspirin in lean, predisposed obese and obese women," *International Journal of Obesity, 20,* 91–97, 1996; Graham T. E., et al., "Caffeine and exercise: Metabolism and performance," *Canadian Journal of Applied Physiology, 19,* 111–138, 1994.
12. "Turkey, gravy, and thermogenesis: Low-protein and low-fat diet keeps pounds off the waistline and increases desire to exercise," Cornell University press release, Nov. 23, 1998.
13. Moore, C. "Caffeine: Grounds for debate," *Navy Health Book: Internally Peer Reviewed,* Apr. 3, 1997. Available: http://www.vnh.org/NHB/HW97126CaffeineDebate.html.
14. Adapted from Nelson and Wernick, 1998.
15. Bonnet, M. H., and D. I. Arand, "Metabolic rate and the restorative function of sleep," *Physiology and Behavior, 59* 777, 1996. See also Van Cauter studies.

16. Ivy, J. L., et al., "Influence of caffeine and carbohydrate feedings on endurance perform-ance," *Medicine and Science in Sports and Exercise,* 11, 6–11, 1974.

17. Bracco, D., et al., "Effects of caffeine on energy metabolism in lean and obese women," *American Journal of Physiology,* 269, E671–E678, 1995.

18. Weir, J., et al., "A high carbohydrate diet negates the metabolic effects of caffeine during exercise," *Medicine and Science in Sports and Exercise,* 19, 100–105, 1987.

19. Conlee, R. K., "Amphetamine, caffeine, and cocaine," in *Ergogenics: Enhancement of Per-formance in Exercise and Sport,* D. R. Lamb and M. H. Williams, eds., Indianapolis: Brown and Benchmark, 1991.

20. McCarty, M. E., "Modulation of adipocyte lipoproten lipase expression as a strategy for preventing or treating visceral obesity," *Medical Hypotheses, 57,* 192–200, 2001.

21. Hetzler, R. K., et al., "Effect of paraxanthine on FFA mobilization after intravenous caf-feine administration in humans," *Journal of Applied Physiology, 68,* 44–47, 1990.

22. Van Soren, M., et al., "Acute effects of caffeine ingestion at rest in humans with impaired epinephrine responses," *Journal of Applied Physiology, 80,* 999–1005, 1996.

23. Sainio, E. L., et al., "Ingredients and safety of cellulite creams," *European Journal of Der-matology, 10*(8), 596–603, 2000.

24. Han, L. K., "Anti-obesity action of oolong tea," *International Journal of Obesity and Related Metabolic Disorders, 23,* 98–105, 1999.

25. Dulloo, A. G., "Green tea and thermogenensis: Interactions between catechin-poly-phenols, caffeine, and sympathetic activity," *International Journal of Obesity and Related Metabolic Disorders, 24,* 252–258, 2000.

11: An Elixir of Life? Caffeine and Staying Younger

1. Evans, W., and Rosenberg, I. H., *Biomarkers: The 10 Keys to Prolonging Vitality,* New York: Simon & Schuster, 1991.

2. Swift, C. G., and Tiplady, B., "The effects of age on the response to caffeine," *Psy-chopharmacology, 94,* 24–31, 1988.

3. Perrig, W. I., P. Perrig, and H. B. Stahelin, "The relation between antioxidants and mem-ory performance in the old and very old," *Journal of the American Geriatric Society, 45,* 718–724, 1997.

4. Evans and Rosenberg, 1991.

5. Swift, C. D., and Tiplady, B., "The effects of age on the response to caffeine," *Psy-chopharmacology, 94,* 29–31, 1988.

6. Edwards, B., *America's Favorite Drug: Coffee and Your Health,* Berkeley: Odonian Press, 1992, p. 71.

7. Julien, R. M., *A Primer of Drug Interaction,* New York: Freeman, 2001, p. 146.

8. Weinberg and Bealer, 2001.

9. Jarvis, M., "Does caffeine enhance absolute levels of cognitive performance?" *Psychophar-macology,* 110, 45–52, 1993.

10. Korkotian, E., and M. Segal, "Release of calcium from stores alters the morphology of dendritic spines in cultured hippocampal neurons," *Proceedings of the National Academy of Science, USA, 96,* 12068–12072, 1999.

11. For a discussion of the dynamics of dendritic spine development, see M. Segal, and P. An-dersen, "Dendritic spines shaped by synaptic activity," *Current Opinion in Neurobiology, 10,* 582–586, 2000. The article states that a new series of observations, using new high-resolution time-lapse imaging of cells, has "provoked a major shift in our understanding of

the dendritic spine, from a stable site of long-term memory to a dynamic structure that undergoes rapid morphological variation." Galea, L. A. M., "The effect of estradiol on adult neurogenesis: Cell proliferation and survival," University of British Columbia, Alzheimer's Society Research Program, grant 2001, 2002. Study currently in progress.

12. Ross, G. W., et al., "Association of coffee and caffeine intake with the risk of Parkinson disease," *Journal of the American Medical Association,* May 24–31, 2000.

13. Interview with A. Lieberman, www.HEALTHSCOUT.com, May 23, 2000. Part of this potential protective effect against Parkinson's disease is probably the result of caffeine's power to combat adenosine's activation of certain adenosine receptor subtypes (A2A receptors) that control motor function. This action affords what investigators have called "the observed extra-striatal neuroprotection afforded by A2A receptor antagonists," possibly affecting the course not only of Parkinson's disease but of schizophrenia as well. (R. A. Cunha and S. M. Weiss, "Patho-physiological role of adenosine A2A receptors in the CNS," 22nd European Winter Conference on Brain Research: www.asso.univ-paris5.fr/ewcbr/Francais/EWCBR2002/Session4.htm.)

14. "The role of inflammation in cerebrovascular and neuronal disfunctions associated with AD, Dr. Edith Hamel, McGill University, Alzheimer's Society Research Program, grant 2001, 2002. Study currently in progress.

15. Veld, B. A., et al., "Nonsteroidal anti-inflammatory drugs and risk for Alzheimer's diseases," *New England Journal of Medicine, 345,* 1515–1521, 2001.

16. Shibamoto, T., "Functional foods for disease prevention: Developed from a symposium sponsored by the Division of Agricultural and Food Chemistry at the 213th National Meeting of the American Chemical Society, San Francisco, California, 1997," *American Chemical Society,* 1998 (ACS symposium series 0097-6156).

17. Both tests are adapted from Walford, R. L., *The 120 Year Diet,* New York: Pocket Books, 1986, pp. 44–45.

12: Caffeine and Good Health

1. "The Vertue of the Coffee Drink: First made and publickly sold in England by Pasqua Rosee," a broadside published in London in 1652, reproduced in B. A. Weinberg and B. K. Bealer. *The World of Caffeine,* New York: Routledge, 2001, pp. 321–22.

2. Heyden, S., "Coffee and cardiovascular diseases: A personal view after 30 years of research," in *Caffeine, Coffee, and Health,* S. Garattini, ed., New York: Raven Press, 1993, p. 178.

3. Sawynok, J., and T. L. Yaksh, "Caffeine as an analgesic adjuvant: A review of pharmacology and mechanism of action," *Pharmacological Review, 45,* 43–85, 1993.

4. Snel, J., and Lorist, M. M., "Caffeine and information processing," in *Pleasure and Quality of Life,* D. Warburton and N. Sherwood, eds., New York: Wiley, 1996, p. 107.

5. Myers, D. E., "High-dose caffeine may be effective pain reliever," *Headache,* Nov. 1997.

6. Sawynok and Yaksh, 1993.

7. Laska, E. M., et al., "Caffeine as an analgesic adjuvant," *Journal of the American Medical Association, 251,* 1711–1718, 1984.

8. Diamond, S., and F. G. Freitag, "Caffeine and migraine headache pain," *Current Pain and Headache Reports, 5,* 472, 2001.

9. Ward, A., et al., "The analgesic effects of caffeine in headache," *Pain, 44,* 151–155, 1991.

10. Snel and Lorist, 1996, p. 107.

11. Sawynok and Yaksh, 1993. "Sawynok and Yaksh point out that, on its own, caffeine may

contribute to amelioration of pain. This may be caused by peripheral action at the level of a local injury or actions within the CNS by modifying nociceptive processing. "Graham, T. E., "Caffeine and exercise: Metabolism endurance, and performance," *Sports Medicine, 31,* 790, 2001.

12. Snel and Lorist, 1996, p. 114.
13. Garattini, S., *Caffeine, Coffee, and Health,* New York: Raven Press, 1993, pp. 161, 163.
14. Caggiula, A. W., et al., "Coffee drinking, coronary heart disease, and total mortality," paper presented at the Tenth World Congress of Cardiology, Sept. 14–19, 1986, Washington, D.C.
15. Grobbee, D. E., et al., "Coffee, caffeine, and cardiovascular disease in men," *New England Journal of Medicine, 223,* 1026–1032, 1990.
16. Wilson, P. W. F., et al., "Is coffee consumption a contributor to cardiovascular disease? Insights from the Framingham Study," *Archives of Internal Medicine, 149,* 1169–1172, 1989.
17. Heydens, S., et al., "Coffee consumption and mortality: Total mortality, stroke mortality, and coronary heart disease mortality," *Archives of Internal Medicine, 138,* 1472–1475, 1978.
18. Wilhelmsen, L., et al., "Coffee consumption and coronary heart disease in middle aged Swedish men," *Acta Medscand, 201,* 547–552, 1977.
19. Willet, W. C., "Coffee consumption and coronary heart disease in women," *JAMA, 275,* 458–462, 1996.
20. Grobbee et al., 1990.
21. Garattini, 1993, p. 184.
22. Yano, et al., "Coffee consumption and coronary heart disease," *New England Journal of Medicine, 316,* 946, 1987.
23. Reed, D. M., et al., "Predictors of Arteriosclerosis in the Honolulu Heart Program," *American Journal of Epidemiology, 126,* 214–225, 1987.
24. *Sixth Report of the National Institutes of Health's Joint National Committee on Prevention, Detection, Evaluation and Treatment of High Blood Pressure,* NIH Publication No. 98-4080, 2000.
25. Wakabayashi, K., et al., "Habitual coffee consumption and blood pressure: A study of self-defense officials in Japan," *European Journal of Epidemiology, 14,* 669–673, 1998.
26. Denaro, C. P., et al., "Effects of caffeine with repeated dosing," *European Journal of Clinical Pharmacology, 40,* 273–278, 1991.
27. Robertson, D., et al., "Caffeine and hypertension," *American Journal of Medicine, 77,* 54–60, 1984. See also Robertson, D., et al., "Tolerance to the humoral and hemodynamic effects of caffeine in man," *Journal of Clinical Investigation, 67,* 1111–1117, 1981.
28. Garattini, 1993, pp. 161, 163.
29. Heyden, S., "Coffee and cardiovascular diseases: A personal view after 30 years of research," in Garattini, 1993, pp. 177–193.
30. Izzo, J. L., et al., "Age and prior caffeine use alter the cardiovascular and adrenomedullary responses to oral caffeine," *American Journal of Cardiology, 52,* 767–773, 1983; Ammon, H. P. T., et al., "Adaptation of blood pressure to continuous heavy coffee drinking in young volunteers: A double-blind crossover study," *British Journal of Clinical Pharmacology, 15,* 701–706, 1983.
31. Grobbee et al., 1990.
32. Wilner, A. N., "Could alcohol and caffeine put a brake on stroke?" *Neurology Reviews.com: Clinical Trends and News in Neurology, 8,* 2000.

33. Adamson, R., "Evaluation of coffee and caffeine for mutagenic, carcinogenic, and anti-carcinogenic activity," in T. H. Parliment et al., eds., *Caffeinated Beverages*, Washington, D.C.: American Chemical Society, 2000, p. 75.

34. Adamson, 2000, p. 75.

35. Adamson, 2000, pp. 75–76.

36. Giovannucci, E., "Meta-analysis of coffee consumption and risk of colorectal cancer," *American Journal of Epidemiology, 147,* 1043–1052, 1998.

37. Adamson, 2000, p. 74.

38. Carrillo, J. A., and J. Benitez, "Clinically significant pharmacokinetic interactions between caffeine and medications," *Clinical Pharmacokinetics, 39,* 127–153, 2000.

39. Nikolajsen, L., et al., "Effect of previous frequency of headache, duration of fasting, and caffeine abstinence on perioperative headache," *British Journal of Anesthesiology, 72,* 295, 1994; Hampl, K. F., et al., "Perioperative administration of caffeine tablets for prevention of postoperative headaches," *Canadian Journal of Anesthesiology, 42,* 789, 1995.

40. Higginbotham, E. J., N. A. Kilimanjaro, J. T. Wilensky, R. L. Batenhorst, and D. Hermann, "The effect of caffeine on intraocular pressure in glaucoma patients," *Ophthalmology, 96,* 624–626, 1989.

41. Leitzmann, M. F., et al., "A prospective study of coffee consumption and the risk of symptomatic gallstone disease in men," *JAMA, 281,* 2106–2112, 281.

42. "Guidelines of care for atopic dermatitis," *Journal of the American Academy of Dermatology Association, 26,* 485–488, 1992.

43. McLennan, C., and W. D. Evers, "Caffeine not found harmful to health: The North America Branch of the International Life Sciences Institute told FDA," *Food Chemical News,* p. 28, Oct. 12, 1998.

44. Rapuri, Prema B., et al., "Caffeine intake increases the rate of bone loss in elderly women and interacts with vitamin D receptor genotypes," *American Journal of Clinical Nutrition, 74,* 569–570, 694–700, 2001.

45. Bara, A. I., and E. A. Barley, "Caffeine for asthma," Cochrane Database of Systematic Reviews (computer file), (2):CD001112, 2000.

46. Carrillo, J. A., and Benitez, J., 2000.

47. Lima, D. R., "Cigarettes and caffeine," *Chest 95,* 255–256, 1989.

48. James, J., *Caffeine and Health,* London: Harcourt Brace Jovanovich, 1991, p. 339.

49. James, 1991, p. 22.

50. Kerr, J. S., et al., "Separate and combined effects of the social drugs on psychomotor performance," *Psychopharmacology, 104,* 113, 1991; Rush, C. R., et al., "Acute behavioral and cardiac effects of alcohol of caffeine alone and in combination in humans," *Behavioral Pharmacology, 4,* 562, 1993; Hasenfratz, M., "Antagonistic effects of caffeine and alcohol on mental performance parameters," *Pharmacology, Biochemistry, and Behavior, 46,* 463, 1993.

51. Lima, D. R., and R. M. Santos, "Effects of coffee in alcoholics," *Annals of Internal Medicine, 115,* 499, 1991.

52. Watson, J., and Kerr, D., "The best defense against hypoglycemia is to recognize it: Is caffeine useful?" *Diabetic Technology and Therapeutics, 1,* 193–200, 1999. Some people suspect that caffeine affects insulin sensitivity, which, if true, would probably mean that it affects blood sugar levels and therefore long-term outcomes for diabetics. Unfortunately, there is no agreement whether caffeine increases this sensitivity or decreases it. Most studies show that caffeine has little or no effect, and a few show that it increases insulin sensitivity. For example, a recent study of the effects of caffeine in combination with ephedrine

on nondiabetics' insulin response improved in all the groups studied after taking the drugs. Greenway, F. L., et al., "Pharaceutical cost savings of treating obesity with weight loss medications," *Obesity Research, 7,* 523–531. One recent study of twelve people has shown that 200 mg of caffeine administered intravenously reduces insulin sensitivity by 15 percent in healthy people. However, there are no studies that show if caffeine has a similar effect on diabetics or whether it might contribute to raising the blood sugar of someone with diabetes.

53. Joesoef, R. M., et al., "Are caffeinated beverages risk factors for delayed conception?" *Lancet,* 136–137, Jan. 20, 1990.
54. Dlugosz, L., and M. B. Bracken, "Reproductive effects of caffeine: A review and theoretical analysis," *Epidemiological Reviews, 14,* 83–98, 1992.
55. Thomas, D. B., "Neonatal withdrawal symptoms after chronic ingestion of caffeine," *Southern Medical Journal, 81,* 1092–1094, 1988.
56. Brazier, J. L., and B. Salle, "Conversion of theophylline to caffeine by the human fetus," *Seminars in Perinatology, 5,* 315–320, 1981; Cnattingius, S., et al., "Caffeine intake and the risk of first-trimester spontaneous abortion," *New England Journal of Medicine,* Dec. 21, 2000, pp. 1839–1845.
57. Armstrong, B. G., et al., "Cigarette, alcohol, and coffee consumption and congenital defects," *American Journal of Public Health, 82,* 91–93, 1993.
58. Yang, S., "Small doses of caffeine may not increase miscarriage risk," CNN web site, Nov. 24, 1999, http://www.cnn.com/HEALTH/women/9911/24/caffeine.pregnancy.wmd/index.html.

Appendix B: Drug and Food Interactions

1. Carrillo, J. A., and J. Benitez, "CYP1A2 activity, gender, and smoking as variables influencing the toxicity of caffeine," *British Journal of Clinical Pharmacology 41,* 605–608, 1996.
2. "CYP1A2 is the major enzyme responsible for the metabolism of many drugs and estrogens"; Kadlubar, F. F., "Molecular epidemiology," available: http://www.fda.gov/nctr/science/96–97%20Research%20Plans/organizations/molepid.htm "Theoretically, estrogen should also inhibit caffeine metabolism"; Graham, T. E., "Caffeine and exercise: Metabolism, endurance and performance," *Sports Medicine, 31*(11), 785–807, 2001, p. 794.
3. Jeppesen, U., et al., "Dose-dependent inhibition of CYP1A2, CYP2C19 and CYP2D6 by citalopram, fluoxetine, fluvoxamine and paroxetine," *European Journal of Clinical Pharmacology, 51,* 73–78, 1996.
4. Julien, R. M., A *Primer of Drug Action,* New York: Freeman, 2001, p. 147.
5. Jeppesen, U., et al., "A fluvoxamine-caffeine interaction study," *Pharmacogenetics* 213–222, 1996; Rasmussen, B. B., et al., *Pharmacological Toxicology, 83,* 240–245, 1998; Rasmussen, B. B., T. L. Nielsen, and K. Brosen, "Fluvoxamine is a potent inhibitor of the metabolism of caffeine in vitro," *Pharmacological Toxicology, 83,* 240–245, 1998.
6. Carrillo, J. A., and J. Benitez, "Clinically significant pharmacokinetic interactions between caffeine and medications," *Clinical Pharmacokinetics, 39,* 127–153, 2000.
7. On-Line Continuing Education for Pharmacists, National Community Pharmacists Association, educational series sponsored by Pfizer, by Daniel S. Streeman, Pharm.D., "Cytochrome P450 Enzymes," ACPE Program Number 207-000-99-001-H01, Dec. 1998.

8. Fuhr, U., et al., "Inhibitory effect of grapefruit juice and its bitter principal, naringenin, on CYP1A2 dependent metabolism of caffeine in man," *British Journal of Clinical Pharmacology, 35,* 431–436, 1993.

9. Carrillo, J. A., and J. Benitez, "Clinically significant pharmacokinetic interactions between dietary caffeine and medications," *Clinical Pharmacology, 29,* 127–163, 2000.

10. Birkett, D. J., and Iners, J. O., "Caffeine renal clearance and urine caffeine concentrations during steady state dosing: Implications for monitoring caffeine intake during sports events," *British Journal of Clinical Pharmacology, 31,* 405–408, 1991.

Appendix C: Caffeine and Children

1. Koelega, H. S., "Stimulant drugs and vigilance performance: A review," *Psychopharmacology, 111, 1,* 1993; Tyajala, J., et al., "Perceived tiredness among adolescents and its association with sleep habits and use of psychoactive substances," *Journal of Sleep Research, 189,* 1997.

2. Rappaport, J. L., et al., "Behavior effects of caffeine in children: Relationship between dietary choice and effects of caffeine challenge," *Archives of General Psychiatry, 41,* 1073–1079, 1984.

3. Snel, J., and M. M. Lorist, "Caffeine and information processing," in *Pleasure and Quality of Life,* D. M. Warburton and N. Sherwood, eds., New York: Wiley, 1996, p. 111.

4. Cines, B. M., and P. Rozin, "Some aspects of the liking for hot coffee," *Appetite: Journal for Intake Research, 3*(1), 23–24, 1982.

Acknowledgments

We gratefully acknowledge the advice and guidance of Eric C. Strain, M.D., professor, Department of Psychiatry and Behavioral Sciences, Johns Hopkins University School of Medicine; Harris R. Lieberman, visiting professor, School of Nutrition and Policy, Tufts University; Roland R. Griffiths, Ph.D., professor of psychiatry and behavioral biology, Behavioral Biology Center, Department of Neuroscience, Johns Hopkins University School of Medicine; Paul Kulkosky, Ph.D., professor of psychology, Department of Psychology, University of Southern Colorado; and Andrew P. Smith, Ph.D., professor of psychology and director of the Centre for Occupational and Health Psychology, Cardiff University. Each of these men has conducted important original research that has increased the understanding of the way caffeine works and how it should be used, and each was kind enough to read our manuscript and offer suggestions for how it might be improved.

We thank the staffs of the BioMedical Library, University of Pennsylvania; the Thomas Jefferson School of Medicine Medical Library; and the Free Library of Philadelphia, for providing patient and considerate research assistance in gathering material for our book.

We also thank Ed and Cate Bigler, Beth Cavanaugh, Forrest Murray, Barbara Sobey, Kate Anderson, and others for listening to our findings, spreading the good news about caffeine, and reporting to us about the experiences of friends and family members who tried our suggestions successfully. And special thanks to Antony Francis Patrick Vickery, our dear friend, for always being available to talk and provide emergency computer assistance that speeded our work and repeatedly saved it from extinction.

Our thanks as well to the professional and hard-working staff at Simon & Schuster. We are grateful for the careful attention and correction of Edith Lewis, copyediting supervisor, and Beverly H. Miller, copyeditor, whose exigent scrutiny both smoothed and sharpened our text. Finally, our warmest thanks extend to Fred Hills, our editor, who immediately recognized the importance of our project, championed it, and advised us on content, organization, and style, guiding us wisely in the creation of a book of which we are proud.

Index

About the Authors

Bennett Alan Weinberg is a medical and science writer, a health researcher, and a pharmaceutical educator. He is the head of his own consulting firm specializing in pharmaceutical and medical communications, serving many of the Fortune 500 companies. His work includes continuing medical education programs to train physicians in disease entities and developing materials in support of research, safety, and purity testing. A graduate of Columbia College and New York University School of Law, he has taught at Temple University. He is a seasoned speaker and has wide experience in broadcast and print interviews, including a feature appearance on *Weekend Edition,* the NPR morning news show with Scott Simon.

Bonnie K. Bealer is a researcher, writer, and editor. She holds degrees in psychology and anthropology from Temple University and has studied management and finance at Wharton Business School of the University of Pennsylvania.

Weinberg and Bealer are the authors of the critically acclaimed *The World of Caffeine: The Science and Culture of the World's Most Popular Drug* (Routledge, 2001), the first book in any language to comprehensively treat the natural, cultural, and social history of the most popular drug on earth, from ancient Chinese medicinals to the colas and coffeehouses of today. This book was the subject of a feature article in *The New Yorker,* widespread national radio coverage, and favorable reviews in *The New England Journal of Medicine, Wall Street Journal, Wired* magazine, *Food and Wine,* and the *Washington Post,* and many other national and international publications. It has been nominated for a James Beard Award for 2002 and is the recipient of the Andre Simon Memorial Highly Commended Prize for 2002.

This publication contains the opinions and ideas of its author. It is intended to provide helpful and informative material, for adults in normal health, regarding caffeine. It is sold with the understanding that the author and publisher are not engaged in rendering medical, health, or any other kind of personal professional services in the book. The reader should consult his or her medical, health, or other competent professional before changing caffeine doses or adopting any of the suggestions in this book or drawing inferences from it.

The author and publisher specifically disclaim all responsibility for any liability, loss, or risk, personal or otherwise, that is incurred as a consequence, directly or indirectly, of the use and application of any of the contents of this book.

THE FREE PRESS
A Division of Simon & Schuster Inc.
1230 Avenue of the Americas
New York, NY 10020

THE FREE PRESS and colophon are trademarks
of Simon & Schuster, Inc.

For information about special discounts for bulk purchases,
please contact Simon & Schuster Special Sales:
1-800-456-6798 or business@simonandschuster.com

Book design by Ellen R. Sasahara

Manufactured in the United States of America

1   3   5   7   9   10   8   6   4   2

Library of Congress Cataloging-in-Publication Data

Weinberg, Bennett Alan.
The caffeine advantage : how to sharpen your mind, improve your
physical performance, and achieve your goals—the healthy way /
Bennett Alan Weinberg and Bonnie K. Bealer.
p. cm.
Includes bibliographical references and index.
1. Caffeine—Health aspects. I. Bealer, Bonnie K. II. Title.

QP801.C24 W447 2002
615'.785—dc21   2002027115

ISBN 0-7432-2896-0

The Caffeine
Advantage

How to Sharpen Your Mind, Improve Your
Physical Performance, and
Achieve Your Goals—the Healthy Way

BENNETT ALAN WEINBERG
AND
BONNIE K. BEALER

THE FREE PRESS

New York London Toronto Sydney Singapore

*f*P